CW00920082

Picture: Brian Evans

JOSS

The life and times of the legendary Lake District
fell runner and shepherd Joss Naylor

KEITH RICHARDSON

Colour photography by Val Corbett

This book is dedicated to fell runners.

'If their sport lent itself to being held in a stadium surrounded by television cameras then they would be known the world over.' – Chris Brasher.

JOSS

The life and times of the legendary Lake District
fell runner and shepherd Joss Naylor

KEITH RICHARDSON
Colour photography by Val Corbett

RIVER
GRETA
WRITER

River Greta Writer
Windebrowe Avenue
Keswick
Cumbria
CA12 4JG

www.rivergretawriter.co.uk

JOSS
The life and times of the legendary Lake District
fell runner and shepherd Joss Naylor

First River Greta Writer edition: 2009

A catalogue record for this book is available from the British Library.
ISBN: 978-0-9559640-1-5

Printed and bound by The Amadeus Press, Cleckheaton, West Yorkshire.
Design and pre-press by Walker Ellis Associates, Threlkeld, Cumbria.

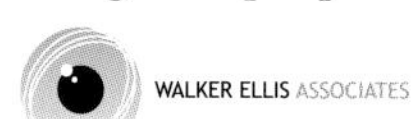

CONTENTS
Joss

FOREWORD
'Training advice from The Legend'

Somehow you get the feeling that the trappings of the modern day sporting idol wouldn't count for much in the Wasdale Valley where down the centuries the men were as rugged as the mountains that enclosed them and they were judged by the quality of the Herdwick sheep they kept and the longevity of the dry stone walls that they built.

The extravagancies of the world never really entered into the equation. Not that Joss Naylor has ever sought such extravagances, unless you count winter holidays in Spain, where the sunshine eases his considerable legacy of old injuries, as one of his few concessions to modern day living.

'Legend' is not the first word that comes to mind when people, who don't know of the man and his remarkable list of long distance running records, first meet him.

The arrogance and inflated self-image of the modern sporting icon don't figure in Joss Naylor's make-up. He's more interested in other people and what they do than to start reeling off his own remarkable catalogue of successes.

Mind you, give him half a chance and he will start listing a veritable medical dictionary of injuries and complaints, none of which seems to have prevented him from reaching the peak of his chosen sport, a sport that places almost inhuman demands on mind and body.

He's a phenomenon of course. He's never stood on an Olympic Games podium. Much of his record breaking has taken place in his own immediate environment where, after 24 hours slogging remorselessly over the Lakeland fells in all weathers, he's been home in time for tea and to milk his cows or to gather sheep.

Where does Joss stand in the pantheon of great athletes? One knowledgeable writer once called him 'the world's greatest long distance runner.' But it's impossible to make comparisons. How good could Naylor have become if he had set his sights on international fame and been professionally trained? Is he the sort of man who could have clocked up endless miles on the road and track and got any sort of satisfaction away from his beloved native hills? The answer to that last question is probably not.

But then you never know where Joss Naylor is concerned.

In life, as well as in his running, Joss has always been a head down and get on with it sort of man. Keith Richardson, in this remarkably insightful book, and in his extensive interviews with Naylor, has uncovered uncomfortable elements in a tough upbringing. But life in the remoter valleys was raw in a way that today's young people would find intolerable. It made them or it broke them. In Joss Naylor's case it coloured the man he became; single-minded, determined, with no side to him and inherently a decent and dignified man who has brought nothing but honour to his sport.

One of my first encounters with Joss came at the end of an Ennerdale Race in the early 1970s. He had just smashed the record. I trailed in, bloodied and broken, dripping wet after falling in the river, nearly two and a half hours later.

Joss, who had probably been home for a cuppa and done the day's farming chores, was at the finish line to greet stragglers. There was no mention of his performance.

"How'd it ga, then?" he asked.

"A struggle," I gasped back. "Fell coming down Kirk Fell and took all the skin off my arm and knees, took a bad route off Crag Fell at the end and then went head first into the beck."

"Aye," said Joss, looking me up and down. "A few mair miles in them legs wouldn't ga amiss. Git some mair training in noo t'lang neets is here."

Training advice from The Legend. I couldn't bring myself to explain to him that I was already running 120 miles a week, using practically every hour of daylight. And still it wasn't bringing me a second nearer to The Great Man's times. I suspect it simply wasn't in my genes, whatever Joss thought about my perceived lack of training.

What attracted me to fell running was the individual nature of the sport, the friendliness of fellow sufferers in the masochistic self-punishment of races like Wasdale, Ennerdale and the Mountain Trial, and the eccentricity it positively encouraged. One regular competitor always took his pipe with him and had a reflective smoke at the highest point in the races. There were teachers, scientists, shop assistants, farmers,

university professors and a fella who used to train by pounding up and down a tower block in Liverpool. All of them seemed to have that slightly off beat, rebellious, individual cussedness that you needed to run the fells.

Joss Naylor was, for many years, the beacon of his sport. He was the best and in the eyes of many people always will be. Yet I never saw him wearing a single item of running kit that looked remotely new. Sitting next to him on a freezing Spring morning at Edale in the Peak District I watched him pull on a pair of his wife's discarded tights, a fashion complement to his moth eaten shirt and tatty shorts. Perfect, apparently, for keeping the legs warm while wicking away the sweat.

No one has done more to raise the profile of mountain running than Joss Naylor and, through it, to raise substantial sums for various charities. He embodies the spirit of those who have pushed back the boundaries of record breaking in the British hills over the decades. And he was still running at an age when most people had donned their slippers and were taking a nap in front of the television.

He reached for the summit and he got there. But then again, he's a top man is our Joss.

Ross Brewster, journalist and former fell runner.

Overleaf: Joss with Titch and Spy at Dore Head.

A WASDALE CHILDHOOD
Black Sail and a boy called Joss 1

Imagine, if you will, a small boy barely five years old in short trousers, woolly jumper and clogs, venturing out from the farm where he lives at Middle Row, Wasdale Head, to meet his father and a hired hand returning from the fell where they have been gathering sheep. The year is 1941 and the country is at war. The boy thinks that he will meet the shepherds, dogs and sheep on the intake land just a few hundred yards from the farm. But there is no immediate sign of them so he advances further into Mosedale on the path high above the fast-running beck of that name. When they still fail to come into view he goes higher still, onto Black Sail Pass with the crags of Kirk Fell to his right and the dauntingly massive Pillar to his left.

He is high, high on the fell, this small boy in search of family, his senses sharp to the cry of the shepherds, the bark of dogs and the sound of sheep on the move. He is not for one moment fazed at the height he has climbed and how far he is from home. He has never been this high on the fell before and is on his own. But this small boy is called Joss Naylor and he is not afraid. For him the fells hold no fear. They are his home, always have been and always will be.

Joss, with his dog Titch, sitting on the very same rock where he sat as a boy of just five waiting for his father and the sheep to return from a gather in and around Ennerdale.

The old metal gate that Joss went through as a young boy when he climbed the fell, the top of Black Sail, to look for his father.

He goes through the metal gate and fence (the remains of which are still there) at the apex of Black Sail Pass before the descent into Ennerdale and climbs still further to his left towards the crags of Pillar Rock. The sun shines out of a clear blue sky and it is a hot day although the soft breeze on the ridge makes it more bearable after the long climb out of the valley bottom.

Young Joss sits on a rocky outcrop, looks around him at the surrounding fells and waits . . . almost 70 years later and that small boy is an elderly man, albeit one with a youthful mind and an optimistic outlook on life, and we have returned to exactly the same place on the mountain to reawaken his memories of that journey up the fell all those years ago. We stand on the self same spot where Joss sat as a boy and he recalls: "I think mother must have thought they would be coming down Mosedale intek so

Joss's father Joe as a young man in the days when he lived at Caldbeck.

Joss's father Joe with a hound and sheepdogs.

it would be aw right for me to ga and meet them. Well they weren't and I got to the top of Black Sail before I met any sheep. I was sitting on top of this laal crag when they started to come. It's good to watch sheep coming towards yer. The Mosedale stock were marked with three stripes on the far side. They looked great, they were fit and ready for clipping. I got on this rock – I like to call it Sail Crag now because it's at the top of Black Sail – and I thowt to missell 'this is great.' It's the first thing I can remember about being up here on the fell and looking down into Ennerdale. I know I was only a little kid, but it's a memory that's always bin wid us."

Joss's father was working with a hired hand called Alf Moore and it must have been fantastic for the young Joss to hear and see the shepherds, the dogs and the sheep approach across the fell from the direction of Pillar.

"One thing about father," says Joss, "he would always tek us to the fell when I was very little. It was a fine summer's day and I wouldn't have started school, but I had gathered sheep from the front of Mosedale. That evening I sat here in the sunshine and the sheep cem in ones and twos and they had been comin' for half an hour or so before the shepherds and the dogs arrived. The dogs wouldn't be very well fed because it was war time – mebbe just fed on a flake maze and Indian meal and a drop of milk - and they might be suffering a bit in the heat."

I wondered what sort of reception he received when he was spotted on the rocky outcrop so high on the mountain?

"I divvent know," replies Joss. "I can't remember but it wouldn't be very complimentary."

In that remark is the suggestion that Joss had a hard upbringing, one that was perhaps indicative of the times.

But if it was a tough time to be a lad on a working farm it was also a time that had its fair share of fun and enjoyment. People in those days had to rely more on providing their own entertainment, especially in the home, while the great outdoors offered all manner of opportunities for boys. When they were not working on the land they could cut loose, run wild and use their imagination and the environment to full effect. Parents in those days did not have any fears – as they do in the early years of the 21st Century – about letting their children roam free, witness Joss's foray to the head of Mosedale and Black Sail Pass at the age of five.

Wasdale Head in the late 1930s and 1940s, when Joss was nobbut a lad, was a place of character occupied by more than its fair share of characters and Joss's amazing memory for people, places and the events of his childhood and of his youth bring it all vividly back to life. Joss was born at Middle Row Farm, just along from the Wastwater Hotel, on February 10, 1936. His parents, Joseph and Ella, had four children, James, Scott, Margie and Joss – Joss being the youngest of the four children and the last surviving member of that group. The Naylors were originally farmers at Fellside, Caldbeck, and came to Wasdale in 1926.

The baby Joss puts in an early appearance in the farmyard at Middle Row. He is being held by his sister Marjorie and alongside her is Joss's brother Scott stroking a sheep dog. Note the postman, George Braithwaite, with his pushbike in the background. The year is probably 1936 and Joss is in his first year.

Joss's first memory of the valley was in 1939 when he was three and was taken, in a pram pushed by a maid, to see the results of serious flooding. The water in the beck raged in full spate, gathering force and momentum as it crashed into the valley on its descent towards the lake, pushing large boulders before it along the stream bottom and carving great gouges out of the landscape. Joss has amazing recall of the extent of the damage. A year later and he has equally sharp memories of a particularly hard winter when the ice had to be broken to give the cows a drink and he failed in his attempt to save the life of a thrush.

"This old thrush was about knackered because it couldn't find any worms to eat," recalls Joss. "I fetched it in and put it in a laal box and I was kind till it. It died about an hour later, but you always had visions of doing some good."

There was a school in the valley at Nether Wasdale. A Mrs Shepherd ran it – appropriately enough in a farming community where sheep ruled – but that school had closed some years previously and Joss and other children from the valley were taught at St Mary's in the nearby village of Gosforth. The children were transported to and from Wasdale to school in Jack Allison's old Chrysler car. Jack ran a garage and taxi service out of Gosforth and the school run to and from Wasdale was part of his daily round. Today's health and safety inspectorate would have had a dicky fit at Jack's concept of the safe passage of children 1940s style.

"He used to get 14 in that car," says Joss. "We were put in like sardines. He would be coming out of Gosforth for the big hill and he would change down to second or third gear, put his foot down and tek a run at it wid aw us kids in. Well, I can remember the car door flying oppen three or fower times when he did that and we lost a couple out on that fust corner."

Were the children all right?

"Oh aye," replied Joss, as if it was an every day occurrence and nothing to worry about. "They got up, shook themselves down and got back in and Jack would reverse down the hill, rev the old Chrysler up again and have another ga. You would nivver have got away wid it today."

Clockwise from far right: A right little band of urchins. From left to right they are Marjorie, Betty Sim (the daughter of Teddy Sim who was a shepherd for J.R. Whiting) Jim and Scott in the yard at Middle Row.

Busy little bees in the Middle Row farmyard. Scott, Jim and Marjorie.

Scott and Marjorie at the gate to Middle Row.

Before Joss had even entered the world. His brother Jim and sister Marjorie on the old packhorse bridge at Wasdale Head. Note the clogs.

Jack Allison was a character. One night he was making his way back from Wasdale, after dropping off Joss's mother and father, when the snow and white out conditions became so severe that he spun off the road and had to abandon his car.

"And the moment he set foot on the road to walk back to Gosforth he looked round and there was this fox at his heels," says Joss. "He said it followed him all the way to Harrow Head Farm and he went into a byre, sat down on a milking stool and had a cigarette. Any way, when he come out the fox had gone. He reckoned it was true, he telt us two or three times about that. He didn't say whether the fox saw him as a meal or was just plain curious. He was always coming up with these daft stories."

The old school at Wasdale Head. The building is still there and is used to store sheep pens and equipment for Wasdale Show.

Occasionally, if the schoolchildren wanted their arrival at school to be delayed, they would put a couple of studs, of the type then used in walking boots, onto the road leading out of Wasdale, in the hope that the car would get a puncture.

"Sometimes Jack wouldn't have a spare wheel and there was nee telephone so it was a longish job getting to school," recalls Joss. "We didn't do it varra often because they would have twigged otherwise."

Joss positively hated school in Gosforth and the 10 years he was there were like a life sentence.

"It was terrible," he says. "It was like going to jail. I hated the bloody spot."

Joss can still remember, as if it were yesterday, his very first day at school. He spent most of it standing in the corner. Unused to being in a controlled environment he apparently wouldn't shut up.

"It was war time," Joss adds, "and it brought reality home when we first went there. Lads used to bring in old iron implements and pieces of scrap iron for the war effort. The school shed was full of newspapers and cardboard boxes for the same thing. Somebody brought an old bloody trumpet in. There was a big lad cawd 'Puck' Tyson, His real name was Norman but he got 'Puck' and he used to sneak out and put this trumpet to an air vent – we were aw laal kids in the infants – and he used to give it one awful blast. It used to echo right through the school and we thought it was great. You

Joss, Marjorie and car.

could see him nip ower the wall and then go back into his own class as though nowt had happened. He got away wid it for ages before they catched him."

Joss was clearly not of an academic nature and can recall sitting an exam, possibly the 11-plus, at Bookwell School, Egremont.

"Nowt ivver come of it," says Joss. "Well, I could write mi name and ah larnt enough. But it was bloody monotonous, I just used to watch the clock go round. I wanted to be home and amang sheep and doing jobs. Middle Row was a really good Lakeland farm with a lot of really good sheep. You had jobs to do before you went to school and then when you cem back yam.

"There was ya morning I went to let the hens out and there was this hen coming towards the farm gate with its wing trailing on the ground. And ah thowt 'bloody hell – ah nivver shut them hens in last night.' There was feathers and hens all ovver the orchard. We must have had 60 hens and the foxes – there'd be mair than yan - had killed the lot of them, apart from about three that had survived. The hens were abed but I hadn't shut the slide. It was a big loss in them days and anyway I got a bloody whipping for that and when I come back from school it was straight to bed. There was discipline for ivverything and that was summat I had just slipped up on. The old lass was rough on us if you did owt wrong and she gev us a bloody good hiding. She was very severe on us."

Tasks around the farm when Joss was just a boy also included milking the cows, separating the cream so that it could be made into butter ("the old lady did cream teas and she used to do well that way") putting out crockery for visitors' breakfasts, and stacking fleeces on sheep clipping days.

"You had the wool to cart away," recalls Joss, "and there was mebbe three fellas

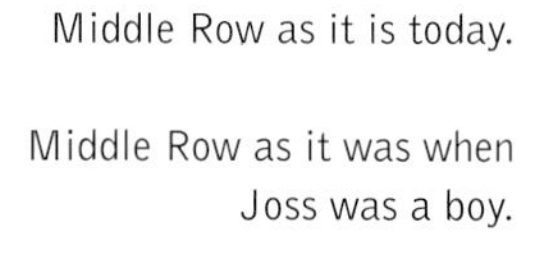

Middle Row as it is today.

Middle Row as it was when Joss was a boy.

clipping away aw day and there would be a bloody big stack of fleeces by the time you got yam at night frae school. I was only a laal lad and they were mebbe clipping them as fast as you were putting them away. It seemed to ga on for ivver. The fleeces were tekken by hoss and cart to the goods yard at Seascale. They would fetch a cartload of coal back to Wasdale and the fleeces would ga to Bradford to be graded. They were bloody long days, trailing down there and then loading coal with a shovel and back up to Wasdale Head."

A happy band of hikers at Middle Row.

Below right: Outside Middle Row are (from left) Bill Cowperthwaite, Joss's cousin Mary Pearson and a friend complete with ciggie and suitcase.

Joss's father Joe peeling potatoes.

Visitors were important to the farm and the Naylor children would often have to sleep in wooden huts in the orchard so that the farm could take in extra visitors at peak periods. In those days there were no subsidies or grants and the farm was more labour intensive with hired hands to pay as well as four children to feed. Fortunately farms tended to be largely self-sufficient when it came to food.

Joss certainly realised fairly early in life that he was well off in comparison to other youngsters of his age who lived in Whitehaven. A visit to the town with his father had quite a marked effect on young Joss.

"Father used to go to a wholesalers called Sibsons in New Street for various supplies," Joss recalls, "and I can always remember seeing these three or four kids on a street corner. They were as black as the ace of spades and had no shoes on or owt and very little clothing. Times were hard, there was a lot of consumption and TB was rife. I always think about them laal kids. It brought reality home; them poor kids had nowt. I always wore clogs, short trousers and a laal sweater and we were fairly well

Joss on a wall at Middle Row with Great Gable in the background. He is pictured with Thelma Whittaker, a visitor to Wasdale Head.

Joss's mother Ella with prize marrows.

dressed compared to a lot of people in them days. Father had a car and at ya time he was the only farmer in the valley who had yan. That day I went to Whitehevven with him in the car it was like a ghost town. It was wartime and there was nobody much about except those kids. We didn't see another car all the way from Wasdale Head to Whitehevven and back, just two or three hoss and carts at Bigrigg."

The black out operated during the war years and there were clearly designated hours during which a light could not be shown in a home and equally strict limitations on the lights displayed on vehicles. Breaking the law could result in an appearance before the local magistrates and a fine.

Cumberland and Westmorland style wrestling was popular and practice sessions were held during the winter at the village hall in Gosforth.

"They had a tremendous following during wartime," says Joss, "and lads from Wasdale and area used to go to the practices on their bikes. The biggest job was going out in the black out because you would have a laal torch on the bike, but if you went by car you would have one headlight completely covered and the other half oppen, so the planes couldn't pick you up sort of thing. I can always remember coming back ya night and there was this old Herdwick tip comin' marching down the middle of the road – it was one of Tot Noble's – and he walked right into the headlight and knocked it out wid its horn. We were in darkness."

They weren't a lot better off in the home where there was no electricity (it did not

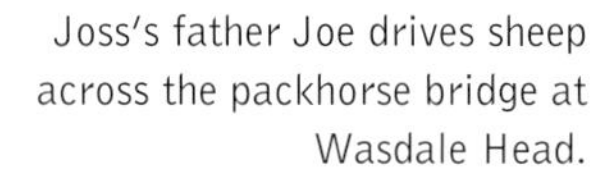

Joss's father Joe drives sheep across the packhorse bridge at Wasdale Head.

Cumberland and Westmorland style wrestling at Wasdale Show.

reach the valley until the 1970s) and illumination was provided by old paraffin lamps and, after 1941, Calor Gas.

"But it was stinking stuff was the gas," says Joss.

There were no tractors on the farms as yet and horses were used for the heavy labour. When Joss was a boy Middle Row had two Clydesdales, Jewel and Peggy.

"They wucked well as a team," says Joss. "They did ivverything from ploughing to cutting grass. I used to git up of a morning, even as a laal lad, and follow the mowing machine, an old Banford, round the field with a rake. You could see the blades in the grass, there was no fertiliser in them days. You went a long way for a lot of hay, they weren't varra big crops, but it was an interesting time because a lot of hay was turned by hand. We had an old turner that would turn it an'all but the dyke backs were always turned by hand and shook out. A lot of work was done by hand in them days and nearly ivvery farm had a couple of men. There was a mass of flowers in the hay meadows, ivvery wild flower you could think of. When nitrogen cem along it gradually did away with them, which is a pity really because it was summat to see."

Joss was never afraid of hard work and he loved being on and about the farm and the surrounding land.

"Ivver since I was about four year old I went to the fell," he recalls. "And I can

Farm work at Wasdale Head. Harvesting bracken.

Joss's father Joe (on the left) with the horse Peggy raking hay.

always remember going up Yewbarrow with mi brother Scott when I was only a laal wee fella. I got most pleasure out of lambing time and gathering sheep."

The Wasdale Head of Joss Naylor's boyhood revolved around the increasingly important benefits of tourism and a thriving farming community – there were many more farms and farm workers on the go in those days. And at the centre of it all – as it is to this day – was the distinctive white walled building of The Wastwater Hotel (now The Wasdale Head Inn). Not only was the hotel a magnet for visitors, walkers and rock climbers, the bar was also a social centre for locals at the head of the valley. It was 'home' to many characters and a place where drink, darts, dominoes, singsongs and banter were the order of the day.

When Joss was a lad the hotel was owned and run by one J.R.Whiting Esq who saw himself as something of a lord of the manor and would parade around his empire in plus fours, long coat and deerstalker hat. The J.R. stood for John Ritson and he was in fact related to Will Ritson (his great uncle), a former owner of The Wastwater Hotel in the mid 1800s who was renowned in Wasdale for his tall stories. He was part of that Wasdale Head holy trinity – the smallest church, the deepest lake and the biggest liar. It became four if you added England's highest mountain, Scafell Pike (3,209ft).

"J.R. liked to think he was the master of the valley, the local squire," says Joss. "He was quite the gent and he had a little black dog, a cocker spaniel called 'Bonzo' which he got off George Abraham (George and Ashley Abraham, pioneer photographers and mountaineers were regular visitors to The Wastwater Hotel)."

Young Joss outside Middle Row.

J.R. Whiting's unfailing pomposity and self-importance, although he was a decent old lad, led to him becoming a natural target for Joss and his brother Jim.

"Jim had a bit of mischief in him," says Joss, "and we used to do all sorts of things when we were bits of lads. We used to mek our own entertainment, especially on a Sunday when we had the day mair or less to ourselves. Anyway, we had a rubbish tip at Middle Row – we used to lead all the old tin cans away of a winter time - and we used to caw it 'Round the Back.' There was this hash plant (Joss means ash but actually pronounces it hash with an 'h', many older rural Cumbrians will invariably add an 'h' to a word) growing right up the back of the barn and it was no thicker than your arm at the bottom. It went straight up. And Jim said 'ah bet that bugger can't half hoy cans.' So he climbed half way up the wall and pulled it ovver. Then I went up past him and between us we hauled the top down to ground level and held it theer. We took aw the side branches off and cut about 16 inches off the top. Jim said 'you hod it' and then said 'no, I'll hod it, ah's heavier than thee. You ga and put a tin on'."

Master of all he surveys. J.R.Whiting of The Wastwater Hotel.

Joss can hardly contain his laughter as he relates the story.

" . . . so I got this old empty bean can. There was this hull window in the barn and the barn door at the other side was half oppen so we could see reet doon the pub yard. Anyway Jim let go and this bloody tin shot reet up in the air. I'd say it went two or three hundred metres up. It didn't half ga a long way and it landed reet at the pub front door about 150 metres away . . ."

Joss is now beside himself with laughter and can barely speak.

"We put half a dozen cans on to the front door of the hotel and just as another bugger landed old J.R. stepped out of the front door and it just missed his bloody nose end by about two inches. Hell, it was funny . . ."

Did old J.R. know where the cans were coming from?

"He'd a bloody good idea," Joss replies. "It wasn't long 'till he looked round the corner and shouted: 'You boys! Get round here and get those tins picked up!' So we buggered off. Anyway we sneaked away did me and Jim and we cem back to the farm at about three o'clock for our teas and as soon as we set foot inside the door father says: 'You two boys know what you can deuh. You can git the saw and git that bloody tree tekken down . . . and you're nut gitting any tea 'till it's done.' So we went and we cut our laal hash tree doon. But what a bloody thing it was. It couldn't half hoy tin cans."

Later in life when Joss and Jim were young men they became acquainted with a visitor to the valley who, for reasons that will become apparent, had the appropriate name of Bill Blewett. On the River Bleng were some deep pools that it was virtually impossible to fish, but which used to hold sea trout.

"Otters used to live on them during the summer," says Joss. "There was ya summer we looked down and there was some beauties in the first dub and Bill said he would have to have a go at them. When he found that fishing was nee good he said: 'I'll tell you what, my mate'll mek us a laal bomb.' Any way he come back about three weeks after and he went ovver and staked up the pool, lit the fuse and scopped it in. There was a hell of an explosion and the watter went reet up in the air about 50 metres and he had one fish that was hardly big enough to put in the frying pan so it wasn't a particularly successful outing. But it was a great experience."

Joss and Jim were good friends as well as brothers.

"We were the greatest mates ever," is how Joss puts it. On most of their Sunday outings as lads they invariably crossed the path of one J.R.Whiting Esq of this parish

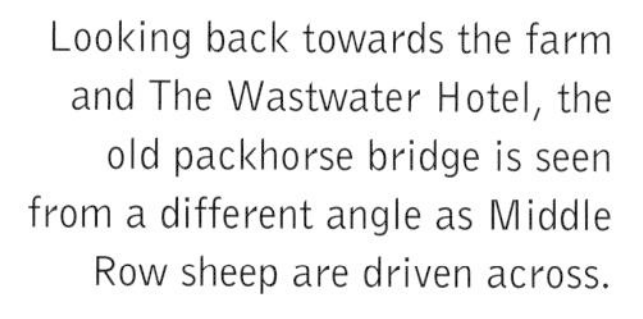

Looking back towards the farm and The Wastwater Hotel, the old packhorse bridge is seen from a different angle as Middle Row sheep are driven across.

and he happened to share, with Joss and Jim, a love for trout fishing. But there the compatibility ended. The lads fished with worm while J.R. used the more refined art of fly fishing, working his way down Mosedale Beck and casting out his line in a graceful arc to land precisely on a likely run of water just beneath the far bank, tempting the fish with wet flies that were popular at the time like Greenwell's Glory, Snipe and Purple, Partridge and Orange or Woodcock and Yellow. Joss and Jim's worm fishing was less sophisticated, but more effective when it came to catching fish, especially on a spate beck when fishing with fly was out of the question because of the height of the river and the muddy-brown water.

"If you went fishing and old J.R. was there you hadn't to pass him," says Joss. "And it was the same at Crab Dale (an area of land near Middle Row) where there were quite a lot of rabbits. We hadn't to ga in theer of a Sunday afternoon because old J.R. would be theer. He was big mates with Willie Newell. He was the Editor of The Whitehevven News and he wrote this column 'Let's Have a Crack' by Copeland. He used to spend quite a lot of time at the pub with J.R. He had two laal Jack Russell

Joss's father Joe with Scott.

Joss, on the right holding the cat, with his cousin Vera Howard and brother Scott.

terriers, yan was called Snowy and the other Smudge or summat. Ivvery Sunday they used to ga in Crab Dale for rabbits – J.R., Newell, Bonzo and the two Jack Russells – and father wouldn't let us ga in because they'd be in there, chessing rabbits and 'aving the crack.

"He had ears and eyes ivverywhere. If you pinched an apple or two from his orchard or burnt a gorse bush or summat like that – once they got a hod they didn't half go up in flames – he would be bloody watching you would old Whiting and you mebbe wouldn't see him for three weeks and then he'd meet you face to face ya day and he'd say: 'You boys should NOT burn gorse bushes. Make that your last one!'"

Joss with hound.

But while J.R. was most definitely on their case, the Naylor brothers (that has the ring of ne'er-do-wells from the Australian outback about it) would exact their revenge from time to time.

The farm at Row Head was part of J.R.Whiting's estate and Billy Birkett was shepherd for Whiting at the farm.

"Old Billy didn't care what you got up to, within reason," says Joss. "On a Sunday morning about half past 10, old J.R. religiously walked up the road, through our yard, up the beck edge, through Kirk Fell gate and then he'd follow the Black Sail path 'til the gate at the bottom of Mosedale intek and then he'd mek his way back. It was his Sunday morning ritual. When he went up theer me and Jim would bag a few white hens and ga in the barn. Old J.R. had to pass the barn on his way back and when he got level wid us we would push these white hens – mebbe fower of them - out of the laal slit holes in the side of the barn and they would fly at him. He got a hell of a shock. He used to snap his fingers he was that bloody mad. And then he would come into the barn and he would say: 'You boys – come down off that hay!' He couldn't git up theer so we would just sit quiet and say nowt. Then he would go and see Billy and say: 'Bill, you must take more care of Row Head. Those Naylor boys are running wild. They're up on your hay mew and they've just thrown some hens at me. It's got to stop!'"

Apart from being on the receiving end of tin cans raining out of the sky and white hens flapping out of slits in the barn, J.R.s life at Wasdale Head and The Wastwater Hotel must have been fairly idyllic. Jack Thompson, who was handyman and driver for the hotel, and not one of this life's more optimistic, energetic or enthusiastic souls, would chauffeur J.R. around and also collect and return hotel guests to the nearest railway station at Seascale. Jack, incidentally, once had a problem with a knee that was badly swollen and went for treatment at the old Whitehaven hospital.

"In those days they had a belief that heat treatment was great and a cure for all ailments," recalls Joss. "So Jack would ga for heat treatment and there he was wid his trouser leg rolled up under aw these lights and you could turn the machine up until you bloody roasted. So they turned it on and said to Jack: 'Is that alright Mr Thompson?' He said 'Aye, ah can stick that.' Anyway, it got hotter and hotter and Jack said he thowt that the hotter it got the more good it would be doing him. So he said nowt. Anyway it took aw the bloody skin off his knee."

But let's get back to J.R. Whiting.

"He was a clever fella," adds Joss. "He was on the old Ennerdale Rural District Council which had a good reputation and he was a very good councillor. Jack Thompson would chauffeur him around to the meetings (held in the council chamber in a building known as The Flosh, at Cleator) and ivverything was given free in them days, there were nee expenses or owt like that. The rates were managed and you weren't burdened like we are today and they didn't feel the need for bonding weekends. They didn't have to tek them to a flash hotel and spend £3,000 of ratepayers' money to introduce Tom to Bill and have a booze up."

Talking of the evil drink, Joss reckons that The Wastwater Hotel did not take off as a really popular centre for drinkers until the arrival of Wilse Pharaoh as landlord in 1951.

"Before that they had an old wooden hut with bench seats in and that was sort of the bar," says Joss. "But we weren't allowed to drink in them days because we were too young. If you went in for a bottle of pop or owt you would ring the bell and five minutes later old Jack (Thompson) would come trailin' in."

Jack, while a very kindly man, did not have the strongest work ethic in the world.

"He was really good at doing nowt," recalls Joss. "There was neebody his equal when it come to gittin' away wid doing nowt. If anybody wanted a pint they would be sobered up by the time they got the next un because Jack didn't move varra fast. But he meant well . . . anyway old Jack would come trailin' in and he'd say 'huh, what the bloody hell does thoo want?' And he would ga and git you a bottle of lemonade and a packet of crisps, and you would have thowt you were asking for the bloody crown jewels the way he went about it. Ivvery night at half past five on the dot he would come out to the front of the hotel for a pipeful of bacca. After a while Miss Edith (Edie) Long (J.R.Whiting's sister in law) would come looking for him and she would call out 'Jack . . ! Jack . . !' in a really screechy voice and he would say 'huh, what the hell does she bloody want now?' Edie would have to come out about three times before Jack finally muttered 'huh, I suppose I'd better bloody ga . . .' tap out his pipe and make his way very reluctantly back inside to wuck."

Joss Naylor was a young man when old Jack made his exit from this world. After suffering a heart attack Jack was bedfast for many weeks.

"I used to ga and see him ivvery night," says Joss. "I would ask him 'how you doing today Jack?' and he would reply 'huh, might as well be bloody deed.' And this went on for ages. And there was ya night I was garn somewhere else and ah didn't git across to see him and you would have thowt I'd committed a mortal sin. 'Where's Joss? He's nivver come to see us . . .' But when I did go to see him he would just lay theer and say nowt. Old Edie used to say till us 'Jack wants you to go and see the solicitor because he wants to leave you something in his will.' And I said 'that's bugger aw to do wid me, I can't go and see his solicitor.'

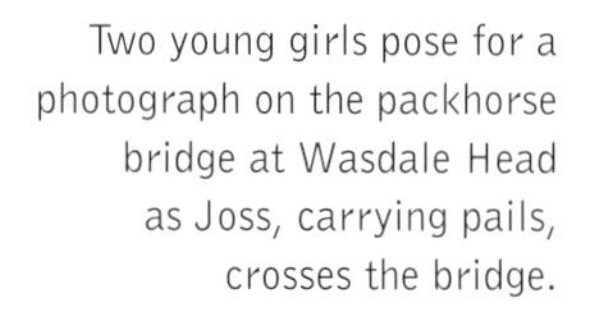

Two young girls pose for a photograph on the packhorse bridge at Wasdale Head as Joss, carrying pails, crosses the bridge.

"Anyway I went over ya morning and old Jack had deed. Big Oaksie was theer and I said 'give us a hand.' He was a big fella was Jack and his knees were up. I said 'we'll have to straighten him out or we won't be able to git him in the box.' So we got him on the floor and straightened him out. From then until the funeral ivvery yan kept garn on about how Jack was gonna leave us summat in his will and ah kept saying 'ah don't want owt off Jack'."

The funeral came and went. And Joss loaded up his van and took old Jack's belongings and furniture to a relative in Gosforth who gave him five bob for his trouble. Meanwhile, old Jack had gone to his grave and been consistent about doing nowt right to the end.

Did he leave Joss anything in his will?

"Did he buggery," says Joss. "And after aw that palaver. Hell, it was funny . . ."

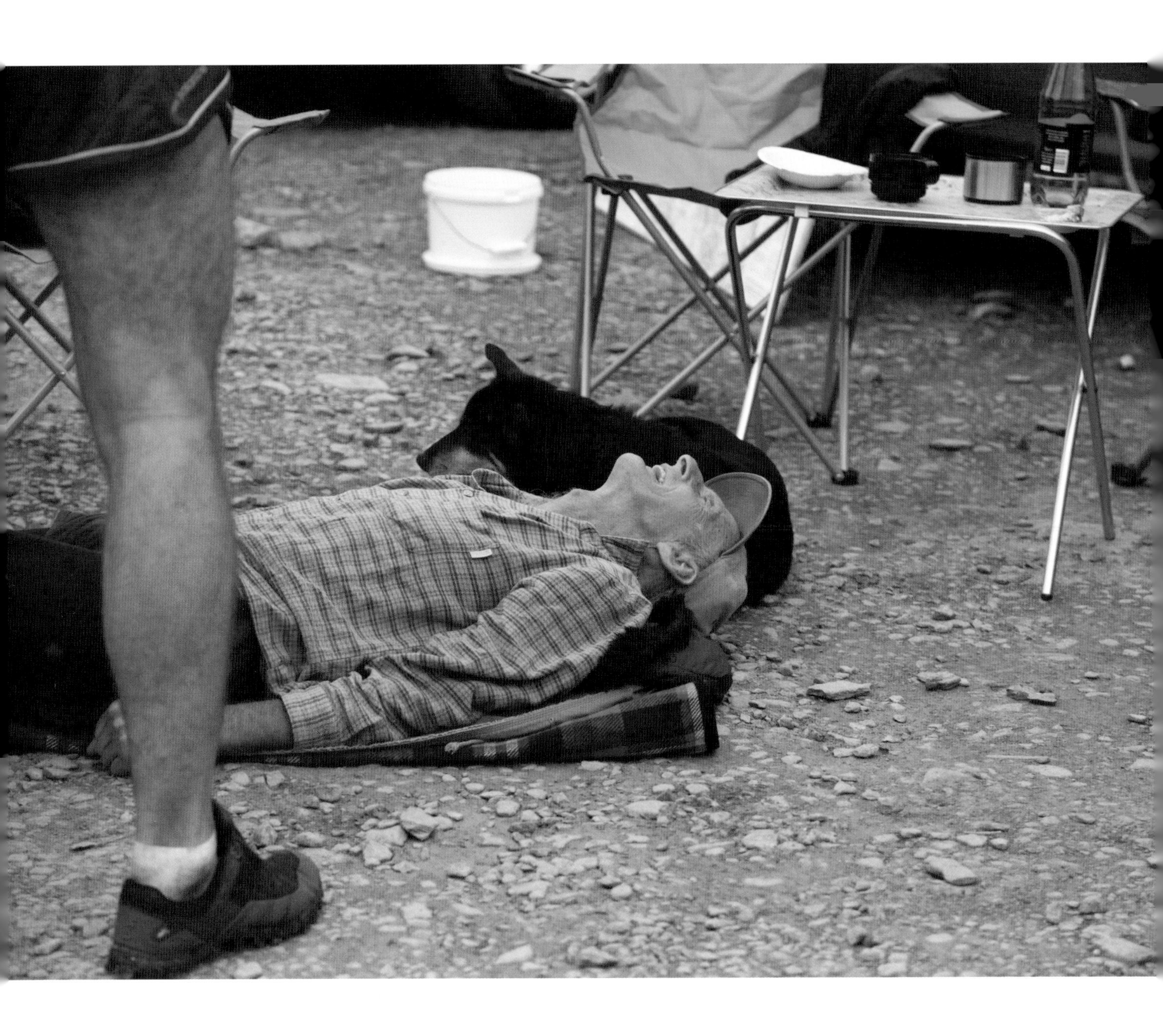

BACK PROBLEMS 2
'When I was right I could catch bloody midges'

When you have a bad back the world is never a happy place. The sense of discomfort is an ever-present affecting your entire constitution and demeanour. It is difficult to raise a smile and when you unexpectedly find yourself off kilter and the back pain kicks in with a vengeance it is accompanied by a grimace, an involuntary groan and an exclamation of 'oh, bloody hell . . .' or language a lot more colourful, as in blue. Fortunately, these conditions are usually temporary, rarely last for too long and even if you are prone to back pain there are long periods when you experience some kind of respite before complacency and a casual posture catch you out and put you back – no pun intended - to square one and more grief.

For Joss Naylor back pain has never really gone away since the age of nine.

It has been his very real tormentor forever and a day and still gives him gip. It is something that he has had to contend with as best he can virtually every day of his life. Unfortunately the condition is made worse because it is a constant reminder of a relationship with his mother that was fraught at the best of times and still affects him emotionally to this day.

You see it was a kick from his mother that caused the problem in the first place.

Joss unexpectedly revealed this to me after we had visited St Olaf's Church and, after our visit, we had gone along the path to the nearby Wasdale Head Inn for lunch. Perhaps Joss's emotions were heightened by the visit to the churchyard where so many of his relatives and friends are buried and where Joss himself has actually dug the graves. In previous interviews for magazine articles and the like Joss had been sketchy about the precise origins of the back injury. There were suggestions that it resulted from a wrestling injury, or a fall while working on the farm.

"I got a kick in the back – off a human," was the nearest he had come to an admission, and I jumped to the conclusion that he had been in a fight in his youth and come off worst. But he didn't elaborate; it had just been left hanging in the air, something that he did not really want to expand upon. So I left it there and did not think much more about it.

Joss, 73, is clearly in agony on his 2009 run across the Lakeland fells when he ran 35 miles and climbed 16,000 feet. Here he is flat out on the rough ground of the car park at Honister. His back caused him problems on the run from Mungrisdale to Wasdale and here he is suffering from cramp. The ever faithful Spy is on guard and is as protective as ever as she lies next to Joss. The runner was soon back on his feet and away again. Photograph: Stuart Holmes.

But over lunch in the Wasdale Head Inn that day, after the visit to St Olaf's, it all came out.

"When did this accident to your back happen?" I asked.

"I had just turned nine when it happened," Joss replied. "I got kicked in the bloody back. We shouldn't say, but it was mi mother who kicked us. I mebbe asked for it. I would have bin up to some sort of mischief and I'd gone out of the back door (at Middle Row) and I'd stepped down off the step and I was probably just at the wrong angle at the wrong time. You shouldn't say these things, but these things happen. And it just got gradually worse and I went to see all sorts of specialists."

Me: "It was unfortunate then, rather than being malicious it was a kick and it landed wrong?"

Joss: "Aye, that's right . . ."

That one kick when he was nine has caused Joss a great deal of pain all his life. The initial blow resulted in serious disc damage that was only partially remedied by surgery to remove two discs when he was in his early twenties.

As a boy he was in agony on the hard wooden benches at Gosforth School.

"As time went on mi back got worse. From nine year old and sitting on a laal wooden seat in school it used to cripple us," he recalls. "I couldn't sleep because of the pain in mi back. I could mebbe git an hour's sleep or summat like that. The pain would come down mi legs. The left leg – it's the best yan I've got now – if I laid down on the floor I couldn't lift it six inch off the ground. If I tried to force it the muscles from mi heel to mi backside would go into spasm. As time went on I used to go to the old Whitehevven hospital. Jack Pharaoh used to tek us from Ravenglass. He had this old Jowett Javelin brek thing. He was a character. He used to have a laal garage and sell petrol and paraffin and stuff like that and he had a taxi service. He used to tek us through and it was the old hospital then. And they had a big belief that heat treatment was great and cured all ailments."

Unfortunately it didn't cure Joss. Or even give him much respite. He had the heat treatment, wore corsets and special straight jackets to support his back, but nothing seemed to do any good. Sometimes, when he had got his body warmed up, he was able to play and even enjoy games of football and cricket and he was always first in cross country races. He even ran in the occasional fell race at a shepherds' meet. But the pain was never far away.

He left school at 15 to work at home on the farm.

Did the back pain not affect his ability to work on the land?

"I nivver missed a day off work wid it," he replies. "You hadn't to because you didn't git any sympathy. Once I got warmed up it was no bother but I couldn't stride out. I used to scuff the soles off mi shoes because I wasn't walking right. It was just one of those damned things. I wouldn't have wished it on anyone. I went to see all sorts of fellas and ivverybody had a different story. And it went on and on 'til the mid Fifties. I was 19 when I went to see a specialist down in Manchester."

A smiling Joss is pictured with Collie puppies at Middle Row. But behind the smile there was the constant pain of his back injury.

Shortly afterwards he underwent surgery to remove the two troublesome discs that had been at the root of his back problem for the last 10 years.

Joss did not take to hospital life.

"I hated ivvery bloody minute of it," he says. "I was theer for about six weeks and I was like a lion in a cage."

The surgeon said that Joss was a one-off, built like a machine, as wiry as any man could be and that he had tremendous stamina. At that time Joss weighed in at a little over nine stone, a weight that has changed only marginally throughout his entire adult life.

Joss and I recalled those days in hospital and his return to Wasdale Head as we walked past the back of Middle Row Farm – where he first suffered the back injury – and alongside the swift flowing waters of Mosedale Beck only a stone's throw from the farm house. Personally I have always felt that the sound of fast flowing water in a Lakeland beck is very therapeutic and reassuring, perhaps a throwback to my own childhood when I lived at Low Briery, Keswick, in a small row of terraced houses next to the River Greta and my constant companion was the sound of the water.

"It's a strange sound, that of running water," said Joss as we walked by the beck and out into Mosedale, heading for Black Sail. "I can always remember 1956 when I cem back from Manchester Royal Infirmary and I'd been lying in there for six week in a ward where there's about 32 beds and there was always a lot of noise and summat going on. I cem back home and when I got out of the hospital and into this car I felt really fit, but by the time I got to Santon Bridge I was just about knackered. I was nearly passing out because mi body likely had no resistance to owt and after travelling aw that way in a car, for mebbe three and a half hours, it just aboot finished us off. I can always remember getting home and going to bed and the only thing you could hear was the noise of that beck.

"We always called it Cobblestone Beck (real name Mosedale Beck). It's the beck that comes out of Mosedale bottom theer. But what a bloody row it seemed to mek because it was so still that night. It was a noise I hadn't heard for a long time and mi mind couldn't git round it. Everything was so quiet and the beck was the only thing you could hear.

"The next morning I goes out and lets the dogs out. And they'd nivver seen us for six weeks and they just sat on their arses in that dog run and howled. They were still missing us and when I went to them they went absolutely wild. I let them out and went back in the house and sat down and I can mind that one of them cem flying in through the kitchen door, landed on the mat and slid on the mat right under the kitchen table. I can always remember mi mother went bloody crackers. The dogs are the one thing you miss when you spend most of your working life with them, I had about six o' them . . ."

The surgery seemed to work for a while and Joss recalls that his general fitness improved and that, for once, he was virtually free of pain.

"In 1958 (when he was 22) that was the only year in mi life when mi reflexes was all right," he says. "I didn't need a bloody dog to catch sheep. I could catch any sheep ah wanted. I could just walk half past it as though I was taking no notice of it and it was mine before it got off its bloody patch. When I was right I could catch bloody midges."

But he later aggravated the problem with a bad fall. Attempting to lowp a fence he placed his left hand firmly on the top post for support as he leapt and his legs and body were in mid air when his resting hand slipped off the post – it was wet after a shower of rain - and he landed painfully on his back. More years of pain and disability followed and it was not until his late twenties that he felt well enough to make his first tentative steps at senior fell running. He ran his first race, at Wasdale, in a pair of old fell beutts and with his jeans clipped off just above the knee to make out they were shorts. The rest, as they say, is history.

Now in his early seventies, Joss reflects on the running style that he has developed as a result of that back problem and also the damage to his right knee where all the cartilage has been surgically removed as a result of wear and tear.

"I couldn't straighten up when I was running," explains Joss. "I'm crouched ovver and that's to do wid mi back being wrecked. I don't think I'm as crouched as I used to be. I've done a lot of work on mi back and run less crouched now. But I used to run very crouched. It was a distinct style and you could see us miles away. I've tried for years to get ovver this thing.

"The way I run is down to the back being wrong and I got to favouring it. Mi back's all right now, but I do exercises for it ivvery morning. I try and keep it right. When the weather's good and warm I feel bloody good, as good as I've done for years. I feel as good as I did when I was 50. I'm mebbe not running as well and I have to do a lot of work on mi knee as well. The alternative's no bloody good, a whole new knee. You can't do bloody much with one of them. You've got to keep hod of what you've got and keep it working and it is at the moment. I can descend and climb well.

"I just need a bit of sunshine to git mi running together again. That's what it's all about. Otherwise you can become a plodder and just plod away. It's nice just to be able to stride out. I was running on a good leg and a bad leg sort of thing and I think that would have had something to do with it. But at the moment I'm getting away wid it and I might get back to running a decent pace again. There's nowt worse than wanting to change your pace, but your knees won't let you when you are running on bare bone, there's no cartilage in the right knee.

"Bone on bone isn't very pleasant. The left un's good and all mi other joints are good. So it just shows running doesn't do any harm if your genes are right. It's the same wid owt. If you want to do something you carry on doing it. What you don't use you lose in this world. And when you go back it's not there. It's a mind over matter thing.

"I don't mind how long it teks us to get fit and to get going again. It doesn't come into the equation.

"I go out with the dogs and tek them for a walk and if I feel like a run then I run with them. If I feel like doing a lot of climbing I do a lot of climbing. It's nice to be able to do that and at the end of the day I think how lucky I am to be able to do those things. And if you can help somebody along the way it meks it all worthwhile."

There have been times when Joss has felt exceptionally good when he was setting out on a long distance run and got into his stride. He knew from the outset that it was going to be a good trip.

"When you get them days it's absolute magic," he says. "I knew I could do what I was setting out to achieve. Mi mind was right and I usually knew after mi first big climb that mi climbing was good. I soon established a rhythm. I used to concentrate on mi climbing and if your climbing was good other things tended to fall in. If you're coming down hill you sort of let your feet drop and try and relax as much as you can. Bend your knees and they act as a shock absorber; look after your joints as best you can. You might say ahs a right bugger for saying that – considering all the miles I've done – but it wasn't through running that I got mi problems."

For every long distance run that went astonishingly well there were others that were always going to be a battle from the outset. Even so, Joss usually prevailed and his high pain threshold and determination invariably saw him through.

For example, Joss wasn't a track athlete. The high fells were his terrain, but in 1984 he went in for a long distance event on the track at Crystal Palace.

"Things went badly wrong," he recalls. "Mi knee went a fortnight before. I was shattered before I went because I knew I was gonna have problems. I was destroyed mentally before I went. I was geared up to do 170 mile. And I would have done it – nee bother. I was 48 year old and running well. Mi mind was right and I knew I could do it but then mi knee went."

It was in the days leading up to the event that it all went wrong.

"I was coming up Ennerdale on the day and had done a hell of a long run. Instead of going over Black Sail and down the road home I just shook mi bloody head and went straight up to the top of Pillar and cem back ovver Red Pike. I knew that mi knee

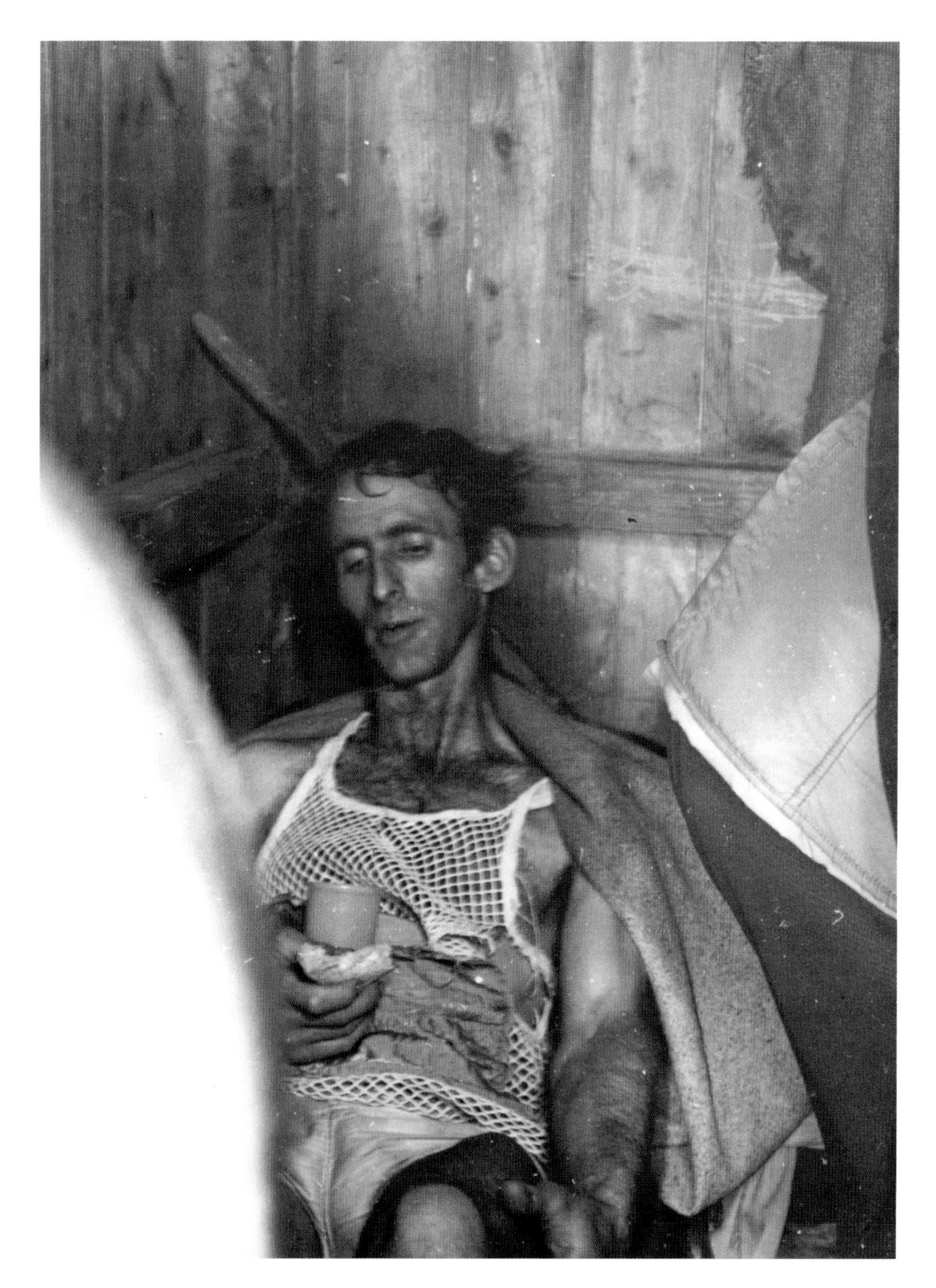

Out on his feet. An exhausted Joss is clearly in some difficulty during the Pennine Way run in 1974. He is slumped in a shed after a bad fall. His supporters thought his attempt on the record would have to be abandoned at this point but Joss recovered and fought through the pain to go the distance.
Photograph: Tommy Orr.

was screaming. It had no cartilage and was full of bits of grime and stuff. And if I'd known and had some anti-inflammatory tablets and tekken summat like that I would have got through no bother."

He had to settle for a mere 134 miles in the endurance event at Crystal Palace.

And for his 70 peaks at 70 years of age he recalls: "It was supposed to be mi last yan that. It was a fantastic day, but I had a very bad start. I had only been going about an hour, an hour and a half or so. I had two lads with mi with flashlights and it was about half past two in the morning. I stepped ovver this bush and there was this hole in the ground with no bottom. Oh I hit the ground and I could see stars half an hour afterwards. I had knocked missell out and it was four or five hours before I had fully recovered. I had a good day after that."

Joss, in fact, had many good days and some of his achievements at home and overseas are recalled in detail in the ensuing chapters and, for those who like to pore over statistics, in a special section at the back of this book.

What the figures and the statistics do not show is the pain Joss went through, the perseverance he showed, the will of the mind to conquer matter and blank out the brain and the body's 'I'm in agony' messages. And then there was the relentless, dogged, almost bloody-minded determination to succeed against the odds and in the face of seemingly impossible challenges.

A youthful Joss with farm worker Willie Monkhouse at Middle Row

Sadly, it would appear that Joss did not have a good relationship with his mother who comes across as a very strong, formidable woman.

"I didn't," he told me that day over lunch in the Wasdale Head Inn. "No, very sad really. It should never be that way. I can't talk about it . . ." and with that he unexpectedly broke down and cried, his head sinking onto the table top in his grief. The reaction came completely out of the blue and caught me by surprise.

Joss's mother Ella with (left to right) her young sons Jim and Scott and daughter Marjorie and a family friend, Betty Simm, the daughter of Teddy Simm, shepherd to J.R.Whiting.

"Sorry Keith," he muttered through the tears as I sympathised with him. A short while later, after he had gathered his thoughts, we continued with the interview and moved on to less emotive areas of his life.

Clearly Joss has always been reluctant to talk about the true cause of the injury that was inflicted on him as a boy and – other than immediate family – has been evasive about what really happened. Equally he will not open up about his feelings relating to his mother (and why should he, it is his concern?) but from his reaction to my question and that on a subsequent occasion when I asked Joss's permission to include the information in the book, it is obvious that the real hurt goes far deeper than the physical pain he has suffered over the years.

What Joss Naylor's mother did to her boy – kicked out at him in her anger – was wrong, but she surely did not intend to cause him the sort of injury that would afflict him for the rest of his life.

Joss Naylor the man has in part been forged out of that incident all those years ago.

It was as much a part of his childhood as walking out to the top of Black Sail Pass to see his father, who he admired greatly, and a hired hand and the dogs return from gathering the sheep. Joss had a tough upbringing on a Lakeland hill farm that was comparable and probably no better or worse than that of other children brought up on the land at that time, the war years of the late 1930s and early 1940s. There are people, including Joss, who will tell you that that sort of upbringing on a hill farm bred character and characters of a type we may never see the like again once they are gone.

As with us all, his childhood experiences and how he related to his parents and them to him, and with the environment and other people around him, helped make him the man that he is today. He is a man who I have come to admire increasingly as I have got to know him better through the writing of this book and I do not simply admire him because of his ability to run the fells. I also think highly of Joss Naylor the person.

Joss has had to contend with some degree of physical pain all his days and as a consequence he has learned to live with it and overcome it in order to run hard and fast and for incredible distances over the Lakeland fells that he loves. If Joss Naylor has any demons from his childhood then, ultimately, they have come second.

Joss could not allow his back problems to interfere with his hard working life on the farm at Wasdale. Here he is pictured shearing a Herdwick at clipping time.

At the end of the day Joss has managed to live with and, to some extent, conquer his back and leg problems. At the age of 73 they certainly did not stop him standing astride a favourite boulder near Dore Head. Spy, as ever, is at his side.

THE THREE PEAKS
The clock is ticking . . . 3

Taking no prisoners, Joss tackles a fell in his usual uncompromising style in a Lakeland event.

Caernarfon Castle, overlooking the mouth of the River Seiont where it flows into the Menai Strait, is massively impressive. And it was there, six minutes before 9am on a misty morning on July 9, 1971, beneath the ramparts of the spectacular Eagle Tower, that Joss Naylor walked down the gentle incline of a slipway, making sure he didn't come to grief on the seaweed and slime left by the tide, and dipped his hand in the water to signify the completion of an epic Three Peaks adventure. It was a journey that had taken in the summits of Ben Nevis, Scafell Pike and Snowdon and all completed within 12 hours (11 hours 54 minutes to be exact) to establish a new record, one that will stand for all time.

The day Joss set out on his journey had started as usual at Bowderdale Farm, Wasdale. He was up and about at the crack of dawn, had milked the cows, fed the calves and taken the dogs for a walk - the equivalent of a day's endeavour for some - before breakfasting and bidding his farewells. He drove out of the farm entrance at 9.30am in a battered old mini van and headed out of Wasdale into Eskdale and up and over the steep bends and almost vertical descents that are the Hardknott and Wrynose passes. His destination was Ambleside where he was to meet up with Frank Davies whose idea it had been to make this latest attempt on the Three Peaks record.

As a great outdoor man and entrepreneur Frank was the charismatic owner of a well-known mountaineering shop, The Climber's Shop (also known as the corner shop) in Ambleside in the days when outdoor shops were the exception rather than the rule. Frank was, in his day, a top rock climber and a leading rally driver. The Three Peaks was already a well-established event and the previous record, of just over 12 hours, had been set by Frank when he drove and Peter Hall ran. This time round Frank was determined to get under the 12 hours.

Frank and Joss set off from Ambleside for Scotland at about 11.30am in a white Ford Capri, its engine specially adapted for speed.

"The weather on the tops wasn't too great," says Joss, who was 36 at the time and now, at 73, seems to have instant recall for the finer details of events that happened the best part of 40 years ago. "But it was still a nice day to have a look at the Lake District. To just sit back and be chauffeur driven was absolute magic."

They drove to Glasgow where the first task was for Frank to work out an exit strategy through the city once Joss had gone up and down Ben Nevis and they were looking for a high speed drive to the Lake District and Scafell Pike at dead of night. Any time lost in making their way through Glasgow on the return journey would have proved costly and wrecked the attempt on the record at the first hurdle. It was important to get it right and Frank had to stick to the inner city speed limits.

"We were trying to memorise the names of the streets and familiar landmarks," recalls Joss. "We had three dry runs through the city and I remember that there was a church on ya corner and a policeman standing theer. He gev us a queer look the third time we went past and I said to Frank 'that bugger'll be tekking our number. We better hadn't come through here again. We don't want them on our tails'."

From Glasgow the white Ford Capri headed further north for Fort William and it was about 2.30pm, near Glen Coe, when they decided to stop for a bite to eat.

"We'd had nowt and were famished," says Joss. "We cem to a lay by and there was an old caravanette with a hatch on the front. They were selling hot dogs and a cup of tea and that was about the only thing you could git. Well, it was the most vile rubbish I've ivver eaten in mi life. The hot dogs weren't hot, they were cold and they were oozing fat. And there was some honions (onions - Joss, in common with a lot of Cumbrians, always pronounces the 'h' on certain words) that had been fried in dirty old fat and they were sticking to the roof of yer mouth. You couldn't git them down. And the cup of tea . . . you would think it had been on the go for three weeks. It tasted sour. I ate a bit of the hot dog and threw the rest away and I said to Frank: 'That's disgusting. That spot wants closing down.'

"Frank nivver said anything. He just turned the car round, backed it towards the open hatch of this caravanette, put it in second gear, put his foot on the accelerator down to the floor and let the clutch out and raced away. I bet he put a barrow load of shale and muck into that hatch. Away we went and they wouldn't be able to see our number because of the cloud of dirt and dust. Frank turned to me as we raced off and said: 'That'll close them buggers down for a bit'."

The next stop en route to Fort William was Ballachulish where the bridge was not to be opened until three years later in 1975 and it was necessary to either drive round the loch or go across by ferry. Frank reckoned it was five minutes quicker by ferry. The arrangements were made via a ferry owner who was a little the worse for drink in a local bar.

"He was about pissed out of his mind," says Joss. "He had a pint in front of him and a couple of whisky chasers and was clearly having a session. When a Scot goes for a drink he goes the whole way and if he can walk out of a pub then he hasn't had a good night. Anyway we OK'd it with his lads later on just to be on the safe side. There would have been nothing worse than gettin' theer at 11 at night and no boat."

Joss did not have a good night's rest on the eve of The Three Peaks record attempt.

"At about 4.30am," he recalls, "these big Herring Gulls went on a tour of the local dustbins and they were taking the lids off . . . crash, bang, wallop! There was such a bloody scale up just as it was breakin' daylight and I couldn't git back to sleep for the bloody things."

Joss and Frank had a leisurely day in Fort William until 9pm that night when they set off for the starting point at the foot of Ben Nevis.

"Eddie Campbell came down to see us off," says Joss, "He watched as I touched the water of the high tide. He was a curly haired fella with a big white beard. We lost Eddie 15 years ago to cancer. He was a really great bloke and he always ran the Ben (he ran the Ben Nevis Race 44 times) in a pair of old galoshes."

Zero hour and the clock is ticking . . .

. . . it is just after 9pm on July 8 as Joss sets off for the foot of Ben Nevis (4,406ft).

"Eddie kicked us off and we went up through Fort William to the youth hostel at Glen Nevis and crossed the bridge," says Joss. "The mist was down to 500 feet and it was pouring with rain. Frank said I did the first 500 in a minute before I disappeared into the mist. It was a job just holding your concentration, especially when you went up the main path to the half way house. I set off to run the paths but the first three or four zigzags seemed to tek you out a long way. There was a wire that cem down the Red Burn and that took you to the skyline so I put mi hands on mi knees and went straight up. It was a filthy night. When I got to the top there were two lads from Nevis Sports who timed us in. I got up in just under the hour (time of departure from the summit is 10.05am).

"My concentration had to be good comin' down because things were really snotty wid the rain aw day. But I had a good run down in 25 minutes. Frank was waiting at the bottom with the engine ticking."

1 hour 36 minutes in and the clock is ticking . . .

. . . it is 10.36pm as Joss and Frank drive south from the YHA at Fort William for Scafell Pike (3,206ft).

Joss takes up the story: "I jumped in the car and had a drink of orange squash. I had put a salt tablet in the drink some time earlier just to keep the cramp away. Unfortunately the salt tablet had killed the citric acid in the squash and it was rotten. I had two or three mouthfuls before I realised it had gone off. I didn't eat anything until 2 o'clock the next day. We got the ferry at about 11pm (the ferry takes about 10 minutes) and then raced through Glen Coe. We had a good trip through Glasgow (00.35). The route was still in our minds and with Frank being a rally driver he could 'vision' the streets. He was concentrating really hard and we went through Glasgow no problem.

"On the more open road beyond that the weather was absolutely storming. I know that at one point we were doing 120mph. We passed this wagon and you could feel the car wanting to stray a bit and I said to Frank: 'There's some power isn't getting to the back wheels.' And he lost his rag. He said: 'If it was a bloody racing driver you wanted you should have got one!' I was only pulling his leg, but he was so bloody tied up with what he was doing. Anyway, I thought I had better keep mi mouth shut after that. But it's surprising when somebody's driving at those sort of speeds the amount of energy they are burning off. And it was difficult conditions." They reach Carlisle at 02.00.

Five hours 45 minutes in and the clock is ticking . . .

. . . it is 2.45am on July 9 as Joss gets out of the car at Seathwaite, Borrowdale. He kick starts his car-weary body into action and sets off up Grains Gill, soon getting into that familiar loping style of run.

"There had been violent thunder storms in the Lakes and it was absolutely bloody roasting in Grains Gill," says Joss. "It was just like running in a hot house with the humidity from the storms. It was so bloody hot the sweat was running down mi legs. Once I got out of the gill and onto Esk Hause, Broad Crag, Ill Crag and up on to Scafell Pike it wasn't so bad. I got over the top of the pike (he reached the summit in an hour at 3.45am) and there was Mike Walford, Alan Evans and Tommy Orr. I didn't learn 'til 20 years later that Alan Evans and Mike Walford were gonna run back to Langdale wid us, but Mike was in his sleeping bag on the pike and by the time he got out they couldn't catch us. I'd gone and they'd lost us. I had a cracking run back to Langdale (the descent took 55 minutes, arriving at 4.40am). I was legging on, going really well.

"The only mistake I med was on the stretch of grass from the top of Esk Hause to Angle Tarn. The light wasn't so good and I was more on the top side of the tarn than the path side so I had mebbe a couple of hundred metres to clip back to get onto the path. But ah divvent think ah lost any time. And then I went down Rossett Gill, back down to Old Dungeon Ghyll and Frank was waiting for us."

Why, I wonder, did Joss decide on the Grains Gill approach to Scafell Pike? Would it have been any quicker to have gone by Styhead?

"It's difficult to say," replies Joss. "Twenty one years later I did The Three Peaks again (for Save The Children) and this time I went up by Styhead, the stretcher box and the Corridor Route. I went straight up the crag face and came out at the cairn and again it took exactly an hour. That was 21 years after, but it was a beautiful day and it wasn't so hot."

I appreciate it's stating the obvious . . . but when you consider that Joss was 57 at the time of his second Three Peaks run and that he still got to the top of Scafell Pike in an hour, I find it amazing that he places such emphasis on the weather conditions.

Joss Naylor accepts a drink from Alan Evans on the summit of Scafell Pike during his successful attempt on the Three Peaks record in July 1971. "There had been violent thunder storms in the Lakes and it was absolutely bloody roasting in Grains Gill," Joss said. "It was just like running in a hot house with the humidity from the storms. It was so bloody hot the sweat was running down mi legs." Photograph: Tommy Orr.

Although he did confess at a subsequent interview: "We had had a good run for an old man."

I am also curious to know how Joss has been fuelling himself at this stage in the 1971 version of The Three Peaks. After all, he has been on the go since 9pm the previous night, it is now in the small hours of the following morning and it is some time since he did his damnedest to poison himself after coming off Ben Nevis by gulping down salt tablets diluted in orange juice.

"I had eaten in Fort William before we set off," replied Joss. "During the run – apart from that gulp of orange juice – I had a drop off Alan Evans on the top of the Pike and got that down. But I nivver used to drink much in them days when ah was running. I'd mebbe have an odd mouthful of watter. Not like folk today. They've got to drink two bloody gallon ivvery 20 miles sort of thing. It's like filling their car up wid some on 'em. I don't know whether it's a good or a bad thing, it's just what your body gets used wid I suppose."

Seven hours 40 minutes in and the clock is ticking . . .

. . . it is 4.40am as Joss and Frank drive out of Langdale for Wales and Snowdon.

"They were doing quite a lot of work on the old M6," says Joss. 'We went down through Liverpool. With all the rallying Frank had done in Wales he knew the route and it didn't seem all that long until we were in Wales. There were no hold ups or anything. But as we went through Betws-y-coed we got into a real thick mist. It was clagged right down and we just couldn't believe it. I was going to go up the old pit track, which would have been faster, but I said to Frank: 'Put us on the bloody railway track and I won't get lost.' So we went down to Llanberis (7.30am) and up to the railway line which put a bit extra on." It has taken Frank and Joss 3hrs 10 minutes to get from Langdale to the foot of Snowdon.

Ten hours 30 minutes in and the clock is ticking . . .

. . . it is 7.30am when Joss sets off up Snowdon (3,560ft):

"Frank let us off and I went across this field onto the line. The mist was really bloody thick. You couldn't see a thing. I took mi top off and tied it to the wire (so Joss would know where exactly to come off on the return journey). I had a cramp in ya leg, but it was just with sitting in the car and I soon got shot of that. I got a rhythm going and I was fair knocking the sleepers off.

"I was running well and med good time. When I left the line I had only gone about 10 foot when I cem out of the mist and into sunshine. All 14 of the 3,000 footers were in a sea of white mist. You couldn't believe it. You would have thought that you could have jumped in and swam to them. It was a creamy-white mist with brilliant sunshine on it and there wasn't a cloud above. It was absolute magic.

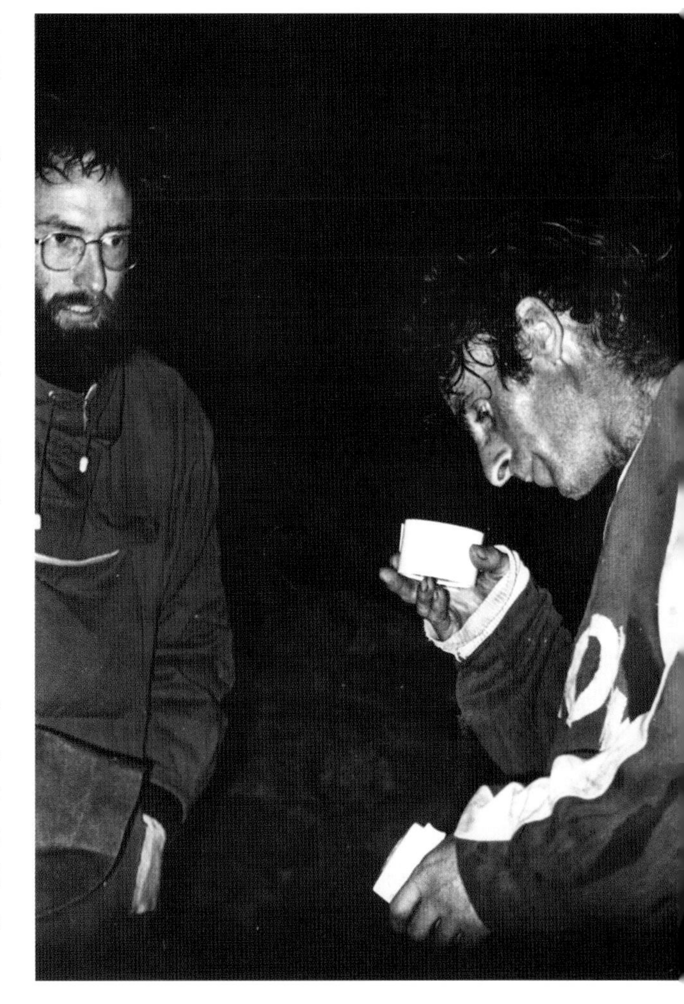

"Eddie Hammond was on the summit to time us in (time of arrival on the summit 8.14am) and he said he could pick up the roar of the car at Betws-y-coed. He could hear it all the way over the mountain pass and down through Llanberis. Anyway, he signed mi card and I dropped in and had a good run down the railway, across the field and Frank was there sitting in the car, engine ready for the off."

Joss had, to use his own phraseology, 'legged it' up and down Snowdon in 1hr 5 mins (44 minutes for the ascent and 21 minutes on the descent).

11 hours six minutes in and the clock is ticking . . .

. . . it is 8.35am when Joss and Frank set off from Llanberis for their final destination, the water's edge at Caernarfon Castle. They have 25 minutes in which to beat the previous record for The Three Peaks. Joss takes up the story once again: "I got in the car and Frank says 'great, we've got everything in hand now. The kids are going to school so we're just going to take it easy from here'."

11 hours 54 minutes in and the clock is ticking . . .

. . .it is 8.54am and there are six minutes to spare as Joss walks down the slipway beneath Caernarfon Castle's awesome Eagle Tower and touches the water to signify the completion of his successful attempt on the Three Peaks record. The distance covered is 474 miles with a driving time of 7hrs 24 minutes and a running time of 4hrs 30 minutes.

"We could have tekken another five or six minutes off that time if we had pushed it going into Caernarfon, but Frank said he wasn't going to take any risks," says Joss, who adds that his record set in 1972 can never be beaten, simply because the geographical situation has changed so significantly.

"They can't reconstruct that route," says Joss. "For starters there's a bridge at Ballachulish and even if someone got a boat the road structures all the way have altered significantly. The roads are faster. Something is only a record when it is achieved over a certain route. That particular route can never be done again – it's been altered so much that any attempt can no longer be authentic in comparison with my original record. The fell times have never been beaten. There's a few lads had a go at the fell times and they've never been beaten."

In the immediate aftermath of his Three Peaks epic Joss was clearly feeling generous because there was an AA man parked near the castle and after he made Frank and Joss a cup of tea, Joss joined the AA.

"I must have bloody weakened," he laughs.

The pair then had to make their way back to the foot of Snowdon because a television crew wanted to film Joss running off the mountain for a special news bulletin to go out that night. No rest for the wicked. This was to prove to be the beginning of another epic return journey to Wasdale for Joss, one with very little sleep; but more on that later. They then went to a friend of Frank's in Bangor and had 'breakfast' at about 2 in the afternoon.

"I'd had nowt to eat aw bloody day," says Joss. "I went upstairs and had a bath and freshened missell up and I got on the bathroom scales and I was 8st 2lbs – I'd dropped about 12lbs," and this for a man who has always hovered at 9st wet through for his entire adult life. That evening they had a beer in Bangor and watched the news bulletin on TV. Then it was back in the car for the return journey.

The Ford Capri was dropped off in Manchester on the way up north and Joss and Frank were given a lift from there to Cumbria.

"We were in a little Hillman Imp," Joss recalls. "Frank got in the back and was soon snoring his head off. He slept all the way to Ambleside. I was sitting in the front in this bloody laal Imp and mi knees were bloody near up under mi chin. It was the weariest bloody journey I've ivver put in in mi entire life. We got back to Ambleside and it was about half past three, four o'clock in the morning (on July 10). I got in mi mini van and drove yam, but by the time I got theer it wasn't worth garn to bed."

Joss had arranged to help out with an attempt on the Bob Graham round that day.

"So I fetched the cows in and milked them, grabbed a bit of breakfast and Joe Long picked us up at half past seven," says Joss. George Rhodes and Donald Talbot were on the Bob Graham and Joss was to meet them at the top of Honister at 11. His task was to pace the runners on the stretch between Honister and Wasdale Head. Despite what he had just been through, Joss fully intended to honour his obligation to the runners. Talbot had a bad patch, but Joss stayed with him while Rhodes went on ahead. When Joss and Talbot got to Wasdale Head there were no other pacemakers.

"So I had to go on with them," adds Joss, "and when we were going up Steel Fell the bloody moon cem up. So that was three nights that I'd had no bed, no sleep nor nowt."

Joss concluded his Bob Graham Round support effort at Dunmail Raise and succeeded in getting a lift back to Seathwaite – a place, you will appreciate, with which he was already very familiar having only recently been there as part of The Three Peaks! So we find our hero at Seathwaite, endeavouring to make his own way back to Wasdale Head over the fells. Let's pause for a while, get our breath back and recap in order to fully appreciate the magnitude of Joss's run.

Joe Long pictured in celebratory mood. Joe picked Joss up at Bowderdale at 7.30am on his return from the Three Peaks event so that he (Joss) could support two runners on the Bob Graham round. No rest for the wicked. Photograph: Tommy Orr.

Here goes:

It's the middle of the night yet again. You've just run up and down the three highest mountains in Scotland, England and Wales in record time and in under 12 hours. You've had little or no sleep for three nights and on finally reaching home after a journey that would have tested the resolve of a saint and the endurance of a metronome, you've done some farm work and then immediately set off on the Bob Graham Round to help out some other runners in their hour of need.

For the record, you actually left Wasdale to begin your Three Peaks epic at 9.30am on July 7 and it is now late on July 10 and you still haven't really got yam; well, you've got yam once, but not to your bed. Now, at long last, you are finally heading for home for the third time in the last 24 hours (the second time was on the Bob Graham) with a view to getting some sleep, or not as the case may be?

But the story doesn't quite end there. Oh no. That would be far too simple for the formidable Joss Naylor as he stands at Seathwaite in the dead of night. Anyone else would have given up the ghost long ago, lost the will to live, been in dire need of hospital treatment, approaching a state of delirium while looking over your shoulder for men in white coats, suffering from recurring nightmares or, at the very least, experiencing a fleeting Seathwaite déjà vu moment.

Not our Joss.

"You do them things and you don't think owt about it," he says, a remark I have heard him make more than once in response to questions about his achievements on the fell. Meanwhile, back at Seathwaite: "I thowt I'll not go up the farmyard because it'll mek the dogs bark," Joss continues. "There's a laal cut through the buildings

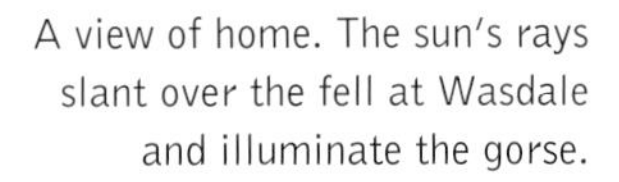

A view of home. The sun's rays slant over the fell at Wasdale and illuminate the gorse.

that fetches you out on the bridge that teks you up the backside to Taylor Gill so I thowt I'd nip up theer. In them days Joe Edmondson (who farmed at Seathwaite) had about 500 Aylesbury ducks in this laal paddock and I was sneaking through when a bloody fox jumped the wall and went amang 'em. The ducks all flew into a corner and squawked together. The hecko (echo) went right round Borrowdale. What a bloody din! I didn't half leg it – I thowt some bugger'll be out here and give me a barrel.

"So anyway I legged it up Taylor Gill and over Styhead to Wasdale. And it was strange going up towards the tarn. There were strands of mist hanging about through Great End and Great End itself looked like the bloody Matterhorn. It looked enormous and the moon was shining over it. It was some kind of optical illusion and it was the same with Gable, but it didn't look as impressive as Great End. Anyway I legged down Styhead and the road and I was just ready for being yam."

I feel exhausted just at the thought of it all. And that clock is still ticking . . .

Schedule for Three Peaks: 8 – 9 July 1971.

Fort William (Sea Level)	~~21.30~~ 21.00	21.00	21.05 YHA.
Ben Nevis (Summit)	~~22.30~~ 22.00	22.05.	
Fort William (Y.H.A. Glen Nevis)	23.00 22.30	22.36	
Glasgow	01.00 00.30	00.55	
Carlisle	02.30 02.00	02.00	
Seathwaite	03.15 02.45. 249 miles	02.45	249 miles
Scafell (Summit)	04.15 03.45	03.45.	
Gt. Langdale	05.05 04.35.	04.40.	
Kendal	05.25 04.55	05.05.	
Queensferry	06.50. 06.20	06.30.	
Llanberis	08.00. 07.30	07.30.	
Snowdon (Summit)	08.45 08.15.	08.14.	
Llanberis	09.15 08.45.	08.35.	
Caernarvon	09.29 08.59 (11.59)	08.54.	474 miles
	~~9.56~~ Max. 09.26 MAX		

Average speed 64.05.

	H mins
Driving time	7.24
Running time	4.30
	11.54

BEN NEVIS:

Time of Arrival: 22.05.

Signature: [signature]

Date 8.7.71.

Fort William:

Time of departure:- 21.00

Signature:- [signature]

SCAFELL PIKE:

Time of Arrival: 03.45

Signature: [signature]

Date: 9.7.71.

SNOWDON:

Time of Arrival: 8.14 a.m.

Signature: [signature]

Date: 9.7.71.

Caernarvon.

Time of arrival:- 8.54 am

Signature:- [signature]

9.7.7.

The actual signed records of Joss Naylor's epic 1971 Three Peaks run with the overall schedule and the dates and times of his arrival on the summits of Ben Nevis, Scafell Pike and Snowdon.

Joss Naylor's route for the 27 Lakes, Meres and Waters.
1983: Circuit of 105 miles in 19hrs 20 mins 14 secs.

LAKES, MERES AND WATERS 4
'A master of the understatement'

Of all the runs in which Joss Naylor has taken part, the numerous mountain trials, the Bob Grahams, 72 peaks in under 24 hours, his forays into foreign lands and his other spectacular endurance epics in the Lake District, running the Wainwrights and 70 summits at 70 and all the rest, he will struggle to tell you which single run was the most rewarding. That is possibly because he tends to enjoy them all to varying degrees but he can, when pushed, get it down to two. These are the Three Peaks in 1971 (as detailed in the previous chapter) and his assault on the lakes, meres and waters of the Lake District in the early 1980s.

Put him further on the spot and ask him which of those two gave him the most satisfaction and he replies: "It's very difficult to say because that time we did the Three Peaks was so unique . . . but the day we did the lakes, meres and waters it was something else."

It certainly was.

For starters it involved running for more than 100 miles, visiting 27 assorted stretches of water at far-flung as well as central areas of the Lake District and it was all achieved in a staggering 19 hours 20 minutes and 14 seconds. The run was in aid of the Mayfield Special School, Whitehaven, for the mentally and physically handicapped and it is typical of Joss that his only thought – apart, clearly, from wanting to achieve his objective – was to raise money for good causes and those less well off than himself.

The previous best time for the run, by Alan Heaton, was 26 and a half hours.

Joss's preparation for the event was thorough. He was always a great believer in being properly prepared and ensuring that everything was in place, the exact route, fuelling stations and the change over of pacemakers. The lakes, meres and waters was no exception and he embarked on a training run, in two sections over two days. It took him a combined total of 19 and a half hours and he was pleased to realise that he could complete the run more or less in daylight. In describing these runs Joss employs an interesting choice of words that make it seem as though distance, ascent and descent are mere hops, steps and jumps. For example: "I nipped ower

An illustration showing the route of Joss Naylor's Lakes, Meres and Waters run in 1983. Joss ran 105 miles and covered the 27 assorted stretches of water in 19 hours 20 minutes and 14 seconds.
Illustration by Walker Ellis Photography and Design.

the top of Red Bank and dropped into Grasmere and back to Rydal and down to Windermere . . ."

Ken Ledward and Dave Elliott were immensely helpful with the dummy run that soon identified the later stages of the run (Keswick – Bassenthwaite – Over Water) as a real ball breaker and not simply because Joss would be feeling exhausted at this stage after running for more than 100 miles.

Joss studies the contents of a bottle while Fred Rogerson is highly amused during an event in Lakeland. Fred, while a great admirer of Joss Naylor and his achievements, reckoned that Joss's projected time for the Lakes, Meres and Waters, was optimistic, to say the least.

"This was the most worrying part of the route because it involved running on the road," Joss explains. "There were no kerbs and you were very exposed to the traffic."

As a result of his training run Joss was convinced that he could do it for real in less than 19 and a half hours.

"I thought I had better let Fred Rogerson know because he had done the groundwork for Alan Heaton," Joss adds. "Fred asked me 'how long's it gonna take?' I said 19 and a half hours and Fred said: 'There's some bloody hope of that' or words to that effect."

Fred, incidentally, has the highest regard for Joss Naylor and his achievements and says it was a privilege to be involved in the organisation of fell running events.

"The camaraderie was second to none," he said. "It wasn't monetary, it was purely mind over matter and very personal and that's the way it should remain."

On the morning of the actual run everything was ready with no stone left unturned in the planning. Dave Elliott and Phil Coulton had ensured that support runners were in the right place at the right time.

"Dave Elliott took us to the start at Loweswater," recalls Joss, "and we kicked off there at five o'clock in the morning. It was a beautiful morning, some sunshine and bits of cloud here and there. I had a cracking run from Loweswater to Crummock and then up the back of Crummock to Buttermere. In Ennerdale I was just coming away from the lake when John Wild picked us up and he ran through to Wastwater wid us and another three or four lads joined in and ran to Devoke Water wid us. . ."

Overleaf: Wastwater and Joss's favourite view of the lake.

At this point in writing *Joss*, I reached for an inch to a mile Ordnance Survey map of the Lake District to follow with a line in blue ink the entire route of Joss's Lakes, Meres and Waters run. As I traced the route from its beginning at Loweswater to its conclusion at Over Water I could only shake my head in disbelief at the enormity of the task. This surely was beyond the pale and I can fully appreciate Fred Rogerson's immediate gut reaction to Joss's projected time.

I would go a lot further and suggest that to attempt such a feat, never mind in less than 20 hours, is tantamount to a death wish. The mind might be willing, but surely the body cannot prevail over such a distance, with so much ascent and descent? It is too much and does not bear thinking about. But then I'm a mere mortal and there are runners out there who think nothing of ticking off the miles over and beyond the 100-mile mark. Personally I don't think they are for real. They must be aliens from another solar system who have been sent to earth to conduct a series of endurance tests designed to gauge the quality of the atmosphere and the air we earthlings breathe.

The route takes in Loweswater, Crummock, Buttermere, Ennerdale, Wastwater, Devoke Water, Goat's Water, Low Water, Lever's Water, Coniston, Esthwaite Water, Elterwater, Grasmere, Rydal Water, Windermere, Skeggles Water, Kentmere, Blea Water, Small Water, Haweswater, Hayeswater, Brothers Water, Ullswater, Thirlmere, Derwentwater, Bassenthwaite Lake and, finally, Over Water.

Generally it was a smooth run in good conditions that Joss, for the most part, enjoyed. But there were one or two problems to overcome along the way. En route to Goat's Water there was some difficult bog land to negotiate near Crosbythwaite.

"Big bogs with no bottom to them," says Joss, "and you've got to get it right to get across them safe." Dropping into Wallowbarrow the intakes proved something of a problem and the bracken was high. But a dog that had come along for the ride with one of the pacemakers gave greater cause for concern.

"There was a fella wid us cawd Richard Eastman and he had this boxer dog," recalls Joss. "Well, it was runnin' three feet in front of yer aw the time and it was a bloody nightmare because you couldn't see where you were putting your feet. The only thing you could see was this dog's tail and its arsehole lookin' at yer aw the time.

Anyway we dropped in at Wallowbarrow and went up the footpath along the beck edge (River Duddon) and crossed over at Turner Hall. We went through the fields there and there's a stile you go over to pick up the Walna Scar track. There was a hornets' nest on this stile and this bloody great dog had gone ovver just in front of us and it sort of half slipped garn ovver and disturbed them and these bloody things cem at yer. There wus only yan stung us, but you thowt they were still chessing yer and they were buzzing in your clothing. You don't want to be stung by them damned things."

Tony Jewell joined Joss at Lever's Water and he (Tony) "didn't half leg it down that path into Coniston." The hornets safely behind him Joss ran into a dead end cul-de-sac in the heart of Coniston, but eventually made his way to the lake where they had time to relax and enjoy an ice cream.

Moving on towards Grizedale and Hawkshead there was a confrontation with a pair of householders who had apparently tried to divert a footpath.

"In the finish I lost mi head with them and gev them the bloody round up," says Joss.

Joss somehow also lost his ongoing support team at Windermere for a while before heading out to Kentmere.

"It was really beautiful at the reservoir there," he adds. "I laid down for about 10 minutes just to tek it all in. You're looking up at Ill Bell and the sun is shining in. I was on this green-cropped part of the dam and it was just like lying on a good bed. I thowt I was in heaven and I had to give missell a shek and git on wid it. I jumped up and went ovver the top to Blea Watter and Small Watter."

Haweswater, Hayeswater and Brothers Water followed. Brothers Water was previously called Broad Water, but the name was changed following the tragic drowning of two brothers.

"Just as we got to Brothers Water," says Joss, "a chap cem out of a cottage and said 'I've got a bath full of water for you, come on – get in it.' So I just stripped off, nipped upstairs, jumped in and had a good bath. It freshened us up no end."

From Ullswater the runners climbed out and over Sticks Pass to Thirlmere and from there to Keswick on Derwentwater. They stopped just outside The Theatre by the Lake (it was the Old Blue Box on the car park in those days) and Joss "had a laal cup o' tea and loosened mi legs off."

And then it was out on the road to Bassenthwaite and what proved to be the most demanding part of the entire run.

"The day was just starting to deteriorate," says Joss. "The mist was coming down and there was a hint that it was gonna drizzle. We had had a fantastic day until then. A little bit of drizzle doesn't do any harm though, it freshens you up."

The terrain was not so runner-friendly at this stage. The light was fading and the field leading down to Bassenthwaite Lake was muddy and heavily rutted by cattle.

"I had a team of three lads running wid us, one had a flashlight showing the best route and another always had a gate open. I touched Bass Lake and cem back up the field and from there it was bloody purgatory," says Joss. "There's nothing worse when you've run over 100 mile than to be running on bloody stones."

The road had been resurfaced about a fortnight before and all the loose chippings were towards the edge where Joss and his team had to run to avoid the traffic. It did not get any easier when they turned off the main road and headed uphill towards Over Water.

"It's a mile or two up there and there's a lot more elevation than you are aware of. It's all switchbacks," Joss continues. "But the end of the journey was almost in sight and I was determined to keep going and to keep running. When you're doing something like that you've got to keep it in your mind that you're gonna run it all the way. The body's got to have that little bit of toughness in it. When you run 100 mile there's always a patch you go through when it won't be very pleasant and that's got to go out of the window otherwise you won't bloody do it.

"More and more people are running longer distances like the Bob Graham now and have gone through that stage – I know it's only 70 mile (the Bob Graham round) but it's given them a foundation to build on.

"If you've got 100 mile or so in and you start walking you've a hell of a job to git running again. Your legs seem as though they want a different stride on them and it's very difficult to put your head down and say 'right, I'm gonna run' after you've been walking. But it's strange. I've run through 100 miles a lot of times and it depends if

Bassenthwaite. The section of the Lakes, Meres and Waters run from Keswick to Bassenthwaite Lake and then to Over Water, proved the most arduous – not only because it was the last leg but also because it was almost entirely on the roads.

you are running correctly, letting your feet drop and keeping the tension out of your legs. Your legs mebbe don't tek as much harm as people think they do."

Joss reckons that the way in which you descend is equally important on a long run.

"When you are coming downhill and you are doing a lot of distance you've got to run with your knees slightly bent," he says. "This keeps the jarring out of your body. If you are running poker-legged when you are coming downhill and especially if you are descending at speed, it's bound to take its toll. It's putting a lot of tension through your body and it tells later in the day."

I suggest to Joss that for most people the thought of running a marathon is bad enough let alone the equivalent of joining four (yes four!) marathons together, without any respite, which is effectively what he did for the Lakes, Meres and Waters run.

"Aye, that's right," says Joss. "It's a different ball game. But it's strange, distance doesn't come into your mind when you are doing these long runs. You are looking ahead, tekking things in and when we did that run that day a lot of the sights were absolutely magic."

Absolute magic, just in case you hadn't guessed it, is one of Joss's favourite sayings.

"It was beautiful to start with," he continues. "You go into areas you know and you've worked in. I've gathered sheep in Ennerdale since I was a small kid and it was just like coming home. And then you go away from it and you see areas you would never go into unless you had been on this run. It's marvellous to be able to do this. You mebbe don't appreciate it at the time and it's only when you sit down afterwards and reflect and go through it all that you think 'how the hell did I do that then?'

"I did 134 miles once on the track at Crystal Palace and mi bloody knee went a

fortnight before. I was floating along and distance didn't come into it. And I'm sure that if mi knee that been right I would have run 170 mile that day on the track."

But let's get back to Over Water where Joss is nearly at the end of his epic Lakes, Meres and Waters run.

Joss was working at British Nuclear Fuels Sellafield – as well as farming at Bowderdale – when he completed the Lakes, Meres and Waters and many of the runners who helped him were also employed in the nuclear industry.

"As I ran down to Over Water all the apprentices were standing down the field with torches shining to light the way. It was just a long line of lights. We sprinted down there and touched the water . . . It took 19 hours 20 minutes and 14 seconds. Nobody's

Wasdale Heed Athletic Club's one and only member. Cartoon by Trevor Green.

Looking out over Wasdale through low cloud from the Corridor Route ivver got near that and I don't think anybody ivver will."

And how did he feel after running for that length of time and touching the water at all 27 lakes, meres and waters in the Lake District and running more than 100 miles up hill and down dale?

"I didn't feel too bad really," he replies. "Aye, you know, just ready for relaxing more than owt else."

As ever, Joss Naylor is a master of the understatement.

THE RUNNERS
'The Greatest of Them All'

The book cover shot. Joss is photographed by the late Brian Duff in 1973 as he leaps across the rocky outcrops on the shores of Wastwater with Great Gable in the background.

Joss looks pooped. Either that or he is working his way through a mouthful of rock bun, with cherries.

All fell runners share a common bond, united by whatever it is that possesses them to head for the hills and put themselves through agony, risk of injury and, in extreme cases, the possibility of death in order to pursue their love / hate relationship with fell running.

But what is it that drives them on? It can't always be the prospect of winning a race. For example, some of the contestants you see grinding their way up Skiddaw in the annual event on that formidable, purple heather-covered mountain and the unremitting climb that is Jenkin Hill – now a snake-like, hard-packed and unforgiving 'motorway' after a JCB was let loose on the old eroded path - haven't a hope in hell of actually winning the race or even an age category.

But it doesn't stop them from taking part. For the youngster brought up on a Lakeland hill farm running up and down fells and taking part in the guides race at the local show is a tradition, but it's not compulsory. There is Cumberland and Westmorland wrestling and a variety of other sporting pursuits which, while undoubtedly hard, are unlikely to be quite as demanding as the pain that comes with attempting to climb a steep fell as fast as you can and then hurtling down it at breakneck speed. The use of the word breakneck is particularly appropriate here.

And if your objective is to train and to stay fit there are easier, less destructive ways than running up and down hills. A love of the Lake District and its scenery doesn't necessarily wash with me either; it is always more appreciated, I would have thought, in a state of relative calm and not with your body aching, your lungs fit to burst and your heart attempting to thump its way out of your rib cage.

So it must all come down to a sense of personal fulfilment, of competition, achievement and the strong camaraderie among the fell running fraternity. Either that or there are inner demons to burn.

For the long distance fell runner – as opposed to the short, brutal race that is Grasmere - there can, apparently, be a time on the run when something else takes over, when pain and fatigue, while not entirely dismissed, are put to the back of the mind and the runner feels on a high, elated at their physical and mental ability. They enter what might be termed 'the zone' and they fly like the wind over the tops.

That there is a special bond and mutual respect between runners, as well as intense but friendly competition, is undeniable. Whether you are running against the clock, trying to set a new personal best, striving to get one over on an opponent, are the first or the last over the line, there is admiration and empathy from your fellow runners. Joss Naylor is certainly one who takes as much, if not more, interest in what might be termed, perhaps unfairly, the 'lesser' runners as those who are blazing a trail and setting new standards. Joss says there is a bond among fell runners that simply does not exist in any other sport.

Some runners have attained god-like status among the running fraternity and Joss Naylor is up there with the best and arguably at the summit. He is The Man. And his appeal stretches beyond the band of runners. Anyone with a love of the great outdoors, and specifically the English Lake District, will most certainly know or know of Joss Naylor and hold him in high esteem. The name Joss Naylor is recognised by a much wider circle and the brevity and succinctness of the name perhaps adds to the appeal. It is not unlike those words in the Cumbrian dialect that convey their meaning without need for explanation. My favourite word is lish, meaning fit, supple, active or athletic. The name Joss Naylor, were it descriptive, would mean down to earth, hard, determined and uncompromising; for want of a nail.

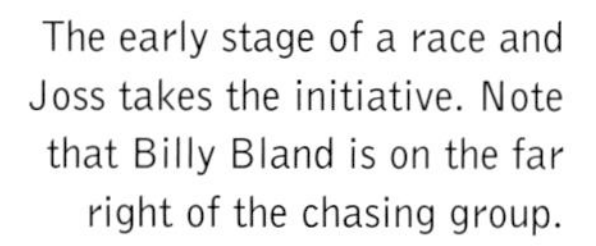

The early stage of a race and Joss takes the initiative. Note that Billy Bland is on the far right of the chasing group.

In the autumn of his life it is almost as though Joss has been elevated to the status of some kind of guru of the high fells, a sage without a beard, but with whiskers aplenty who, if given the opportunity, would wave his hazel walking stick and right the wrongs, very real or imagined, that affect the Lake District today and also bring his influence to bear on such universal issues as environmental pollution, climate change and the balance of nature and how it impacts on wildlife.

As much as he hates the newspaper headlines 'King of the Fells' and 'Iron Joss' and despite his fierce independence, I sense that Joss thrives on the publicity and – without gloating about it –the recognition it brings. And so I turned to some of the runners who know Joss personally with a view to flushing out further views, observations and information on the lad himself.

My first call was to a terraced house in Threlkeld and Kenny Stuart, still relatively wafer-thin in his fifties, a gardener by profession and a former GB marathon runner and, before that, an exceptional fell runner whose burgeoning career – as he approached what should have been the height of his powers - was brought to a sad end by a recurring mystery illness that sapped his energy and left him totally lethargic. Medical tests were inconclusive, but the problem appears to have been related to his immune system and sounds very much as though he had, quite simply, burned himself out through excessive training and his body and mind were telling him so in the only way they could – by failing to co-operate and switching off at the mains.

Although there is a significant age difference between Joss and Kenny, the two have an empathy with each other that is based on a mutual understanding of their individual determination to succeed against the odds.

"Whenever I have met Joss he has always been a very likeable sort of person and there is a lilt to his conversation that makes you want to listen to him," Kenny says. "He is a very sensible chap, knowledgeable and as interested in local life as he is in running itself. Another thing that strikes me is that he seems as interested in the poorer runners as he is in the top runners; he'll always give everyone a cheer on. He's a very sociable fella, likes a crack with folks and is very sincere in what he believes and what he says. I couldn't find a bad word about him.

"He appeals to me because he's a local fella, a shepherd and a countryman. And it's everything that I've wanted to be in my lifetime. He's an ambassador for a lot of things, life in general . . . he's got a good outlook on life. He's very humble and he doesn't look for gratification. In short he's a decent character. He's a raconteur, a storyteller and it's all part of his character. Comin' frae Wasdale there's a hell of a lot of history of that sort of thing. After his day, when these fellas go, there won't be that type of bloke ever again. You won't ever get people like that. You won't get kids being brought up as tough and as hard. I think that's why we're lacking in sportsmen in this country at the moment. They're mollycoddled today."

Kenny makes an interesting observation about one event in his own childhood that has stayed with him and is perhaps indicative of a sense of determination. Apart from that I think it's a damn good story and one worth the telling even if it is marginally out of context in this biography of Joss.

"There was a set of wooden gates garn into where mi Uncle Sid lived," he recalls. "They had a slate step and out of this step there would grow a single poppy, a laal yellow thing. Garn to school of a morning, me and Kevin Booth, we would git to within 20 yards of that bloody poppy and we each wanted to pick it for Mrs Moore, the schoolteacher. We were mebbe seven or eight year old and we would run as fast as we could to be the fust to git to that yellow poppy. Nine times out of ten we squashed it in our hands and then we would start to fight on the bloody road. And this happened ivvery morning that yellow poppy grew. And I look back and I think about

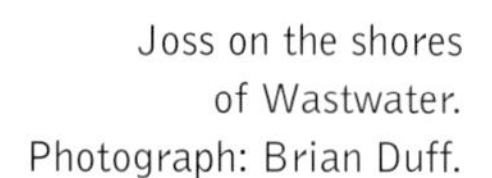
Joss on the shores of Wastwater. Photograph: Brian Duff.

that . . . we used to always look for it, daft things like that. I don't think kids would ivver engage with that sort of thing nowadays."

The same Threlkeld kids were dab hands at tickling trout.

"We'd practice catching this bar of soap in the bath. Every little beck we could get on we would tickle trout, we were experts in our field. Kenny Hebson at Guardhouse was one of the best I've ever seen. He could tickle trout up Guardhouse Beck and another fella who lived at Scales, John Wilson's brother, 'Twiddler' Wilson, he was good at it anaw."

Threlkeld was also renowned for its nicknames:

"Mi grandfather was laal Gi'. He was my height, but he was broad and very strong so he wasn't a big giant, he was a little giant and he was known as Laal Gi'. Apparently he used to give demonstrations at bait time working at the quarry, lifting things on chains with his teeth."

Kenny and I realise, entertaining and informative though it is, and indicative of a different time and a way of life that has closer links to Joss Naylor's childhood than those experienced by the children of today, that we are getting a bit off the beaten track and so we return to the subject of Joss and fell running.

"I did run against him in some races," Kenny continues, "particularly long races in the latter stages of his career. But you couldn't actually say we raced against each other because I was in my prime and he was past his racing best, although he went on at a greater age to do other extraordinary things. As a runner he never seemed to come into his own until he had gone about two and a half hours.

"His back's very straight and I'm sure he had a hell of a lot of trouble with it and it's amazing that he was able to run at all when you look back. He's obviously developed an economical running style and he's very distinctive in the way he runs. Mebbe that's why he didn't go into marathon running – he might not get warmed up until after the 26-mile mark. If it was a double marathon he'd mebbe come into his own in the second half!

"Every runner's just as good as the era and the time he ran in. The long distance running lent itself to the lifestyle he led in so much as he was mebbe lambing for so many weeks and hay timing and then he had to jam his training in. So he just started to do long runs, one after the other. A normal mortal, any runner, could never ever have done anything like that. I could never have a lay off for two or three weeks and then start banging out four and five hour runs on the fells. It would have killed most people. He must have had a hell of a lot of stamina and his constitution must have been like leather. Tremendous. He'd wall for a day and then he'd go for four hours up the fell. Sometimes he didn't know hissell where he was garn and he'd just set off and run. And if he felt like doing another two hours he'd do it. It's absolutely amazing what Joss did because he almost led two lives. The life of a shepherd which is 24 hours and the life of a top class athlete. It teks doing."

If he had been running at his peak now, in the early years of the 21st Century, what could he have achieved?

"He'd have been up there," replies Kenny. "If he had had a slightly different lifestyle, an opportunity to rest as a lot of athletes do nowadays it would have given him the opportunity to train differently and a little bit harder. And I don't see any reason why he couldn't have been absolutely at the top. There's no reason why he couldn't have been a tremendous, world-class athlete.

"He's got that inherent toughness, just like the Billy Teasdales of this world. Some of his long distance epics (like the Lakes, Meres and Waters or the Wainwrights) were done with very little scientific or technical back up. He just went out and he ran every day as long as he could and as hard as he could. He was virtually unbeatable and unstoppable. One of the great qualities he had was that even when he was having a bad time he'd still bray on. Tremendous stubbornness."

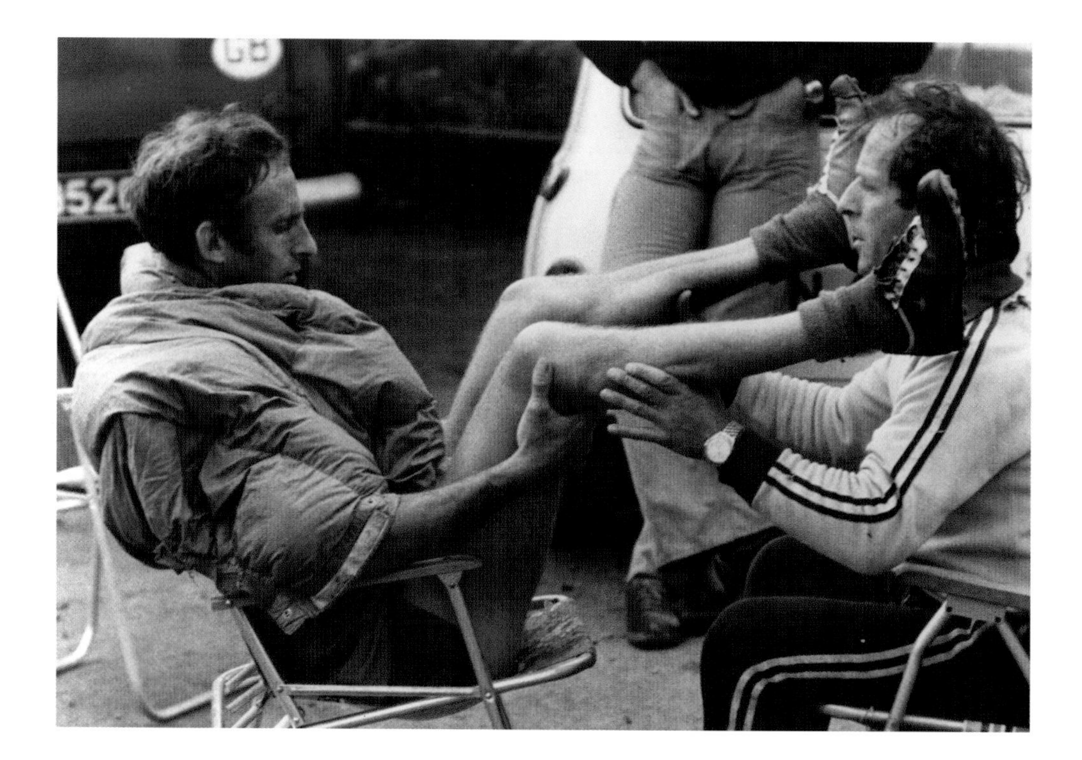

What drove him?

"A determination not to give in. It's typical of a lot of fells men and countrymen and farmers and shepherds, sometimes to their own detriment, that they are determined to go on with an idea they've got. I tend to be that way missell. Once I've set off to do something I'm determined I'm going to see it through if I believe it's right. If Joss had agreed to do something for charity he's the sort of fella that'll want to do it. Full stop. He'll want to achieve the best for that charity."

Ken Ledward, of Uzzicar, near Keswick, first came across Joss Naylor in the farmyard at Wasdale Head, as you do. It was July 1959 and Ken had earlier left the Forces and come to the Lake District looking for work. He first took a job at a youth hostel in Borrowdale before joining the Outward Bound in Eskdale. He now runs his own company KLETS , testing mountain equipment. An accomplished climber, skier and fell runner – although he leans towards self-deprecation when talking about his own achievements – he leads and has led an active life and in 1963, when he was Chief Instructor at the Loitotik Outward Bound Mountain School, below Kilimanjaro, he set a record of 13 hours 20 minutes (one that still stands) for running to the 19,340 foot summit (Uhuru Peak) of Kilimanjaro, a distance of 26 miles, 41.8 kilometres and a total ascent close to 26,000 feet.

Ken is a lively character with a gently wicked sense of humour.

Ken Ledward tends to Joss.
Photographs: Tommy Orr.

"My first meeting with Joss was at the end of a walk over with a group of students to Brackenclose campsite and I would go out for a run," he recalls. "I went through the yard at Wasdale Head and met Joss and his brother, Scott. That was the first meeting I had with him and he wasn't really into running then. There wasn't much of a conversation because I found it extremely difficult to understand him. He and his brother were talking about sheep and sorting sheep at the time and they were speaking in broad Cumbrian. Anyway I just asked which was a good route for a run, and he said he wasn't sure about running, but pointed me in the direction of Dore Head and I went up the side of the scree.

"Next September the fell race (the Lake District Mountain Trial) was actually based in Wasdale Head and he entered and he wore a pair of boots, farm boots. I don't think he even wore shorts that day, I think he wore long trousers (Joss in fact cut the trousers with a farm knife at the starting line to make them into shorts). I don't remember too much because once we got started I didn't see much of him after that. But he didn't win it, I know that much.

"But then he really got into it and he used to run from his house out over the Scafells round the Crinkle Crags, over the Coniston fells, down through the Duddon, back through Eskdale and back to Wasdale. He set a gentle running pace all the time, not really fast, but he'd do something in the order of six or seven hours. And a six or seven hour run for Joss Naylor was a 12-hour run for most of us.

"When I left Outward Bound in Eskdale I went to live in the Duddon Valley and almost every Sunday when there wasn't an event Joss would run from Bowderdale

down to the Woolpack in Eskdale, up over Harter Col and arrive at my place, have a cup of coffee, a shortbread biscuit and then we would leave there and we'd go Walna Scar, Brown Crag, Dow Crag, Coniston Old Man, Brim Fell, Three Shires, Crinkle Crags and then we'd either go to Scafell Pike and go our separate ways or go to Bowfell and split. From Bowfell I could run right down into Cockley Beck and back home. But he would do all that and it would just be a gentle training run.

"Mike Short became one of the fastest of the 15/16 mile fell race runners. And he said to Joss once that he'd like to do one of his stamina days. Joss brought him over to my house and we had the coffee and the biscuit and we set off up the fell (Ken starts to laugh). On the way back after I had left them Mike was praying for a short cut. Short wanted a short cut! So they dropped down onto the old pony track off Styhead to get back into Wasdale. He said he'd never ever do a run like that again. He was regretting he hadn't dropped off with me . . .

"Joss runs in a very sloped style because of his lower back problems. Even when walking around the yard he would stoop from the lower back, well forward and his hands used to hang. And he was a bit like an Alpine skier with his knees bent all the time. No one would ever think he was six foot, even as a young man he always looked shorter than he was."

Ken still gets a lot of fun out of remembering some of the remarks that Joss would come out with and he gives another of his hearty laughs as he recalls one particular occasion.

"The great thing about Joss was that he never put on a show," says Ken. "I always

Joss on The Pennine Way. Photograph by Brian Evans.

Far left: Joss on the descent, arms flung wide for balance, with Buttermere and Crummock in the distance.

remember I took a friend of mine who was an instructor at Eskdale over to the Langdale race – Rob Pashley his name was - and I introduced him to Joss in the yard outside the Old Dungeon Ghyll as we were warming up. Rob pointed down to Joss's foot and said: 'D'you know you've got a hole in that shoe?'

"'Aye, lad,' replied Joss, 'that theer toe's got claustrophobia.'

"He had a hole in his shoe that time and I can't remember a time when Joss had any running gear that was 100 per cent complete, that didn't have a hole or a tear in it. We once went into Eskdale and did a bit of a recce around the Harter Fell and the Border End crags. The rain was torrential and Joss finished up with a plastic farm bag over himself as a waterproof. And I know of another occasion when he was going for the start of a fell race, I think it was the Ennerdale, and the day before a bullock had stood on his foot and flattened the bones out. He found another shoe that was about two sizes too big and he won the Ennerdale. None of us that have been around Joss know everything that he did. A lot of the things that he did he just went out and did them off his own bat."

Ken recalls that the first major event he helped Joss with in a support role was the Pennine Way in June 1974. Joss was 38 at the time. Bill Bird, of Ranelagh Harriers had previously completed the run from Kirk Yetholm in Roxburghshire to Edale in Derbyshire in four days eight hours. In 1973 Alan Heaton lowered the record to four days five hours. Joss intended to do it in three days . . . that's 270 miles, near as dammit, in just three days. The maths is elementary and while the information slides off the tongue the enormity of the objective is unbelievable and, as with so many of Joss's long distance epics, the initial reaction is to say 'that can't be done, surely?'

As it was Joss did not quite manage the three-day target. He failed by just over four hours. He covered the 271 and a half miles in three days, four hours and 35 minutes and knocked 24 hours off Alan Heaton's record. The current record is held by Mike Hartley and was set in July 1989. Mike did two years of research on the Way and peaked his training at 170 miles a week. He ran without stopping for sleep and, in fact, stopped only twice, 18 minutes each time, and one of those was for fish and chips in Alston; an Alf Tupper, Tough of the Track, moment if ever there was one.

The late, great Chris Brasher, a tremendous admirer of Joss Naylor who supported him on some of his major long distance runs and helped bring Joss's achievements to the attention of a wider public, wrote in *The Observer* newspaper: ' . . . every three hours there is Joss's mentor, Ken Ledward, with a meal ready, a change of clothes and shoes and some wintergreen to massage his legs . . .

'He will never be an international athlete, never wear a British vest for he has little speed and can be beaten by many men in races up to two or three hours. But once you venture beyond that time, when ordinary mortals are wilting into exhaustion, Joss goes striding on, covering the ground with a silky, effortless stride . . . what he does have is an astounding ability to whisper over rough country without seeming to expend any energy. It is the supreme quality of relaxation.

'Two years ago (1972) I saw him come down off the Langdale Fells in a rain storm, at three in the morning. He had already been running for 17 hours and had traversed more than 40 peaks. He ate and drank and then set off again into the rain and dark to raise his own record (61 peaks in 1971) for the Bob Graham 24-hour run to 63 peaks (later enhanced to 72 peaks in 1975).

'Those few hours when I tried vainly to stay with him as the rain drummed on my hood, so fiercely as to obliterate all thought, are still a memory equal to any of the greatest Olympic races that I have seen. But this Pennine Way surpasses them all . . .'

Chris Brasher, CBE, was a pacemaker for Roger Bannister when he ran the first sub four-minute mile at the Iffley Road stadium in Oxford. Chris paced Bannister for the

The support team (left to right): Chris Brasher, Pete Trainor, Milne, Bond and Bull on the Pennine Way run.
Photograph: Tommy Orr.

Above and above far left: Joss on the Pennine Way.
Photographs by Brian Evans.

first two laps while his friend Chris Chataway paced the third. Two years later at the 1956 summer Olympics in Melbourne, Chris Brasher won the gold medal in the 3,000 metres steeplechase. He went on, of course, to become a sports journalist of some renown, a successful businessman who designed the innovative Brasher walking boot and was a co-founder of the London Marathon. He died in February 2003.

On another occasion, he was helping to pace Joss on one of his successful attempts to raise the standard on the number of Lakeland peaks covered in 24 hours.

Chris had the easy section from Honister to Newlands and he wrote in *The Observer* and in his preface to *Fifty Years Running. A History of the Mountain Trial*: 'The moon was full behind us but it still seemed very dark at half past one in the morning as we climbed out of Honister Pass towards the summit of Dale Head. The pace was fast enough to keep me silent, but out of the dark came the voice of Eric Roberts, a good athlete and a great man of the mountains. "I was thinking," Eric said, "of how to equate this effort of Joss's with any known performance. I thought of Ron Clarke when he first ran under 13 minutes for the three miles – great performance but not great enough. I thought of Emil Zatopek and his three gold medals in one Olympic Games – still not good enough. And then I decided that there was only one man in athletic history who is in this league – Wilson of the Wizard." 'And then Eric laughed': "A man of fantasy for a fantastic performance."

'For those of you not old enough to have come across Wilson of the Wizard he was a comic book hero, a Yorkshireman who slept in the bracken on Dartmoor, climbed Everest alone, bowled out the entire Australian cricket team and then scored a double century. He also won just about every event in the Olympics – all in the pages of the weekly comic *The Wizard*.

'That, I hope, illustrates the calibre of these men and women who every year run prodigious distances at a prodigious rate over the fells of the Lake District. If their sport lent itself to being held in a stadium surrounded by television cameras then they would be known the world over.

'I myself keep coming back to compete. I know not why – I passed my peak several decades ago. There must be something magnetic and it is not just the beautiful mountains of the Lakes but also the companionship of some of the most tough and genuine characters – competitors and officials alike – that you are ever likely to meet anywhere in the world.'

I think that is a wonderful tribute and could not be bettered. Wilson of the Wizard would probably be quite chuffed as well. For the record, Wilson also ran barefoot and wore a bodysuit that was clearly ahead of its time, ran the 100 metres in 4.7 seconds, climbed the great pyramid of Cheops in eight minutes, spent a lot of his life in a cave – shades of Millican Dalton, Lakeland's very own Professor of Adventure – and trained on a herbal formulae diet. And, oh yes, he was gifted the secret of eternal life by a hermit and was reputedly born in 1795.

Wilson is, of course, still alive and well, roaming the wilderness and surviving on a diet of berries and sweet stream water and preparing himself to save the world and humanity from itself.

Also for the record, Chris Brasher referred to Joss Naylor as 'The Greatest of Them All,' a title he bestowed upon Joss when he ran 72 Lake District mountains inside 24 hours in 1975.

'Joss,' he wrote, 'has sinews stronger than any man-made substance and his will is harder than a diamond.' And on another occasion he wrote: 'We drove west to find Joss Naylor. I have always believed that he is the toughest runner in Britain, which inevitably makes him the toughest runner in the world, for there is no other nation with such depth of talent on those events which really pull the stamina from a man's heart.'

Joss at a checkpoint on a Mountain Trial.
Photograph: Tommy Orr.

Ken Ledward takes up the story of The Pennine Way run: "I was with Alan Evans, Pete Trainor and Tommy Orr. It was desperate on the first two sections. Hardly anybody could stay with him. Chris Brasher, who went in to do the second section, turned back and dropped out within the first two miles. He said he couldn't keep up with him."

Chris Brasher also at one point set up his camera against a dry stonewall to await the arrival of Joss near a fell top. Unfortunately, Chris fell fast asleep propped up against the wall, Joss sailed through, the photo opportunity was missed and Chris, for once, failed to meet his deadline with *The Observer*.

The attempt on the three-day objective suffered a major setback when Joss – who appears to be accident prone at the best of times – took a serious tumble.

"Coming in off the Cheviots I got mi leg in a hole, just went right in to the top, right up to mi arse and I hit the ground," Joss recalls. "It was terrible. I ran 106 mile that day easily and should have done the same the next day, but I got up and could hardly walk, the leg had all seized up, muscles were torn and I had to mair or less walk to Edale. It took just over three days four hours, whereas I should have been finished in two and a half days when I was running right. But these things happen. Things aren't going to be sometimes are they?"

In a general observation on Joss and his running, Ken Ledward adds: "He was before his time. Some of his times and records have been broken and this is because people have dedicated themselves to training specifically for those events, which Joss didn't do. He'd go out and he'd run for a day. He did it almost out of a natural ability. God had given him a gift. He didn't do any contrived exercises except, before I knew him, when he was given some for his back. He was a natural phenomenon. He didn't actually do any training as such and I don't think he ever had anything you could remotely call a diet regime . . ."

On the subject of Joss's diet it is a fact that he has hovered around the nine stone mark all his adult life and this despite a passion for his wife Mary's shepherds pie, rock buns, apple pie and custard, fruitcake and virtually anything with a cherry in it, and that very definitely includes rock buns with cherries. Whenever I have been out on the fells with Joss (walking I hasten to add, not running) his staple has been what I would call the sandwich made in heaven. This, I am reliably informed, contains tongue, beetroot, chutney, onion, garlic, mayonnaise, tomato, a big slice of cheese and, as Joss puts it "what the hell do you call that fancy margarine?"

Joss's favourite sandwich.

"It's a very luscious sandwich," says Joss. I agree totally. And that, as such, is Joss Naylor's dietary regime. Joss also appreciates a glass or two of red wine, the occasional Draught Guinness or a dark beer and, of an evening after dinner, a glass of brandy and four squares of chocolate. Finally, he is also inordinately fond of what he describes as the "really cold, good sweet water" that is freely available from all the fresh running little becks on the Lake District fells.

"Joss didn't drink much water," says Ken Ledward. "When we went on long runs we tried to go as long as we could without water to get the system used to doing without water. It was only many years later that we became enlightened and realised the reason why we were sometimes getting cramp wasn't because we were losing too much salt, but because we hadn't drank enough."

Ken remembers the time when he finally had to commit to running the Bob Graham round: "When I decided I was going to do it in '77 Joss said 'you've helped me out such a lot I'm going to pace you, you don't need anybody else.' And he did, he came every step of the way with me. I'd been putting it off over and over again and he kept badgering me saying 'next weekend looks good.' Eventually I said 'when I'm the same age as Bob Graham I'll do it' and, of course, that year came. And he didn't forget, so he rang me on a Wednesday and said 'we're going, on Saturday.' That was it, I couldn't get out of it. I had to do it then," laughs Ken. "And do you know it was just like going out with your dog. He'd race ahead and he'd look at the views and he'd run back and then he'd start away again. So I was on mi own for an awful long time!"

Joss on the Pennine Way.
Photograph by Brian Evans.

When it came to the people who accompanied Joss on his long distance, record breaking runs, Ken says that Joss liked to be in charge of who was going to be where and when on the route.

"'You're in charge of the safety aspect,' he'd tell me, 'so I don't want anybody out on the high tops in bad weather or in the dark that isn't really competent.' A lot of fell runners who are willing horses can't navigate, don't know mountain safety, and wouldn't know which was the best way to get off if anything went wrong. You've got to have the right people in the right place and at the right time and Joss would check and vet everybody. He was meticulous in his preparation.

"There was one time on the Wainwrights when two quite experienced outward bound instructors got lost, took a terrible route, and Joss had gone on record as saying that I should have done that particular route. But I was looking to keep myself back for the higher peaks and the next morning we set off and we went up from Eskdale on to Whin Rigg and Ill Gill. He hadn't said it to me directly but I knew there was a wall between us the next morning. He never spoke to me until we got all the way up to the top and the view was unbelievable. And he said: "Will you look at that fucking view!" And that was the first time he spoke to me. I must have worked it out of his system by not talking to him on the way up . . ."

Apart from the occasional navigational problem the support team had also got to keep Joss right physically.

"When we were doing the Wainwrights," Ken continued, "we had a real problem at the Buttermere end when he had gone through a night of driving cold rain and his hands had started to swell and we couldn't get anything over his wrists. Everything had to be cut to get it over his hands which were badly swollen because the blood had been running down all the time . . ."

But nothing seemed to deter Joss from continuing, whatever the state of his body. It would appear that he was putting into practice his philosophy that the mind could overcome matter and blank out the pain and the conditions and run through it.

"He was incredibly determined," Ken adds. "Whether or not he didn't want anybody to think he had failed at something I don't know, but once he had said something to somebody he'd do it. I think he felt duty bound to do it; not for any really serious psychological reasons but because it was a physical challenge that he could do. It all comes back to his natural ability.

"His one failing would be that he was like a young man at every single event. He'd get psyched up and he'd over run to start with. He always did the first section of every run far too fast. We were never able to rein him in. He always tried to blast it out to start with and it was almost like a youthful exuberance. But once he got settled into his stride it was still at a pace that was beyond everyone else. Even when he was much older, doing the Wainwrights, that was one of the problems. In the first two days we were going too quick and we couldn't slow him down. Only nature slowed him down eventually.

"I have seen that man's feet when a medic would say 'no, you can't go out on those.'

"Barbara Nelson, a qualified medic, had been bandaging his feet for two days and she had to go back to work. And so Joss's daughter Gillian watched how to do it and then did it. But the feet were an unbelievable mess. A fully qualified medic was saying 'this is ridiculous,' but Joss wouldn't take a blind bit of notice."

A successful completion of the Pennine Way run and Joss holds a pint of beer that looks as though it needs a pick-me-up. The picture caption in Joss's own hand and words, tells the story.

Joss Naylor descending screes in Wales. The oil painting is by Jonathan Trotman, of Threlkeld. Based on a photographic image by John Cleare.

Joss himself recalls that particular situation on the Wainwrights: "It went wrong early on because I had a new pair of shoes and they were wrong around the ankle bones, they were too high and cut into mi ankles. They were very very sore. Barbara Nelson used to come out of a night to dress mi feet, they were that bad. And then I got an infection in mi throat and I couldn't eat. For the last two days I was just running on empty, I couldn't get any food down. And where I should have been finished inside of seven days easy it dragged on a laal bit. Then there was the heat. We come through Hartsop one morning and it was 73 degrees at half past seven in the morning. And it just got hotter and hotter.

"When I did 72 peaks it was a tremendous achievement at the time because I was never under any pressure, I ran well all day and all night. It was just too hot towards the finish. It was burning mi feet comin' off Grisedale Pike. The road was burning but it was a great thing to do. And when I did the Hadrian's Wall that morning we were just flying right through. No bad patches. It took nine hours 25 minutes running time and 10 hours 25 minutes altogether."

For most people Hadrian's Wall is a 10-day walk.

Ken Ledward continues: "The reason we have got outstanding endurance mountain runners now is because they've chased after what Joss has done and realised that the way they have got to go is slightly different from Joss because they are not God blessed with natural ability. They've got to train. If Joss arrived on the scene today as a young 20 year old and nobody else had set those sorts of standards, which is very unlikely, he would have gone in at the top echelon again.

"He would also have done it, I think, had he been committed to road running. Kenny Stuart made the switch quite clear, coming off the fells and going onto the road and was almost the best marathon runner Britain has ever had. Joss could have done that. Had he said 'right – I'm going to dedicate myself to marathon running' he would have done it. Because I think Joss could have gone through the pain barriers. But would he have enjoyed the monotony of running along a road with thousands of people? His whole physique and the way he had developed his muscles and tendons were for mixed ground. He is an entirely independent person who likes nothing better than to be on those fells on his own with his dogs."

THE PATHFINDER 6
'He would have done quite well with Genghis Khan'

While Joss is very much his own person and clearly appreciates being on his own on the fell with just his dogs and the world and its wildlife around him, he is also very much a social animal in his own environment. Out on the fell he will talk with anyone and everyone he comes across and in some instances will virtually adopt people and walk and talk with them for quite a distance.

In fact he can be wonderfully and cheerfully direct in his initial encounter with folk on the fell and he invariably gets people onboard straight away and has a way of engaging them even if they are sometimes at a loss to understand precisely what he is saying or are, in truth, a little in awe of him. Walkers who know the name Joss Naylor and who are aware that he is a legend of the Lake District fells, are quite made up to find themselves in his company. It makes their day.

And while runners will tell you that Joss loves to converse on the fell during a long distance run, and if he is not talking he is usually whistling away to himself, this is not always the case. One of the runners who Joss most appreciated for his support was former Whitehaven building society manager Allen Walker.

"Allen was Joss's first choice when two day mountain marathons started," explained Ken Ledward. "Allen is an experienced mountaineer and he doesn't talk unnecessarily and chatter away, which Joss likes. When Joss is out running he doesn't like banter all the time. Allen is also the sort of person who if he says he's going to do something then he'll do it. And that's where Joss clicked with Allen.

Joss receives attention at a makeshift refuelling / medical station on his Pennine Way run.

Above: Allen Walker.
Photographs: Tommy Orr.

"Allen was the same sort of mould as Joss, not quite as strong a runner. But, like Joss, he was a good pathfinder. He did the Bob Graham and those of us who knew him said 'Brilliant, well done,' but the hierarchy in the Bob Graham said the run could not be validated because of a lack of witnesses. Allen said he wasn't worried, it didn't worry him if he didn't go on the list. He knew he had done the Bob Graham and that was all that mattered to him. But the whole business really annoyed Joss and that put him against some of the establishment people."

Allen Walker, who lives in Whitehaven on an estate high on the hill overlooking the town and the Irish Sea, accompanied Joss on sections for many of his record-breaking long distance runs and describes Joss as "a very hard man." He says that he first came across Joss when he (Allen) was out for a run in Ennerdale in the early Seventies and Joss stopped for a chat and invited Allen to join him in a run. It was the first of many.

"There was one Sunday before we started out from Bowderdale that we went down to Greendale where he had some cattle," Allen remembers. "One of them was lying in the gutter, sort of legs up in the air. Together – but not with a lot of effort from me – we somehow got this beast on its feet and then we went for a run. It took about an hour to get it on its feet and I think on that occasion, more than any other, I was impressed at how hard and strong he was. He's as strong as an ox and I've seen him carry a sheep under his arm and lift boulders onto dry stonewalls as if they were pebbles.

"We used to go for long runs on a Sunday and run as far as the Duddon Valley and back. On one of his record breaking runs I joined him at Wasdale and went with him over Great Gable. Joss had already run for perhaps 16 hours and I was fairly fresh and very fit, but Joss was going up Gable faster than I could.

"He used to train for a mountain trial by running virtually a mountain trial every day for a week in the week immediately leading up to the event whereas somebody like myself would put in a long distance run and then rest for a week to build up my strength. From his background as a hill farmer and the son of a hill farming family, he had the kind of hardness and character background that perhaps these days you'd only find among the Turkish peasants or somewhere in Outer Mongolia, Serbia or Croatia. He would have done quite well with Genghis Khan!"

There is a photograph by Tommy Orr of Joss approaching the finish of a mountain trial. Joss has a big grin on his face while Allen Walker, in the background to the side of the track, is also enjoying the moment (right).

"It was a Mountain Trial at Newlands in the Duddon Valley," says Allen. "Joss won every year for several years and there were many occasions when he set off last and finished first. He had passed the whole field. On that one occasion at Newlands I actually finished before him, but I had set off quite a bit in front. I finished third on that occasion, and Peter Walkingshaw was second. As Joss ran past I just asked him 'what kept you?' One expected to be overtaken. My view of him was usually of his back."

Joss is all smiles as he runs in to the finish. Allen Walker, on the left, is also amused because he has just said to Joss "what kept you?"

Tommy Orr and his wife Audrey, of Moor Row, are good friends of Joss and Mary Naylor. Tommy has an extensive photographic record of Joss-related running events, and has also supported Joss on many of his epic runs. He and Ken Ledward sometimes felt the sharp end of Mary Naylor's tongue if they failed to phone Bowderdale at an appointed time with the latest update on Joss's progress. In fact on one run they failed to make contact on two consecutive days. Mary was not amused.

Several of Tommy's superb images show Joss in various stages of exhaustion and he recalls: "On the first day of the Pennine Way he did 104 miles and came in absolutely shattered. We thought that was going to be it and he would have to retire. When you look at the pictures of Joss running, his ankles are like puddings hanging over the side of his running shoes. He was obviously really suffering and had badly swollen ankles.

"Everyone said that was the finish and we would have to abandon the attempt. We got him in a hut, I put some cold bandages on Joss's ankles and his feet up on a suitcase. Someone gave him a couple of sleeping tablets and the next morning, hey presto, he was as fit as a fiddle and was off. Joss has a very high pain threshold. I once asked him what he did if he got a stone in a shoe on the Ennerdale Horsehoe and he said 'Oh I just keep going and it beds itsell in.'

"He hasn't got any cartilage left in one knee and has suffered so much pain with his back that everything else, in comparison, is nothing. And because he runs with his arms down the blood is flowing continually into his hands, the blood accumulates and his fingers are swollen like sausages. Half way through the Wainwrights we thought he was going to have to abandon it. There were times when he was totally exhausted and we seriously thought that if he ran any further he would have a heart attack."

One day Tommy made his own contribution to the Joss Naylor list of injuries suffered in advance of major runs.

"It was a few days before he was due to run and Audrey and me were staying at Bowderdale," says Tommy. "Anyway Joss got me helping out on the farm. I'd driven a car, but I'd never driven a tractor before in my life. 'Git on this tractor,' he said. And before I knew it I was up on this tractor. Joss's farm was on a hill and imagine what it's like driving a tractor on a hill and he had me moving these big railway sleepers; you put them on the forklift at the front and the back wheels were coming off the ground. I managed to move these sleepers and there were one or two that had to be moved manually and it was a bit of a wet day. Joss got hold of this sleeper and I got hold of the other end and we moved a few. They were quite heavy and one of the sleepers dropped out of my hand and Joss couldn't take the full weight himself so he had to let go of his end and it dropped on his foot and broke some bones. He needed hospital treatment for that and I wasn't very popular."

For a long time Joss was unbeatable.

"I remember once in the Ennerdale, Harry Walker and another fell runner Jeff Norman were out to get him," says Tommy. "They were good runners, but Joss had

Joss leads the way with Allen Walker.
Photograph: K Rhodes, Scaleby.

Running on the roads, as opposed to the fell, is not Joss's favourite terrain. But here he appears to be going along at a fair lick with Allen Walker (second right) in close support.

the mountain craft. It was a morning with thick mist and I was on Green Gable. The idea was that Jeff and Harry were going to stick on Joss's heels and then at the finish they were going to out sprint him and win. But Joss got wind of it and had other ideas. They were coming off High Crag down to Haystacks when Joss deliberately ran off the course down Scarth Gap and hid behind a rock. Jeff and Harry came storming down the path to Buttermere and Joss came out from behind his rock and returned to the course. Joss went over Green Gable in the mist and about half an hour later Harry and Jeff came back spitting blood."

Tommy and Audrey Orr and Joss and Mary Naylor went to an annual presentation do for The Bob Graham Club. It was the early 1980s and the event was held at a hotel in Ambleside.

"We went to this hotel and were sitting in reception," says Tommy. "There was this big bowl of fruit and so Joss and I thought we'd eat some. Time went on, we'd nearly finished off the fruit but there was no sign of the others. We thought this was a bit strange so we asked at reception and were told that it was at the hotel across the road."

Ken Ledward has happy memories of the time he spent in Wasdale with Joss and the locals at the pub.

"Joss's old friend Ben Ullock had an Austin Cambridge van. We'd play darts with Wilson Pharoah who was the landlord and the crack was always good. This was the 1960s and after a few beers we always used to see Ben home, we used to stop at the green and Ben would turn up the lane – driving out to Burnthwaite – and we'd see his lights going by the church and then we'd hear this bang bang bang as he bounced off the walls on the way up the lane. And then we'd eventually see the lights hit the barn at Burnthwaite and go out. And we knew that he'd got home safely and we'd go . . . but there were a hell of a lot of scrapes and scratches on the side of his van.

"Sometimes I would be in a tent and other times, if I hadn't got an Outward Bound group, I would stop at Bowderdale. We would sit up for hours. He liked to drink pale ale and sherry. He also liked a Mackeson. Ben Ullock was a huge hole in Joss's life when he died. The funny thing about Ben Ullock was that he married a woman called Maggie who came from Ullock. She used to make drop scones on their Aga and when

we ran into the yard Ben had this quirky sideways sort of mouth and he'd say: 'Right, they're 'ere.' Mary would start doing the drop scones before we'd got our shoes off and by the time we came in they were ready. She was a wonderful, wonderful person was Maggie Ullock from Ullock."

While Ben Ullock was a great supporter of Joss and his endeavours this was not true of other local people.

"There was a lack of credit from the people of Wasdale," says Ken. "It was the same with the Blands in Borrowdale. Most of the people round Borrowdale thought they were lunatics for going out running. Their attitude was that there was work to be done on the farm. What brought Joss into the public eye was a wonderful article in *The Observer* by Chris Brasher. A lot of people had no conception of what it meant to run the fells. Even today some people in the newspaper world don't realise what skills are required for moving across these fells in the dark. They don't understand it, they can't even get the names of the mountains right either."

What was Joss's greatest single achievement?

"I think his record on the Ennerdales was his greatest single achievement in running," replies Ken. "The Ennerdale used to attract the cream of British fell running. Year in, year out he used to win it." In fact Joss won the Ennerdale for nine successive years, from its inception in 1968 to 1976 and may well have won a tenth had he not had to

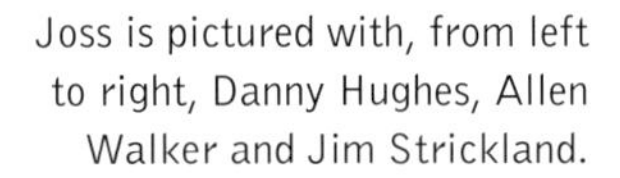
Joss is pictured with, from left to right, Danny Hughes, Allen Walker and Jim Strickland.

miss that year's race through injury. He set a course record of 3hrs 30mins 40 seconds in 1972. Kenny Stuart holds the current record with a time of 3hrs 20mins 57 seconds. And while Joss would not decry someone from away taking one of his records I think he's happier if it's a Cumbrian who has the honour.

"Joss is a Lakeland man through and through," adds Ken Ledward. "What he believes to be good would probably be good for all of us. He could be the spokesman for moving the Lake District forward because in reality everything he wants is what we all want. He doesn't want anything for himself. He's not selfish. Every single run we have done, long distance, there has been a beneficiary at the end."

The final word in this chapter goes to Bill Teasdale. He and Joss are the only two Lakeland fell runners to have been awarded the MBE. But they have other links in that both were shepherds and their fathers – and quite possibly their grandfathers – knew each other.

Bill lives on the outskirts of Caldbeck at Bushby House and, although he is in his eighties, is as bright as a button with a hearty laugh and a good crop of rhubarb in the corner of his well-maintained vegetable plot. Bill won the Grasmere senior guides race 11 times – the last when he was 42 – and won Keswick on 12 occasions, 10 times in a row. Like Joss he also is a legend although he specialised in the shorter, more direct fell running as opposed to the longer distances. His immense success also came at a time when officialdom in the amateur ranks frowned on the so-called professionalism of those who took part in the Lakeland games such as Grasmere and Keswick and accepted cash prizes handed out in little brown paper envelopes; amounts that were pitiful in comparison to the effort and risk needed to win them. It is a shame that Bill was deprived of the opportunity, officially, to display his running ability on a wider stage.

When Joss's father Joe made the move from Caldbeck to Wasdale in the 1920s, Bill's father George gave Joe advice on the farm and land he was considering tenanting.

"I don't know whether they went on bikes or they would have to walk," said Bill.

Many years later young Joss actually went to Bill for advice when he was looking for a sport to pursue.

"I told him that he had just got to mek his mind up and go for it," said Bill. I wonder

There's still no holding him back, not even on a gentle outing around Wasdale. Fast forward to 2009 and Joss, at 73, with Spy and Titch in close attendance, descends towards Low Tarn from Gosforth Crags.

if Bill's father George gave Joss's father Joe similar advice over that farm tenancy in Wasdale all those years before?

Bill Teasdale has vivid memories of running in the Wasdale Fell Race and tackling the steep ascent and descent of Kirk Fell.

"When ah was comin' doon ah catched ya foot behint the other and I think I landed on mi nose and reet back onto mi feet again," he says.

Bill is full of laughter, even if it is at his own expense, and is difficult to stop once he gets started; not unlike his considerable achievements in fell running. He tells me the story of the time he recently decided to buy a car. When he returned home with the new vehicle he drove into his old tin-sheeting garage across the road from Bushby House and discovered that once inside he had difficult getting out of the car. The new vehicle was wider than the old one and was jammed into the garage. So much so that Bill had to cut a door into the side of the garage, in line with the car door, in order to extricate himself.

"I had to a knock a wol in the wall to git out and the tin was harder than ah thowt," he says. After a fascinating hour or so talking to Bill about shepherding, running, the old times and modern times, I leave Bill as he wanders around his garden, waiting for signs of his new potatoes to emerge from the soil.

I bid him farewell as I walk round the corner of the house and with a mischievous glint in his eye Bill Teasdale MBE calls back: "Give old Joss my regards when you see him tomorrow. I always call him Old Joss even though he's a hell of a lot younger than me."

He's a smashing little fella is Bill Teasdale and by hell could he run.

167
MANITOU

PIKES PEAK MARATHON
To hell and back
7

If ever there was what might be called an odyssey in the fell running career of Joss Naylor it would most probably be the time he left Cumbria and ventured across the Atlantic to Manitou Springs, Colorado, to take part – by special invitation – in the Pikes Peak Marathon, a race described as America's Ultimate Challenge.

'There's a reason trees don't bother growing above 12,000 feet on Pikes Peak,' goes the blurb for the race. 'They can't! Makes one wonder if trees are smarter than runners. Above the tree line most runners take 30 minutes or more, some much more, just to cover a mile . . .'

The promoters of the event claim that the marathon will 'redefine what you call running. As you gain almost 6,000 vertical feet, your legs, lungs, heart and mind will be worn to a ragged nothingness. But it won't be until your last three miles, with still over 2,000 ft of vertical to go, that you will realize where the marathon got its moniker – America's Ultimate Challenge. On the descent protruding rocks are waiting to send you crashing to the ground, mangling flesh and only temporarily masking the pain of blood-filled blisters. Meanwhile, the temperature has often risen by more than 30 degrees since the race start. After all, it's always best to cook raw meat.'

With that sort of billing runners will be queuing up to take part and the fact is that they always are. The entry limit for the marathon is 800 and race registration typically fills up within 48 hours. The race climbs over 7,700 ft to the top of the 14,115 ft peak and has taken place annually since 1966. Its origins date back to 1956 when three smokers challenged 10 non-smokers to complete the 26 mile-plus race. The smokers did not finish the race. Hardly surprising really, the initial three miles are very steep, the next seven are more gentle but become increasingly vertical towards the end, and the final three miles are above the timberline and may need rock scrambling to reach the summit. The oxygen levels drop further as the altitude increases, adding significantly to the uphill ordeal. This, apparently, would not be a good time to light up a Woodbine.

Unfortunately Joss Naylor did not have sufficient time to train at altitude, nor did

Bearded locals look on curiously as Joss Naylor walks through Manitou Springs, running shoes in hand.

All pictures of Joss Naylor taking part in the Pikes Peak Marathon are by Carl Iwasaki, Sports Illustrated / Getty Images.

he appreciate that for training runs of 20 miles or so it was advisable to drink as much as 10 pints of water to rehydrate the body afterwards. At this stage in his running career Joss was still having the occasional swig of sweet water if he happened to pass a stream on the Lakeland tops. Otherwise it was no big deal.

It was against this backcloth that Joss flew to America barely two weeks before the race in August 1975. When he left Wasdale in the morning it was, he recalls in a small notebook diary, a typical Lake District day, the cloud was down to 1,000ft and it was raining heavily. His first stop was London where he was met by Chris Brasher and taken to the Regent Gate Hotel. Joss was very impressed with the facilities, 'what a place, telly in the bedroom, bath, wireless phone, the lot.'

The flight to America was the following morning and Joss changed planes at Chicago for Denver. On arrival in Colorado Joss's first visit, as a tourist, was to Central City, the old gold mining town. He still has the copy of the spoof newspaper the *Central City News* (1859) with the imposed banner headline 'JOSS NAYLOR VISITS HISTORIC CENTRAL CITY.' The newspaper's front page carried reports of the Gold Rush; a horse thief being hung; a notorious gunslinger called Jack (Brushhead) Badman being

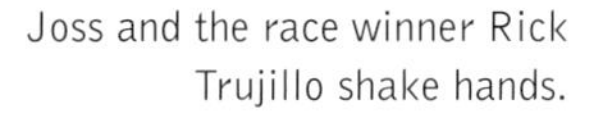
Joss and the race winner Rick Trujillo shake hands.

run out of town; a poker player shot in the back as he walked out of the Red Bull saloon with his winnings; and a Yankee called Kola arriving in town with a notion that he could make more money from opening a bar that sold only sarsaparilla as opposed to strong liquor. This was not, as you may have gathered, an entirely serious publication.

Joss had his first training run on the Wednesday (about a week and a half before the actual marathon) and wrote: 'Did about eight miles along the road and it was far too hot.' He moved to a wooded area at about 1,000 ft on the Friday to step up his training.

'Ran along the forest roads and it soon became very hot, it dried your throat up and there seemed to be no humidity in the air. Ran for an hour and seemed to be going OK.' On a subsequent run he reported that he was again having difficulty with the heat. On the Monday he added: 'Had a better run and my body seems to be adjusting to the altitude. I ran for about an hour. It is really Indian country and you can just about imagine the battles in the old days.'

It soon became clear that Joss was facing a fight of his own and the opposition was

Man at the front. Joss stands out from the crowd at the starting line for the Pikes Peak Marathon.

Joss runs through the streets of Manitou Springs on his way to completing the descent from Pikes Peak.

DRY CLEANING
& LAUNDRY
25¢ CAR
RIFLES KNIVES
ORIENTEERING
167

Joss takes on liquid after an exhausting climb to the summit of Pikes Peak. After a brief rest on the top he recorded the quickest time for the descent.

the mountain, the altitude, inadequate acclimatisation time and his lack of knowledge on body rehydration: 'Made the summit of Pikes Peak today but what a struggle,' he wrote in the notebook. 'I went quite well to 12,500 ft but then the air was so thin I simply could not run.'

Joss was shown great hospitality during his visit and added: 'I am now staying with a Chinese man and living on health foods. Am just about ready for a good feed of rock buns. Roll on home.' The Chinese was in fact a seer called Gia Fu Feng who ran a local commune where Joss stayed for four days. If this all sounds like an American remake of Wilson of the Wizard with Joss in the starring role, the reality was somewhat different.

'I was advised to take vitamins E and C to overcome the low humidity and high altitude and also some kind of oil so I topped up with butter,' wrote Joss. 'I managed to run to the top of Pikes Peak which put me in a better frame of mind. I had no headaches or light-headedness. Yesterday I was about out on my feet but today I ran up in quite a fast time, 2hrs 40 minutes so if I progress tomorrow I should be alright on race day . . . '

But he continued: 'Thursday was the last real training and I died near the top of the peak, it was so hot and the sun shone all the way up. Let's hope for better things on Sunday.'

Joss took time out to relax in Manitou Springs. 'It's like any other tourist town, there are plenty of gift shops and they know how to charge.' However, it wasn't all take.

'I was stopped by a man in a car and he gave me a copy of *Sports Illustrated* which was very nice of him. They're going to do an article on me.'

Joss took himself and a camera on the railway train to the top of the peak on the Friday for a sightseeing tour: 'Some of the film will be unsteady because of the train jumping. I had a nice walk around the back of the peak and managed to find some mountain sheep. I should have them on film but they are as wild as deer and you can't get near them. The wild flowers were very nice and colourful. I stayed on the summit for about three hours.

'I later met the *Sports Illustrated* people and they took me out to dinner. I had one

A gaunt looking Joss Naylor after the highly demanding Pikes Peak Marathon.

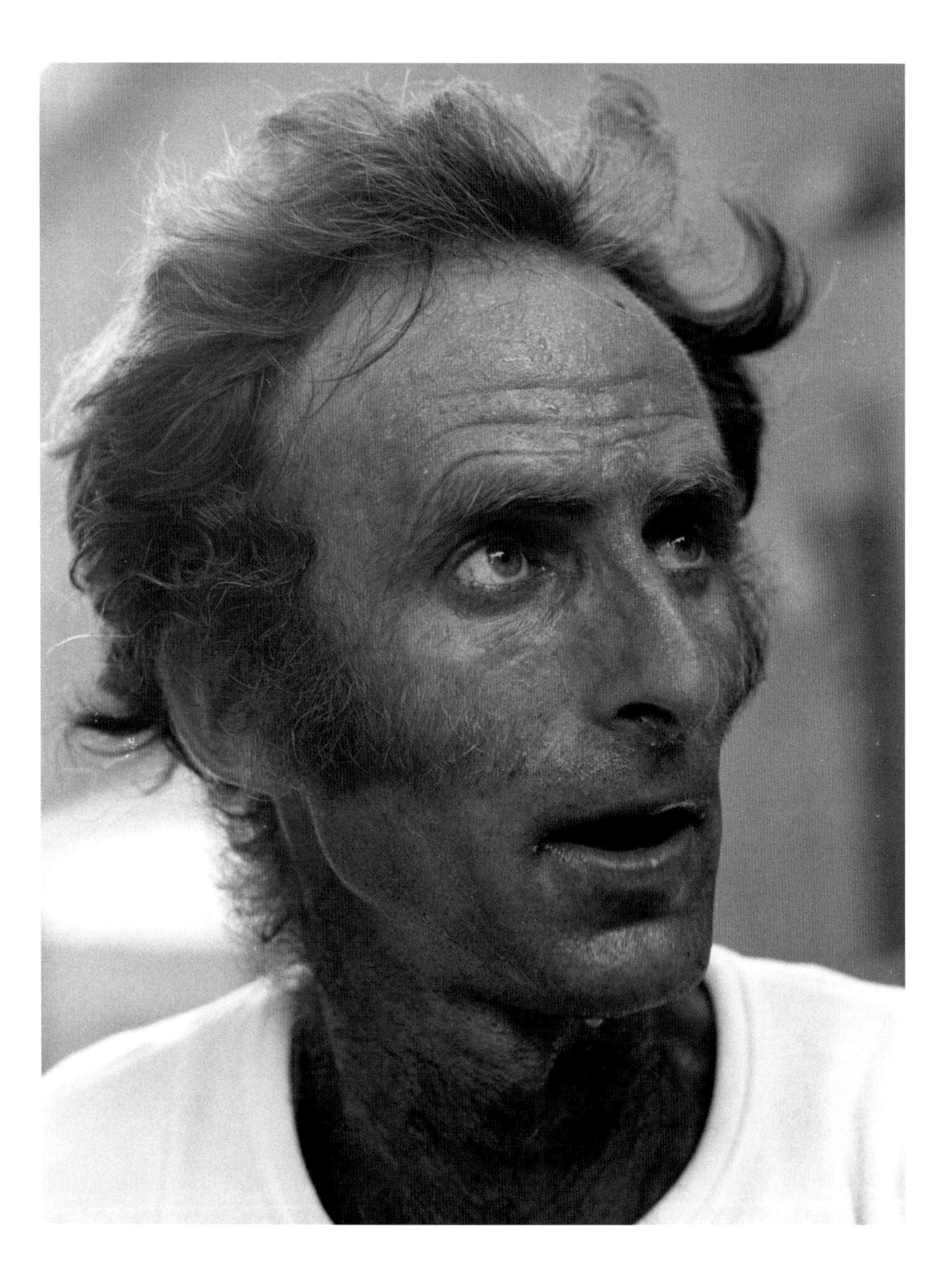

of the biggest T-bone steaks I have ever seen. It must have been off an old bull to be so big but it was good. I decided to have a shrimp cocktail first. The shrimps out here are as big as our black snails and they were a feed on their own.'

On the eve of the race Joss went for a little retail therapy in Manitou Springs and that evening 'had dinner with Simon Winchester from *The Manchester Guardian*. It was the first sports coverage he had ever done and he was very helpful. Then I went for an early night.'

In his report for *The Guardian* datelined Manitou Springs, August 3rd, 1975, Simon Winchester reported that at a pre-race party Joss told him that he doubted he would do at all well: 'The altitude is very bothersome. I'll keep on running to the end but men like Rick Trujillo have been training here for months and they know the form. I doubt if I'll get in the first 10.'

Joss wrote in his notebook: 'I was up at 5.30 on race morning and had an early breakfast. It was a very bright sunny morning. I then got myself ready for the race and by 7am the sun was very hot. At 7.15 I went for a warm up and my legs felt very heavy. I ran about a mile and they seemed to improve. At the start there seemed to be plenty of interest from the TV and Press. The vicar said a prayer before we started. At 7.30 we were off. There were 370 of us. It seemed to be going okay. For about half a mile I was up with the leading bunch and then my legs seemed to go solid and I just could not get plenty of oxygen. Runners were passing by one after another.

'The sun was getting hotter and the sweat was teeming off me. I just could not get going. After about six miles the wind got up and I started to move. I passed quite a few runners after that but at 12,000 ft I started to slow down again, just going rather faster than walking pace. At 13,000 ft I met Rick Trujillo coming down. He was moving really well. I reached the summit 40 minutes behind him, about the time I thought I would. I was very light headed, had a drink and sat down for about two minutes (he was in 18th position at the summit).

'Then I started back down. I was going really well and started to enjoy the race. I was catching runners one after another now. But my heart was still running very fast, making a real thumping noise in the back of my head. Once or twice after I had passed runners I had to look round because I thought they were about to pass me again, but it was just the noise my heart was making. When I got back down to the timberline I was still going strong and getting plenty of encouragement from other runners.

'By this stage it was so hot that I just couldn't get any oxygen out of the air. But I was still making progress and was in tenth place with three more runners in my sights. A determined burst and they were all mine. My feet were beginning to burn but the end was in sight. I went to the start point which I thought was the finish but there was no one there and I found a policeman who directed me down the road. After another half mile of red hot road I found the finish and had to run among the cars to get there.'

Joss did not win the race, but he won the downhill, his descent being faster by three minutes than the eventual winner, Rick Trujillo. Joss came down in 1hr 26 minutes 17 seconds, just under three minutes faster than Trujillo (1hr 29mins 18 secs) and faster than any one else in the race. Not only that, at 39, Joss was the oldest competitor in the first 14 runners home with Trujillo just 27 and the other first six all under the 30 years mark. His finishing time was 4hrs 7minutes 22 seconds compared to Trujillo's 3hrs 31mins 5 seconds.

Had Joss given himself longer to acclimatise – life had been too hectic at Bowderdale where he had sheep to clip – there is no telling what he might have achieved had he put in a stronger ascent. Joss finished in a highly creditable sixth place overall out of the 107 runners who managed to complete the race. There were 370 starters so the event clearly claimed more than its fair share of casualties.

After the race was run Joss 'made to the shade followed by TV cameras and the Press. I took my shoes off to get rid of the stones but had to put them right back on as the road was burning my feet. I did about a dozen interviews and after a beer and a cold shower went to a studio to do a tape for Radio Carlisle back home and another for America.'

Lunch followed with the *Sports Illustrated* people and Simon Winchester but there was still no respite as BBC Radio 4 made contact from London and wanted an interview. In the report he filed for *The Guardian*, Simon Winchester wrote: 'Joss Naylor, the 39 year old Wasdale sheep farmer and fell runner came a triumphant first in his category – and sixth overall – out of a field of more than 300 competing in the world's toughest mountain climbing race, the Pikes Peak Marathon.

'He beat dozens of runners from America and Australia in spite of only having trained at high altitude – Pikes Peak is 14,000 feet high and the round trip is over 26 miles – during the past four days for the 20th annual marathon. He panted over the finishing line here shortly before noon today saying: "I'm absolutely knackered," and went on to give dozens of interviews to reporters clearly astonished at the wiry Cumbrian's cheek and courage.

'"That limey sure is quite a guy," said the overall winner of the race, Rick Trujillo, something of a legend among long distance mountain runners in America. "He was under fantastic pressure and he's only been here a few days. But he did incredibly well."

'Today at 10am, as we waited in the crisp air on the snow-capped summit of the peak, Naylor's fears (about altitude and acclimatisation) seemed well grounded. He limped in, obviously distressed and grey with fatigue. He drank a few ounces of glucose and then turned down for the remaining 13 miles. He was the first man over 30 to reach the summit but this did not appear to cheer him.

'Coming down he overtook a number of runners. Trujillo, a mining engineer who lives at an altitude of over 8,000 ft, set a new record, coming in a full 30 minutes ahead. But Naylor easily won his own category of veteran men 30 to 39 and received a medal and ribbons to carry home. He also carried an enormous amount of goodwill; thanks in part to a lengthy article about him in a glossy sports magazine last week. Naylor is now a famous figure in this part of the world. One girl on top of the peak this morning said she had hitch-hiked all the way down from Wisconsin "to see your sheep herder." She thought he was a "really neat person".'

The tarmac was red hot in the sun and Joss was quick to put his running shoes back on.

JOSS AND HIS DOGS 8
The peak where wolves play

Long ago the flanks of the Lake District fells and the lowlands were thick with forest and scrub, an almost impenetrable jungle – even wild Ennerdale had nothing on this – and it was a land where grey wolves, their soft yellow eyes threading the gloom of a downcast Lakeland dawn, roamed free. The wolves, sadly, became extinct in the UK in the latter years of the 17th Century, but a reminder of their considerable presence in the Lakes is still provided, for example, through Ullock Pike which was known, in the 13th Century, as Ulvelaik. The name of the fell, adjacent to Skiddaw and with commanding views out over Bassenthwaite, is derived from the Old Norse 'ulfr' (wolf) and 'leikr' (to play) meaning the peak where wolves play.

Ullock Pike and a moon for the wolves to howl at.

Sam in his kennel to the rear of Low Greendale.

The wolf, of course, shares a common ancestry with the domestic dog and nowhere is this more apparent today than in the fell hunting packs of the Lake District or on the Lakeland farm where the shepherd may have up to half a dozen dogs at any one time. The pack instinct is as strong as ever, but instead of the leading alpha male wolf there is now the huntsman or the shepherd, the leader of the pack.

The grey wolf that is undoubtedly Joss Naylor, with his distinctive long, loping strides and ability to run endless miles of the wilderness forever and a day, has probably lost count of the number of dogs, principally collies, and the occasional terrier, with which he has shared his working life in Wasdale. Even in his retirement (I am not entirely convinced that old shepherds ever truly retire) Joss has three dogs at his home at Low Greendale. These are Titch, Spy and Sam and each has its own kennel and chain at a different part of the house wall, front, side and back respectively.

I must confess that Titch is probably my personal favourite of this particular triumvirate, although Spy is very affectionate and I haven't, in truth, really got to know Sam very well. It is predominantly Spy and Titch who have accompanied Joss and myself on our walks in the Lakeland fells near Wasdale. Sam occupies the kennel at the back of the house and is kind of out of the way while Spy and Titch are very much on display at the front and side.

I have a soft spot for Titch because she is very much the mongrel of the pack and each year, around the middle of May, suffers the clip out to end all clip outs. For much of the winter, spring and early summer, she is the owner of a thick and over-luxurious, shaggy coat out of which peep a pair of appealing give-me-a-biscuit eyes. But after mid-May, when Joss has been at work with the sheep shears, she is a sheepish-looking nude.

A severe short back and sides results in a complete transformation and you'd be hard pressed to recognise the dog in front of you as being the mighty Titch. Only the area immediately above the paws has retained any depth of fur, giving the impression that Titch is wearing thick woollen socks. The downcast gaze in the eyes is even more profound, as if to say 'look what he's done to me now!' And this at a time when a TV advertisement, promoting a particular brand of spectacles, featured a sheepdog that was left looking decidedly the worse for wear after being sheared by a short-sighted shepherd (don't say that too quickly) somewhere in the Outer Hebrides. The shepherd in question, it must be said, bore a passing resemblance to Joss Naylor.

Joss, who might possibly benefit from a new pair of spectacles himself, was entirely responsible for Titch's diminished coat, but he defended the 'death by shears' trim of

Titch is pictured before and after his May clip out at the hands of Joss and his sheep shears. Note the stylish quiff on the 'after' image.

his unfortunate and sorry-looking charge by proclaiming: "There's only ya thing that separates a good clip out from a bad un . . . and it's aboot two days."

It must be hellish when you're a dog and your owner thinks you're a Herdwick.

Looking back on his life with dogs Joss says: "I had aw sorts of dogs given that folk couldn't handle because they were daft buggers (the dogs, that is). You can soon steady a daft dog up. If it isn't a bloody crackpot you can always deuh summat wid it. It's wuk that meks dogs. I had a laal white dog when I fust started and another cawd Gyp. And this laal white un, Bet, Jim (Joss's brother) fetched us it back from Hartsop Hall, Patterdale, where he was friendly with Harold Iredale. This laal white dog was a short-legged thing and you would think it had a bit of bulldog in it because it had tremendous shoulders. It was the hardest dog ivver ah sen. It used to scuff the pads off its feet when I gathered Mosedale which was a long gather. That laal dog was as hard as iron. You could set off for the fell in the morning and its feet would be sore and it would be about 200 yards behind you going up the path. But the moment you asked it to go by sheep it forgot about that and it would run aw day. And it had a laal bit of temper.

"I used to gather for most folk at Wasdale and so I used to put in a lot of hard days on the fell. But it was the way to mek dogs. You could soon mek a good dog. If you had one that was a thick headed bugger and wouldn't tek much notice, by the time

VEDIMA SOL.

you got gathered round the front end of Mosedale it would listen to what you told it. I used to start gathering at Sail Crags there, right round Black Sail and it's a hell of a lot of ground. Ah tell you what, it would soon tighten a dog up. They were soon listening to you. It's wuk that meks dogs. It's marvellous how dogs learn what to do and where to go. I had yan cawd Fly that was never to train. You would have thowt that dog had been on this earth before it was so clever.

"Willie Monkhouse worked for mi father Joe when he first came to Wasdale Head from Caldbeck in 1926. He went away to farm at Mungrisdale for a while but cem back to Wasdale in the early 1940s to Middle Row. He always had a good dog, nivver two, and he had a big dog called Monty. He was a big fine dog. And the next one he had was also cawd Fly. Real sharp, good dogs, keen o' work and old Willie could really handle them.

"Sheepdogs today don't run for ivver. I've had them uns that would run aw day and aw night. They are few and far between now. Bet wasn't fast, but it could go aw day and aw night. It was slightly daft. It was yan of them that used to like hens. If it seen a hen it had to have it. You had to watch out because it would ga to Row Head and ga wid yan of the old fella's hens. And he used to go bloody crackers.

"Gathering sheep was the most rewarding job. If you had the right team of dogs it was great. I was lucky. I always had half a dozen dogs with one or two comin' on. I loved the freedom of being on the fells and having a pack of dogs. Absolute magic. But I always liked a good terrier wid us anaw. There was ya terrier I had it was a great laal dog. It was so honest. It was cawd Nip and was a laal red thing. And it would

Joss with Spy in Blengdale.

Joss pictured with Bet at Wasdale in 1974. Bet originally came from Hartsop Hall, Patterdale. "If he seen a hen he had to have it," says Joss. "You had to watch it because it would go to Row Head and go wid one of the old fella's hens. And he used to go bloody crackers."

look at a borran and if there was a fox it would be in and bolt it out. There would be Yap! Yap! Yap! And the fox would pop out and the terrier would be 10 yards behind it chessin' it and after another few seconds it would be 150 yards behind."

Walking with Joss and his dog Spy on the northwest flank of Seatallan one September day we came across a sheepfold and as we approached the dog flushed out a fox that must have been sleeping among the reeds in a corner of the fold. The fox leapt onto the top of the wall, in full view, and then made a dash for it in the direction of Blengdale. Within a matter of seconds it was well out of harm's way, far too fast and elusive for the chasing Spy who was soon left far behind.

"Jim liked to go hunting with the fell packs," Joss continued, "but mi other brother Scott nivver bothered much. We had a pack of dogs on the farm that hunted. There was this old dog cawd Bell and it used to hunt foxes. It had pups and Jim had yan and I had the other. And if you let them off in a morning they would tek off and hunt.

"Gyp, Bell and Smart were just like a pack of hounds and they catched dozens of foxes. There was ya morning I let them off and I went and washed mi hands in the sink at Row Head and I was looking out of the window and they had only bin gone five minutes and they catched this bloody great big fox that had been asleep in a sheepfold. I would let them off of a morning in the wintertime and they would just tek off and hunt foxes. Just for fun."

But it was a brutally efficient business.

"They couldn't half catch them and they would kill them in seconds," Joss continued. "Yan got them by the throat and the other just between its four legs and collapsed its lungs. When they first went out yan would come back on three legs where the fox had bit it, but they soon got the job off.

"There's some big bracken on Kirk Fell bottom and ya morning I sent them out onto the fell in search of a fox that had been tekkin' lambs. After a while there was such a bloody howl up. I climbed out to them only to find that they had come across a hedgehog, way up on the fell. I could have kicked their bloody arses. I couldn't believe it. What the hell this laal hedgehog was doing way up on the fell I don't know, but it had rolled itsell up intill a ball and they couldn't mek head nor tail of it and were barking at it."

The dogs had a highly tuned hunting instinct.

"Bell knew if you were on a push bike. It would hunt you down the road. If you had gone somewhere and it wasn't about it would hunt mi feet. As long as I was on a pushbike or the tractor it would find us, but if I was in the car it wouldn't bother. Bell lived until she was 18 years old and it's a strange thing, about two mornings before Bell died it used to sleep in the oppen barn at Middle Row and it was always sitting waiting on the back door step when I went out. And this morning I looked in the barn and there was a dead fox, this old fox had died. The fox would just be done with age, it would just be trailing about. That fox hadn't a tooth in its head. And do you know two mornings later old Bell died in the exact same spot."

Joss with Bet at Wasdale.

All of Joss's dogs down the years had their individual characteristics and he got to know his animals well and felt a deep sense of loss whenever a dog came to the end of its days, not only because they were sometimes difficult to replace, but also because he was extremely fond of them.

"On a personal level you become too attached to them," says Joss. "There was one of them died of a heart attack a few years back while we were out in Spain on holiday. It knew the day before that you were coming back yam. How the hell it knew I don't know, but it was up on top of its kennel and barking. That same dog knew 300 or 400 yards before a car approached Low Greendale if there was a dog in it. If there wasn't a dog in the car it wouldn't bat an eyelid. How it knew I nivver found out, it nivver telt us.

"The day it died I knew there was summat wrong. It had this massive heart attack and had gone down. It hadn't suffered so that was something to be thankful for. But you can't replace dogs like that. It was one on its own. We cawd it Chance. It was a bonnie black and white dog and the reason we cawd it Chance was that its mother wasn't ready to have pups. She had no milk and we lost the other five and it was a miracle that it lived. I used to tek it to the fell when it was six weeks old. I used to pick it up and put it in mi pocket. It was more or less a pet. It was a great laal dog."

Reference the point about Chance knowing if another dog was in a car approaching Wasdale, there is a lot of evidence to suggest that dogs have a sixth sense and I personally believe they can see things which are beyond the reach of Man.

A friend and I were once walking a smashing little mongrel dog called Bob on the path beneath Falcon Crag close to the shores of Derwentwater. Out of the blue and without any apparent reason on an innocuous fine afternoon, the dog suddenly froze on the spot as if it had been electrocuted, its hackles were up in an instant and then, clearly in a state of terror and agitation, it made a bolt for it and did not stop until it had reached the place in Big Wood, several hundred yards away, where we had parked the car at the start of the walk.

I am convinced that the dog was able to see something that we could not and, what ever it was, it was very, very scary and, presumably, not of this earthly world. My instinctive thought was a spirit or apparition of the something-evil-this-way-comes variety. Fortunately perhaps our limited senses could not pick up on the threat, real or unreal.

"I had this dog called Scamp," Joss continued. "And he died when he was young. He was born ya day when we were gathering sheep at Gillerthwaite. It was just lucky that I seen it when mi brother Scott's dog Flip pupped on the fell. The bitch dropped it when it was running and I put him in mi pocket and fetched him yam. I dunno if Scott fetched any mair back, but I put Scamp in mi pocket and he was a beautiful dog. He mebbe wasn't the cleverest but anything you asked him to do he would do it as fast as he could. And when you were hay timing in the fields, going across to the church or summat like that, he would sit on the path and look pitiful and these old ladies would always give him sweets. He was a right bloody cadge. At that time we used to tek the milk ovver to the old lady at the vicarage and if Scamp was with us he would always sit under the window of the room you were in and the moment you got up to go he would be waiting for you at the back door.

"Scamp was a good dog for lambing time. It could catch sheep anywhere. We lost Scamp when he was in his prime. I was gathering sheep over in Ennerdale on the Black Sail side of Pillar Rock and it was coming through under there with most of the sheep when a yow and a lamb shot into the forest. Scamp went after them and it jumped this fence in a hollow, but it caught itself awkwardly on the wire. When he cem out with the sheep and the lamb he was walking stiff. And he was sort of stiff aw that day until we got yam. I fed him at night and he was still the same. Next morning we were going gathering round Mosedale and he was lying dead aback of the door. It was just four year old but it was born on the fell and it mair or less died on the fell. Losing Scamp was like losing a leg. It was one tremendous dog and it couldn't half git sweets off old ladies."

Then there was the legendary Lassie.

"As good a dog as I ivver had was yan cawd Lassie," explained Joss. "Ben Ullock said to me ya day: 'You couldn't handle a wild dog could yer?' I said 'Aye.' He said 'it's just blotted its copybook. Our Hazel was just going to judge the produce at Cockermouth Show and Jimmy (Hazel's husband, Jimmy Phizacklea) was in the house and she'd left her handbag on the table. So she wound the van window down and said 'Jimmy, can you get my handbag off the table.' Lassie was garn by at the time and jumped up on the van and Hazel had greet mucky paw marks on her nice white blouse."

Lassie, it seemed, had to go but Ben's loss was Joss's gain.

"It had a top gear and it would go aw day," says Joss. "You would set it off to gather sheep and it would go flat out. When it went to gather sheep they knew they had to come. And it would terrorise the cows.

"But Lassie was another bloody old cadge. It would mebbe disappear when you were milking and you would go down to Netherbeck Bridge and it would be sitting having a picnic with some old ladies. Old Lassie would put her nose in a tent pitched near the roadside and git half a pound of butter. And it didn't really want it. It would walk along the road to the bottom pasture and there was a heap of leaves. So it just stuck its paw in, pulled the leaves forrard, dropped its butter and then covered it with its nose.

"And if it found a sheep on the fell that was kessen (stranded on its back) and was still alive it would sit and howl. It was very honest that way. . . ."

That mention of a kessen sheep brings to mind Lancelot Noble, or Lant as he was known, who lived in the hamlet of Butterwick, near Bampton Grange in the Eden Valley and who was a farmer all his life, a tenant at Scar View since 1934. When it came to the night sky Lant said it had its uses for determining what the weather was going to do and he placed a great deal of faith in predicting the weather by the phases of the moon.

"There's dry uns and wet uns," he said of the moon. "If it's ganna be wet the moon would be a thin un, upright and all the watter running reet off it. But if it's kessen (lying horizontal) it'll hold the watter and then it'll be dry."

So there you have it, meteorology made easy.

For farming in wet weather (the moon clearly must have been thin and upright the night before) Lant wore a hessian sack over his shoulders, fastened at the neck with a nail. He maintained that it was far better than any modern day protective clothing for keeping off the rain. Lant was clerk of Bampton Parish Council for many years and wrote his minutes in an immaculate copperplate hand. I find it totally fascinating that Bampton children in Lant's day and before were taught to 'plough in Latin' and instructions to the horses were given in that ancient language.

But back to Joss, his dogs and the continuing story of Lassie.

". . . the day that it started to go wrong I was gathering Kirk Fell and there was sheep away in by Sail Crags. So I put Lassie in and it went legging in and as it got by the sheep its back end started to go. It had a job to git home. So ah thowt I'd tek it to Jackson Hodgson, our vet. So that night I was away to Jackson's wid it and he said 'it's knackered – it's discs are all over the place in its back and they're worn. There's no hope. I'll put it to sleep for you.'

"I said 'you won't, it's garn yam and I don't give a bugger if it eats every egg the hens lay.' Lassie knew that if it heard the hen crowing it had laid an egg and it would go and eat it. And it was good at that. But do you know within two days that dog had died. It died of a brokken heart because it couldn't work. It nivver looked up and it could have lived for another 12 months if it had wanted to. But it just said 'no.' Jackson had said there was nowt up with it apart from the back problem and that it would last quite a while. But in another two days it was dead . . ."

What did Joss look for in a sheepdog?

"The dogs I had had no high creep in them. I like dogs to be on their feet and getting on. You want something that's up on its feet with a lot of bark when you are shifting a lot of sheep. It's only yance in a lifetime that you get a dog like Lassie. The sheep were bloody terrified of it. If ivvery thing was going right things were moving and moving fast. I used to gather for Jackson Fearon and his sheep used to go in the front of Iron Crag and you would set Lassie off and it knew exactly where it was going. And it was only away two or three minutes and them sheep would be out of there. And old Scamp and Patch would be away elsewhere before that at 50mph, barking ivvery bloody step and the sheep used to come out of theer like rabbits with their ears back. It was a great feeling when you had the right dogs and old Moss was always with us if there was owt near that wanted shifting."

For the record, Jack Martin gave Moss to Joss when he (Jack) left Wasdale Head Hall.

"I had three litters of pups out of Moss and they were the best dogs you could wish for," says Joss.

Dogs are renowned for their loyalty to their master and in the churchyard at St Olaf's, Wasdale Head, is the grave of young local man John Wilson Brockbank.

"When he died his dog Jess sat on his grave for weeks," says Joss.

In the Lake District there is arguably no greater story of dog's devotion to man than that of the artist Charles Gough who fell to his death on Helvellyn in the spring of 1805 on the crags overlooking the waters of Red Tarn. The story became known as 'The Unfortunate Tourist of Helvellyn and his Faithful Dog.' Gough was crossing the mountain from Patterdale to Grasmere by way of Striding Edge with the intention of fishing for trout on the other side of the mountain when he lost his way and fell to his death from the crags above Red Tarn.

His terrier bitch, name not known, stayed on the fell at the spot where he lay and stood guard over the body for three months until the corpse was reduced to a skeleton. The terrier, still alive, and Gough's remains, were discovered by a shepherd, William Harrison who observed that "the skull was clean picked o' flesh and was a gay good way off frae t'body, but aw rest o' t' body was togidder, and t'beans (bones) was inside t' cleas (clothes)."

Titch, over heating in his luxurious coat, takes a cooling dip in a pool at Dore Head.

Gough's fishing rod and his penknife with his name inscribed on it were found some distance from the corpse, but still on his person was his Claude Glass, broken in the fall and used by the artist to give a new slant on images of the fells and lakes. He also had on him two guineas and a half in gold, and fifteen shillings in silver.

Newspaper reports at the time suggested that the terrier could only have survived on the fell for such a long time by eating the remains of her master. Others, including Sir Walter Scott and William Wordsworth, clearly thought otherwise and Wordsworth, who visited the scene, paid tribute to the loyalty of the terrier in a poem entitled 'Fidelity.' A monument recording the tragedy stands on Helvellyn to this day and carries lines from the last two stanzas of 'Fidelity' as testimony to the terrier's loyalty:

The Dog, which still was hovering nigh,
Repeating the same timid cry,
This Dog had been through three months' space
A Dweller in that savage place.

How nourish'd here through such long time
He knows, who gave that love sublime,
And gave that strength of feeling, great
Above all human estimate.

Scott wrote in his poem 'I Climbed the Dark Brow of the Mighty Helvellyn':
Dark green was that spot mid the brown mountain heather
Where the pilgrim of Nature lay stretched in decay,
Like the corpse of an outcast abandoned to weather,
Till the mountain winds wasted the tenantless clay.
Nor yet quite deserted, though lonely extended,
For faithful in death, his mute favourite attended,
The much-loved remains of her master defended.
And chased the hill fox and the raven away.

You can trace this sense of loyalty in the way Joss describes his dog Spy, a dog that is also fiercely protective of her master.

"Of the ones I've got now," Joss says, "one crawls up over mi bloody shoulder. That's Spy. That laal dog here (Spy) if I put mi jacket down anywhere it'll sit and guard it. It won't let anyone or another dog near it. And if anyone comes near it'll chess them."

But the line between domestic dog and the wolves that once played on Ullock Pike in the heart of the English Lake District is a marginal one.

There are many stories of dogs that have reverted to the call of the wild and killed sheep and lambs on the fells in order to survive. The most famous, or infamous, of them all was probably the wild dog of Ennerdale which caused mayhem in the early 1800s. The dog – which may have escaped from a travelling circus – appeared to be a cross between a mastiff and a greyhound. It was smooth-haired, of a tawny-mouse colour, and was distinguished by dark, tiger-like streaks. The wild dog of Ennerdale would sometimes destroy as many as eight sheep in a single night and was reputed to have killed almost 300 sheep and lambs in the five months he was at large.

A cunning beast he worked and killed in complete silence, would never return to the same killing ground two nights running and was often chased from the fells by shepherds and their dogs and was regularly and unsuccessfully hunted by men and hounds. Men, armed with guns, also took it in turns to sit and wait in hiding, hoping

Joss and Spy in front of one of the old shooting hides built into the side of the fell on Seatallan.

they might get a chance to shoot the wild dog. He was eventually shot by a man called John Steel who came across the dog taking a cold bath in the river after shaking off the attentions of the hounds. He tracked it to Eskat Wood and sent it to oblivion or, more precisely, to Hutton's Museum, Keswick, where the dog's stuffed skin was exhibited.

Special hides, narrow entrances created in the craggy outcrops of rock on the back of Seatallan are almost impossible to make out until you are upon them. Shown to me by Joss they were used by man as he played an uncomfortable waiting game with his gun and attempted to put an end to the stray dog or dogs – like the wild dog of Ennerdale – that had answered the age old cry of the wolf and were now plaguing the shepherd and his stock.

Meanwhile, back at modern day Low Greendale, Titch, Spy and Sam bounce back and forth from the full extensions of their chains by the kennels against the house wall, the latest in a long line of dogs to stand guard over Naylor property and do their level best to keep wolf-like tendencies in check.

A wonderful painting by the artist Patrick Cremer showing Lakeland characters and a larger than life sheepdog. The man in the centre is the late Derwent Tyson who once farmed at Wasdale Head and later moved to Middle Row, Threlkeld, where his son, Willie, now farms.

Joss and Titch on the packhorse bridge at Wasdale Head with Kirk Fell in the background.

SOL

A DAY IN THE VALLEY 9
Bowderdale, Broken Point and the Emerald Pool

Joss looking out from Dore Head into Wasdale.

Val Corbett and I came across this amazing pattern in a piece of volcanic rock on a footpath at Styhead as we made our way over to Wasdale Head from Seathwaite to meet Joss.

Spending a day in the Wasdale valley would not be the same without the company of Joss Naylor and his dogs. It all starts, of course, at Low Greendale where the Hounds of the Baskervilles, namely the collies Titch and Spy are, as ever, delighted to see you drive up with the possibility of a walk on the fells and extra rations. Spy is arguably the most ravenous dog on the planet and is constantly on the look out for food. Until you have seen this dog lick out an empty crisp packet you have never come close to a true definition of cleanliness.

For the adults, the first food comes early. Joss has already been out and about and by the time you rock up at Low Greendale – at about 9am – it's time for Mary Naylor's celebrated rock buns and sponge cake washed down by mugs of coffee or tea. The rock buns are laced with cherries or currants while the sponge cake and / or the Guinness cake are also to die for. How on earth Joss has kept his weight down to nine stones, give or take a pound or two either way, throughout his entire adult life, can only be attributed to his love of the great outdoors and being constantly on the move, almost hyper in fact. He is forever roaming the valley and the surrounding fells and walking or running long distances, working off the calories in Mary's cakes.

For the photographer Val Corbett and myself there is no chance. It all goes straight on the hips. And the stomach visibly bulges as the rock buns hit the waistline like winter boulders crashing out of Great Gable's south-west facing crags, the Napes.

For this particular day, Val and I had a cunning plan – the past tense is significant here – to stay at more or less ground level at Wasdale Head to take a number of photographs, the dry stone walls, the inn, the packhorse bridge over the beck, Herdwicks in the fields, the show poster on the old school house door, The Emerald Pool,

Bowderdale in the morning sunshine and with washing on the line.

Joss on the lake shore with dogs, you know the sort of thing.

But Joss clearly had his own agenda and it appeared that we had little or no say in the matter. What Joss says goes and where he goes you go. He was soon leading the way with Titch and Spy in close attendance; his other dog Sam was left behind at Low Greendale, a bit stiff after accompanying Joss on a run over the fells the previous day.

And so we found our way bouncing up the rough lonning (this possibly had implications later for the nearside wheel on my car) to Bowderdale, the farm where Joss lived and worked for more than 40 years and which is now occupied by his son Paul, wife Jenny and two children Craig and Denise. In the field on the approach to Bowderdale are sheep and their lambs, ewes in waiting and a liberal number of stones, many of which have been constructed into two monuments in the shape of small towers; one is more pointed and taller while the other is circular with a seating area of larger stones around its base.

It transpires that the monuments have both been built by Joss, ostensibly to help tidy and gather the stones in the field, but also to leave them in the same location where they may originally have been old burial cairns.

Joss loves dry stonewalling, it is close to his heart and over the years he has seen it as his duty, and a rewarding one in which he takes immense pride, to maintain the dry stone walls in the valley; a job well done and done right, upholding the tradition of

Monuments Joss has created in the field below Bowderdale. 'Joss himself would probably scoff at the suggestion, but to my mind it is the work of an artist, a sculptor. His creations in the Herdwick pasture at Bowderdale and on the lower slopes of Buckbarrow are something special. They are works of art, intentional or not . . .'

The old school building at Wasdale Head is now used to store equipment from the Wasdale Head Show and a colourful wooden poster, on the old door to the school, promotes this annual event.

the hundreds of miles of walls that sweep not only over the Lake District fells, like armies on the move, but also through time. It is estimated that there are something like 3,000 miles of dry stonewall in the Lake District National Park and it is a generally held belief that for every yard of wall there's a ton of stone. Whatever the precise figure on the mileage front, that constitutes an amazing network of walls and a hell of a lot of stone. Most of the walls are built in the traditional style, in effect two walls in one, built alongside each other, with through stones connecting the two and looser rock and rubble in the centre to enable the wall to settle over the years. Then the wall is crowned with coping stones and, if you want to get really fancy, you can introduce a hogg hole or two to allow the easy passage of sheep from one field to another. Steps built into the wall are another nice, user-friendly touch.

Dry stonewall at Wasdale Head.

Overleaf: A monument built by Joss on the lower slopes of Buckbarrow, not far from his home at Low Greendale. The marvellous view beyond stretches out to the sea and the estuary at Ravenglass.

In recent years Joss has complained long and vigorously about the consequences if the Wasdale walls fall – quite literally in some instances – below the standards to which he feels they should be kept. They are an essential part of the environment in the valley and if they come down then something a great deal more important collapses with them. Riding the backs of the Lakeland fells, seemingly for all eternity, the walls are a metaphor for a standard and a way of life that has survived for centuries.

The early settlers, on clearing the forest, would have found the valley floor strewn with stones left by the glaciers. To work the land they would clear the stones into heaps and, eventually, they would be used for field walls. In his highly informative booklet about Wasdale, *The Vikings: Wasdale Head and Their Church*, Bill Bailey writes: "My belief is that they (the walls) were built when the original field clearances took place, maybe as early as AD1000."

In years gone by farmers considered it tantamount to a serious offence to leave a gap in a wall. And as one old dry stone waller said to me: "If you did that you're neighbours would soon be yakking (talking) about it." It's fair to say that Joss is also upholding the yakking tradition whether it's dry stone walls or the maintenance of footpaths on the fells. Both are issues on which he has very strong views and never misses an opportunity to give vent to his feelings; that and the impact of industrial pollution and acid rain on the high fells and streams.

Joss has developed the outline and structure of what is reputed to be a Neolithic building on Buckbarrow.

Dry stone walling at Wasdale.

"The walls are very important to the Lake District," he says, "and I don't like to see them being neglected. Wasdale is renowned for its dry stonewalls and in my day there wasn't a wall down anywhere. When the frost come out of the ground – and the winters were real in them days – you would hear cobbles rattling down off Yewbarrow and they would tek mebbe five or six metres of wall clean out and some of the stones would end up on the road. Ya spring we put 57 wall gaps up at Wasdale Head. I've seen me work on walls 'till mi finger ends were bleeding. You did it and you did it right. It was an understood thing. But today it's a case of stick a bit of wire in, that'll deuh. Well it won't deuh at aw."

The two monuments Joss has created in the field below Bowderdale, between the farmhouse and the lake, are fascinating. Most shepherds or farmers would possibly just heap the stones in the corner of the field but Joss, mindful of the origin of the stones as markers to the dead of another era, has given them added significance. The monuments are creations in their own right and are carefully made with a great deal of skill and attention to detail.

Joss himself would probably scoff at the suggestion, but to my mind it is the work of an artist, a sculptor. Joss is a one-off and is capable of the unexpected. His creations in the Herdwick pasture at Bowderdale and on the lower slopes of Buckbarrow above his home at Low Greendale, are something special. They are works of art, intentional or not, and they work in this rural setting; unlike many of the monuments and memorials increasingly littering a landscape that, in truth, needs nothing but itself to look spectacular.

A special seat Joss has built into the side of the fell on Buckbarrow.

The Angel of the North is an inspirational work of art in its own environment. To have any kind of equivalent sculpture, big or small, in the Lake District landscape would be completely unnecessary and an eyesore. For example, the white wind turbines near Bothel, while outside the Lake District National Park, can clearly be seen from the summit of Walla Crag overlooking Derwentwater and, to my mind, despite their 'green' qualities and design, constitute a blot on the landscape. But the concept of something made out of stones that have been there since the beginning of time, erected into a monument on the possible site of a burial ground and following the method used for the traditional dry stonewall, is not only innovative it is entirely appropriate.

Joss himself needs no convincing about the beauty of the Lake District and Wasdale in particular.

"This is the most beautiful place in the world," he never tires of telling me. "You see nice places, but this is summat else. You can get the sun shining through the trees onto the lake of an evening and it's magic. And the Lake District itself is my paradise. It's a great place and we don't know how lucky we are to be born and raised here."

Joss appreciates Wasdale, Wastwater and the screes in all their different moods and seasons.

"When you come down the road near the bottom end of the lake you nivver see it in quite the same light twice," he adds. "Sometimes the mist is down and it looks a really evil place. The next time you come round that corner it can be paradise and the tops are shining. Ya winter there was snow on the fells and just before you get to what we call Hunter Close, where the boathouse is, you could look in the lake and see the whole of Great Gable. Gable had snow on it and the lake was really black and evil. There wasn't a ripple. It can be very beautiful or very ugly and the weather has the final say. It can be the most evil-looking lake on this earth."

One morning Joss was given a lift to school by a man called John Pool who was in the RAF and who had a vehicle that was more a shooting brake than a car.

"We got to Smithy Beck fall and the wind was blowing and fetching water out of the lake in great big spouts," Joss recalls. "At one point it covered the car in a great sheet of water and it got hold of the car. It didn't exactly blow it ovver but it blew it across the road and the tyres screamed. He went in bottom gear from that point until we were clear of the lake. We were absolutely terrified. I have nivver seen the lake quite like that since.

Crag at Dore Head.

"I have thowt about it many a time and I saw John in the Santon Bridge pub mebbe 30 years ago and he said 'do you remember that time I took you to school' and I said 'I couldn't forget it.' He said 'I couldn't tell anybody about that morning because I couldn't describe how bad it was and they wouldn't have believed us in any case'."

It is a spectacularly fine day in mid April when we stroll up and around Bowderdale. The sky is a vivid blue and the washing on the line in the garden to the front of the farmhouse is barely stirring in the softest of breezes. Joss's son Paul is at the door at the back of the house and is a man of few words. I shake his hand and introduce myself – Joss, I've noticed, isn't particularly strong on introductions, with anyone – and when I ask Paul what he will be doing today he replies: "Seamme (same) as yesterda' – keeping them alive."

He is, of course, referring to the daily routine of lambing time and ensuring that as many lambs as possible survive their early days on the planet when they are at their most vulnerable. Only the night before he

Joss strides up the fell above Bowderdale with Spy at his heel.

killed two foxes that had been taking lambs. The foxes tend to carry off their prey and eat the body, but for some reason leave the legs on the fell, perhaps cached away for another day when food is scarce. As we walk out from the farm towards Dore Head, in the valley through which runs Over Beck, Titch and Spy are soon picking up the scent and trying to find the remains of the lambs taken by foxes.

Spy, in fact, sniffs out a leg on Gosforth Crag on the return journey and crunches her way through it in double quick time. Everything is bolted down and nothing is left before Spy responds to Joss's whistle and dashes back to fall in at his feet, alongside Titch whose earlier attempts to sneak away and hunt out a lamb's leg he had got a scent of at Broken Point were continually thwarted by his master's voice.

On the outward journey the valley is flanked by the impressive heights of Yewbarrow and High Fell. Over Beck is a beautiful little stream and at one point, not far out from Bowderdale, a massive boulder – not unlike the Bowder Stone but about half as big – has come to rest next to the stream; a beck that is punctuated by those small waterfalls and pools which can make fantastic bathing places on hot summer days in the fells. Val is wearing long black shorts which could just as easily be short black longs, and is clearly tempted by the water in her attempt to remain cool on this unseasonably hot spring day. And to back up her wild swimming credentials she points out that she had a dip in a Lakeland tarn on Christmas Day.

But Joss is bounding ahead and we are clearly on a mission.

It soon transpires that our objective is Dore Head. We scramble along an exposed path looking down onto Dore Head Screes and Mosedale and all of a sudden are confronted by a pinnacle in the crag face that resembles a broken tooth. This is what Joss calls Broken Point and it is spectacular with an equally spectacular drop to the valley below. Joss, Titch and Spy are suitably arranged on the point itself. Joss looks out at the amazing view of Wasdale and its myriad dry stonewalls and Scafell Pike and Scafell high in the distance on the far side of the valley.

Val complains about the light being flat – photographers must be like shepherds and farmers in that climatic conditions are rarely ever to their liking – but I am mightily impressed by the vantage point to which Joss has dragged us for the photo shoot. I am sure that the end result will be some stunning images. Most pictures of Wasdale are taken from Styhead or Gable and Westmorland Cairn, erected in 1876 by two brothers called Westmorland to mark what they thought to be the finest view in the Lake District. The view from Broken Point represents a unique take and angle on a much-photographed scene and Joss and the dogs are impressive against a backcloth – when viewed from my standpoint against the crag – of Kirk Fell and Mosedale.

Kirk Fell, of course, is the mountain used for the fell races at Wasdale Show on the second Saturday in October. The route goes straight up to the summit and then follows the same path down. It is a steep, unrelenting climb, direct and merciless and will leave most people gasping for breath and with searing pain in the calf muscles. To run up the fell is nigh impossible and the experienced will put hands on knees, put their head down, go for it and climb as quickly as they can. The helter-skelter of the descent is strictly for those with rubber joints and the bravery of youth. Joss, who started his brief short-distance fell running career in his early twenties and wore sawn off trousers for shorts and a pair of fell beutts for footwear, tells me that he once decided to, as he put it, "trot up to the top" on his own.

"One night," he said, "I went up there from the old school at Wasdale Head quite comfortably in 28 minutes without really pushing it. The legs were good then and I stopped at the top because I had a laal stone in mi shoe and in 53 minutes I was on the top of Pillar. So that was 53 minutes from the old school to the top of Pillar (2,927ft) via Kirk Fell (2,630ft) and then in an hour and 25 minutes I was back home."

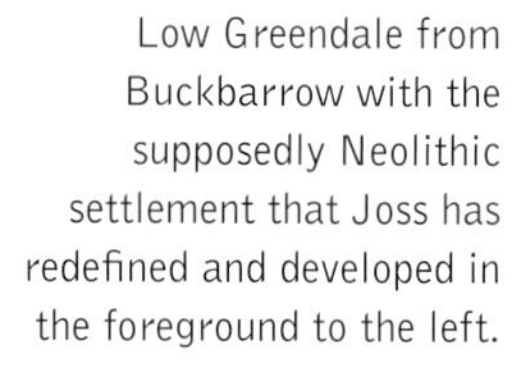

Low Greendale from Buckbarrow with the supposedly Neolithic settlement that Joss has redefined and developed in the foreground to the left.

"Bloody hell, that's going some," I say.

"Aye, but I was young and fit then and running well," Joss replies. "It's nowt when ivverything's right and it's in your legs. But things have got to be going right."

As Joss looks out from the Broken Point into Wasdale Head there is a magnificent view of the patchwork of fields enclosed in the dry stonewalls. The fields are quite unique in the Lake District and they all have names. And while some have been forgotten, Joss can recall a fair few of them: New Close, Goose Lump, Pub Meadow, Priest Meadow, Jopson's intake, The Long intake, Grayson's Riggs, Square intake, Reservoir intake, Top Long intake, Bull Field, Orchard intake, The School Field, The Ashes, The Vicarage Field, Long Field, Pig Field, Crab Dale, Round Field, Gate Riggs, The Wool Walls, Gable intake and Down in the Dale meadows.

Trees on the shore of Wastwater with the screes on the far side of the lake.

Wasdale screes in winter.

"Some of the names are lost," Joss adds as he points with his hazel stick across the valley. "Those at the top of the beck are the Red Brows. And those two top lots of fields, they're cawd the Cobalt Fields. The Ministry (of Agriculture) did an experiment with cobalt. They put cobalt in among the manure that was put on the fields and it was a pick me up for sheep suffering from sowt (a joint problem). Ya fella from the Ministry reckoned that sheep in the cobalt fields were growing faster than the others so we used to kid him on, but their improvement was mair to deuh with going onto a piece of good, fresh ground."

At the start of this book I refer to Joss venturing alone onto Black Sail Pass as a five year old. In fact his father Joe had taken him to the fell when he was only three years old, high into Mosedale, and Joss recalls being left below scree beds at the foot of the fell to watch a sheep while his father went higher to look for two more sheep that

had gone over to Ennerdale. They were the only three sheep missing from an earlier gather of the fells.

Joss recalls his father telling him how certain places got their names.

"Father pointed to a crag on the skyline where the metal fence finishes – which most people call the Wire End – but he said that's what Willie Greenup caws Boot Crag. This hiker had changed into a pair of plimsolls or summat and he left a boot there so old Willie christened it Boot Crag. About 40 years after I was gathering sheep in that area and I was crossing these stones below Boot Crag and this old boot was there. It was the sort that had clinkers in for rock climbing in the early days. It must have been there 50 – 60 years and I reckon it's the same boot that Willie had come across. So there's a little bit of history that nobody else knows owt about."

Willie Greenup, for the record, was another – like Joss's dad – who originally farmed out Caldbeck way but moved to Wood How, Wasdale. Farmers in those days were often on the move with a view to improving their lot in life; sometimes it paid off and other times it was a mistake.

In the early 1940s Joss was again on the fell with his father when a plane crashed up above Bull Crags.

"He was a Polish pilot," says Joss, "and he would know there was no way out for him when he cem past us because he had no height. Whether he had left it too late or what I don't know. There was a bang and that was it. The mist was down. Father and one or two others went up and brought his remains down in a bag. Whether he was on a training flight or what I don't know. The plane had caught fire and it was a sad end to a lad who had given his life to fighting in the war."

Joss, Val, the dogs and I move away from the exposure of Broken Point back to Dore Head. En route we come across a turmoil of tadpoles in a small water hole and in imminent danger of being left high and dry by the burning sun and a lack of rain. Val and I end up ferrying bottles of water from a larger pool of water nearby to the smaller pool with a view to saving countless lives. Joss does not appear to be overly impressed and after a while announces that it's time to move on and heads off for Red Pike with us trailing in his wake.

On the return trip to Bowderdale, via Great Knott, Gosforth Crag (where Spy crunches his way through his lamb leg lunch) and skirting Low Tarn, we descend to Over Beck and Joss and I scan the wonderfully clear pools for any sign of fish life. Sadly there is none and it seems a great pity that there are no, or very few, trout in a beautiful little beck that once teemed with fish. Joss says that industrial pollution and acid rain are to blame.

Back in the valley we head for the Wasdale Head Inn for a drink and a snack and Joss shows me the side of the building at Middle Row where, nobbut lads, he and his brother Jim catapulted a volley of old tin cans out of a bent over Ash sapling onto the front door of the hotel. Spy, still hungry despite that leg of lamb, is on the cadge as we sit at the picnic tables by Mosedale Beck at the back of the inn and does an immaculate job of licking out a crisp packet. Spy has no scruples whatsoever when it comes to food. Titch, on the other hand, is above begging, adopts a more dignified approach and merely sits there with her front paws splayed and a solitary eye peeping out from underneath the wilderness that is her coat. She certainly wins the sympathy vote.

"She's just like a walking wind bush," observes Joss. "She's a scruffy looking dog but she's gonna have a clip out around the 15th or 16th of May and you'll not recognise the hound then . . . it'll be a new dog. In fact it'll be nearly ready to go to Crufts by June. It's time it won it, it's had lots of seconds."

It is now after 3pm, we have been on the fell since 10am and it is time to move on from the Inn to our second destination of the day, a magical place called The Emerald Pool which lies at the head of the valley and at the point where Piers Gill and Spout Head Gill merge to form Lingmell Beck.

But more on the pool later . . . as we make our way along Moses' Trod (named after Moses Rigg, a Honister quarryman who had a sideline in illegally distilled whisky that he used to hide beneath the slates on his pony-drawn sled) we come across a tractor wobbling its way towards us on the rutted track and being driven by Andrew Race, a North-Easterner who runs nearby Burnthwaite Farm. Joss and Andrew stop for the crack. As a buzzard rises in the thermals over Hell Gate scree on Great Gable the conversation moves to the subject of birds of prey and how effective peregrine falcons are at taking wood pigeons out of the sky and training their young to do the same.

Joss says we are headed for the Emerald Pool and Andrew says: "There are trout in there if you sit still enough and long enough," which is good news. Joss says he once saw trout spawning in a beck high on Wasdale Common.

"There were these two little buggers spawning on a gravel bed in an inch of watter and they weren't fower inches long the pair of them," he says. "Nature's a marvellous thing, how it keeps these things going."

The small stained glass window in St Olaf's Church, in memory of those members of the Fell and Rock climbing club who died in the First World War.

What is developing nicely into an interesting exchange between two residents of Wasdale Head, one who has been there since birth and the other for a matter of just a few years, is interrupted by the arrival of a fell walker, a large young man, red of face, a rucksack on his back and carrying a water bottle. He looks mildly agitated and stands for a short while, anxious to make his entrance, a looming presence and no one seems sure who he belongs to.

Eventually Joss puts him out of his misery and opens the door to the conversation.

"Now young fella?" he says.

"Are you Andrew by any chance?"

"I am," says Andrew, from the cab of his tractor.

"There's a couple up there asked me to call Mountain Rescue," says the walker.

Someone on the fell has told the walker that Andrew can contact the mountain rescue from Burnthwaite Farm.

"They were coming down this side of Gable on the screes," the walker adds. "I think she'd slipped down a few times and was panicking. She hadn't hurt herself. She was just sitting on a rock . . ."

A quick recce through my binoculars shows a young couple, a man in white and a woman in blue, making their way slowly down the screes. They are about 100 yards apart and it would appear, as the fell walker had suggested, that they have had something of a domestic over their position on the fell, possibly of the "what the hell were you doing bringing me here for, it's dangerous" variety. They do not, however, appear to be in any immediate danger as they make their tentative way down the scree towards the Gavel Neese path and are certainly not in need of mountain rescue.

"Go and carry her down Joss!" laughs Andrew. But Joss has had enough and we are off again in the direction of the Emerald Pool. Every now and then I pause to take a look through the binoculars at the fell and the couple have made their way successfully off the loose scree onto the firmer footing of the path and are now either having a secondary row, renewing their marriage vows or hoping against hope that the mountain rescue and a helicopter are not on their way.

Wasdale Head has always been considered to be the home of mountaineering. The Wasdale Head Inn, or The Wastwater Hotel as it was previously known, was the HQ for the early rock climbers and there are wonderful images on the walls of the inn showing, for example, boots, ice axes, ropes and rucksacks in the entrance hall. An image of two of the early pioneers of rock climbing, the Abraham Brothers, George and Ashley, from Keswick, stands proud in the dining room. The brothers, following in the footsteps of their father, G.P.Abraham, used an old Underwood whole-plate camera, a heavy wooden box that recorded images on large glass plates. This was the era of hobnailed boots, heavy tweeds and soft hats. The photographs taken by the brothers conjure up a romantic image of the period with men and women clambering up snowy ridges on Great End or clinging precariously to exposed rock faces with fingers, knees and boots; the latter appearing to hinder rather than help the scaling of rock.

Wasdale Head's drystone walls and the yew trees surrounding St Olaf's Church. The earliest reference to the church is 1550.

But it was a deadly business, a great deal more risky than today, and the early equipment used was invariably out of the basic, washing line school of rock climbing favoured by youngsters on their first ventures to the fells. The small graveyard at St Olaf's Church, Wasdale Head, holds the bodies of just a few of those who have lost their lives on the crags in the surrounding area. A tiny stained glass window in the church carries an illustration of Napes Needle and beneath it the words: 'I will lift up mine eyes to the hills from whence cometh my strength.'

In the days before mountain rescue teams were officially formed, the forerunners of today's highly trained and dedicated teams were the local farmers who went out onto the fells to rescue climbers or bring back the corpses of those who had fallen to their deaths.

"Originally the farmers would have no choice," explained Joss. "They had an old canvas stretcher in the shed at The Wastwater Hotel. And if someone came to grief they would try and get a team up and I know mi father nearly always used to ga. It was a question of whoever was available at the time.

"It wasn't so bad if the bodies were fresh. There was a couple who were missing in the late 1920s early 1930s. They were camping at Burnthwaite and disappeared. Three or four days later somebody saw their ropes hanging on the west side of Pillar Rock. They had fallen off and were lying in a waterfall yonder. And they were badly maggoted. It took them two days to carry them back, they just had the old stretcher, and they fetched them and put them in the barn and put sheep dip on them to kill the smell. Jim Wilson (a Wasdale shepherd) said the stench of rotting flesh in the barn was there for ages. Jobs like that weren't very nice. But there wasn't anyone else to do it."

Joss also recalls the extraordinary case of the wonderfully named Cornelius Crump who was staying at The Wastwater Hotel in 1921 and who disappeared on June 21 after venturing onto the fells. Search parties went out repeatedly, but failed to find any trace of him.

"He had likely bin trying to climb through Piers Gill," Joss explains. "But I think he had slipped in this waterfall and brokken his ankle. And he just couldn't get back down and he was stuck at the bottom of this waterfall for 19 days before he was found. He was just lucky someone cem across him. He was a bit hungry and mebbe a bit strange, the water had affected his mind a bit. But in time he got better. Mi mother knew him. He cem to Wasdale Head quite a lot at that time."

A party of climbers found Cornelius as they attempted the first descent of Piers Gill. They came across him sitting sideways and gazing down the gill. He was conscious and able to walk a little, but had had no food for three weeks. He would certainly have died had the weather not been so warm and had he not been so close to fresh water.

In 1946 one climber with a broken leg was successfully brought down by other climbers, including Colonel "Rusty" Westmorland, of Keswick, from Great Gable. After a particularly arduous rescue operation in freezing gale force winds, sleet and in pitch black the injured man was put in front of the Aga at Burnthwaite Farm and the farmer's wife, Maggie Ullock (the wife of Joss's friend Ben) looked at the assembled climbers and said: "You all look gay tired."

"Well, we've been out for 20 hours," came the reply.

"Aye," said Mrs Ullock, "it's far less trouble when they kill thersells." It was a sentiment probably not shared by the injured man recovering in front of the Aga.

The shepherds, of course, had firsthand experience of going into precarious places on the fells. It was part of their working life to try and save sheep stranded on crag faces.

"They used to get in Raven Crag," recalls Joss, "and Proud Knott in Ennerdale was also notorious. On a Sunday I used to have a walk out and tek a hemp rope wid us and a sling or two and I used to go and tek them out. There was ya Sunday I took 25 sheep out from fower different spots but mainly in Ennerdale."

It occurs to me that climbing around on a rock face with a fearsome drop below is bad enough without having the added problem of catching a frightened sheep, tying it to you on a sling and then climbing out. And if you should fall the rocks below do not give on impact and are unforgiving on brain, brawn and bone. The sheep, not surprisingly, are very rarely helpful – on the contrary they are scared rigid and capable of anything – and occasionally develop lemming-like tendencies.

"Ya day there was yan lying crag fast on a ledge," recalls Joss. "I got mi rope out and swung missell in and this thing blew down its bloody nose at us and jumped straight off. It must have gone 200 feet before it hit anything. You can't understand them. As a rule I'd tek a bit of grass wid us and go in slowly and entice them. They are pretty forbidding some of these places and I used to anchor missell in well so they couldn't tek us wid 'em and as I got nearer I'd grab them by a leg. I used to try and get them by the chin and then you had the centre of gravity. If you got them under there you had them. I would hang on to a leg and pull them back to us and tie the legs so they couldn't kick or scuffle.

"Sometimes I used to leave them until they had lost a bit of flesh and you hadn't the weight to contend with. If they were weaker it was easier to get them out. But there were odd places where it's nearly impossible. Just above Robinson's Cairn it was really icy one morning and I couldn't do anything for it. I couldn't get at it. You couldn't get at it from the top and if you went in from the side it would have pulled you off so I just had to say goodbye to it. Sometimes they die on their legs, but mostly the wind blows them off. Nature's cruel. Nowadays it isn't such a problem because there isn't the number of sheep on the fells."

We branch off the path to Styhead, hold fast to Lingmell Beck and walk up a gentle incline alongside the beck and over rough ground, bog and stone to the point where Piers Gill and Spout Head Gill merge to form Lingmell Beck. And it is there that I am genuinely astounded by the vision, yes vision is the only word for it, which meets my eyes. As a lover of water, especially the pure variety (what Joss would call "sweet water") that flows fast over Lakeland rock in beck, stream and river and a great admirer also of smashing little pools that make wonderful bathing places in the heat of summer, preferably with a waterfall that can also act as a shower, I have never, ever seen the like of The Emerald Pool.

It is like something out of a fairy tale.

At the head of this magical, enchanting pool what was presumably once a massive piece of rock has been reduced to a tall, almost wafer thin slab by the force of water

The Emerald Pool.

hitting it from either side for hundreds of years where the two streams meet. That alone is amazing, but nature has also carved its signature into the rock where boulders have gouged out grooves as they crash along with the beck on countless spates. The pool that has formed below the central rock at its head is nothing short of mesmerising. The combined effects of sunlight on the water and the turquoise blue-green of the rocks (the emeralds) on the bottom of the pool are incredible. Viewed from above the waterfall the patterns in the water made by sunlight, reflection and the stream's underlying current appear to be dancing and shimmering; they are almost like phantoms.

This is the sort of place where you would not be surprised in the least if you came across an elf with a fishing rod sitting on a toad stool on the far bank attempting to catch a fish for his tea and wishing you the time of day, or Tinker Bell flitting over the water, this way and that and leaving a trail of stars in her wake. This is a special place but to get the maximum effect you need strong sunlight and to approach the pool at a time when the sun has risen above the slopes of Lingmell and is slanting up the valley. In other words you ideally need to wait until late afternoon or early evening otherwise the charm will be lost and it will be just another pool, a good one yes, but one in need of a kiss from the sun to bring its magic to life.

The name Emerald Pool was actually coined by a man called George Haslam, a schoolmaster who used to visit Wastwater twice every year on holiday. He would tell Joss's old pal Ben Ullock: 'I'll just go and spend half an hour watching the reflections and the colours in the pool before dinner. I think it's magic. It must be a gift from God to have a place like that.'

I now know precisely what he meant. And I hope that those people who love the fells and the Lake District and who will appreciate The Emerald Pool are those who pay it a visit.

Overleaf: Lingmell Beck with Great Gable in the background to the left. The stones are testimony to the force of the water when the beck is in spate.

Hypnotised by the pool it is not easy to drag yourself away, but we must as the light will soon be fading and it is time to leave Wasdale and head for home. At this stage we have been out on the fells for eight hours and Joss and the dogs are still tearing ahead. No rest for the wicked.

The walk back to the car park at The Wasdale Head Inn gives us an opportunity to study the mass of boulders left high and dry by the low water in Lingmell Beck. The amount of stone here is awesome and a strong indication of the force of the water when the beck is running at full tilt on the back of heavy rains. The erosion and great width of the channel and the amount of debris that has been washed off the fells, stone and wood, is quite spectacular. There is also a savage reminder of the cruel, unforgiving nature of this world. Just beyond the wooden bridge where Gable Beck joins Lingmell Beck there are the skeletal remains of a sheep that has presumably fallen into the beck, been washed away and drowned during a flood, its backbone and skull now stranded on top of the stones and arched in such a way that it is indicative of the agony of its death throes.

With the dogs safely ensconced in the back we set off from the Wasdale Head Inn for Low Greendale, but there is clearly something wrong with the car – something appears to be catching on the nearside wheel arch – and a tyre blows about a mile along the road. Bloody hell, this is the last thing you need at the end of a long, but very satisfying day on the fells. All attempts to solve the problem prove fruitless (it is clearly more serious than just a blown tyre) and I call out the help of a mechanic, a friend, Gary Stevens, who kindly agrees to drive from Threlkeld to our assistance. The frustrating thing I always find about Wasdale Head is that you have to drive all the way round via Whitehaven and Gosforth, to get there from my home in Keswick, yet – if you went up Borrowdale to Seathwaite – it's just a hop, step and a jump over the fell. Still, I wouldn't have it any other way. A road linking Borrowdale to Wasdale, as was once mooted, would be sacrilege.

Joss and the dogs have already set off on foot for Low Greendale and Val and I decide to walk back to The Wasdale Head Inn for food and drink. In the rapidly fading light and with the moon and stars starting to appear in the early night sky we trudge along the footpath by the stream to the inn. In our weary state we start to talk about walking at night on the fells. I reminisce about the time I followed in the footsteps of the poet Samuel Taylor Coleridge when he made his way at dead of night over Helvellyn to Dove Cottage and Grasmere to visit the Wordsworths.

The Lake Poets, especially Coleridge and Thomas de Quincey, were not averse to drug taking – it was seen as essential medication for some ailments in the 1800s – and Val and I are clearly starting to hallucinate when we speculate on the possibility of a legally questionable idea for 21st Century tourism in the Lakes. We would call it 'Off Your Heads' – the STC Lakeland holiday experience of a lifetime and beyond, or something snappy like that. Everyone signing up would get a large bottle of Laudanum and there would be a complimentary phial of Kendal Black Spot for every party of 12. Fortunately the Wasdale Head Inn arrives out of the gloom in the nick of time and much needed food and drink helps restore our sense of balance.

Gary arrives an hour and a half later and declares that the car is, to all intents and purposes, dead, a spring has snapped on a wheel arch and cannot be fixed on the spot and it will need to be recovered to a garage the next day. So we head off for Keswick in his vehicle with the reassuring presence of Gromit – out of the world famous Wallace and Gromit – staring meaningfully at us from his perch on the rear view mirror. There is clearly no escape from dogs of all breeds after this long, tiring but happy day in the valley in the company of the inimitable Titch and the ever-hungry Spy.

Not forgetting, of course, the lad himself, Joss Naylor.

The view from Styhead down to Wasdale

CORPSES AND COCKFIGHTING 10
A matter of life and death

The remains of the old peat houses on the Wasdale side of Burnmoor Trod. The peat would be used by houses and farms in the valley.

Imagine, if you will, two distinct scenes of life and death on a Lakeland fellside.

In the first a coffin strapped to the back of a horse makes its way over the trail leading to a desolate Lakeland moor on a harsh winter's afternoon. The horse labours up the fell path and in its wake comes the funeral cortege, the family dressed in black, bent over and huddled together against the driving sleet and rain that slashes into their faces as they crest the rise. If the mourners lift their eyes from their cold, sodden feet – the water streaming off the fell has turned the path into a beck – they can make out the grey and sombre Burnmoor Tarn that lies ahead in the middle distance and, beyond that, the sea to the west where a sailing ship struggles through turbulent seas on the distant horizon, its destination the port of Whitehaven further up the Cumbrian coast.

In the second the scene changes to a warm summer's evening. There is a small grouping of stone houses, peat houses, about 10 in total, on the side of the self-same fell and on the high side of the trail. In the lee of one of the houses a group of men gather furtively in a circle. Not far away, on either side, two of their number keep a careful eye on the approach routes to the fell. As a shout goes up the two men hurriedly make their way back to rejoin the group. The men, cloth-capped and fell beutted with rough trousers and off-white shirts, become animated as they form a tight-knit ring around the cockfight, shouting and bawling in a hubbub of noise as, in the centre of it all in the main, two game cocks, razor sharp spurs attached to their legs, start a fight to the death.

The birds come together in a whirl and frenzy, wings beating as they clash, leap into the air and then retreat momentarily before flying at each other again, a flurry of feathers and aggressive intent. Splashes of blood soon lick the grass and there is a smear of red on a blade as one of the birds begins to flap helplessly on the ground and the other goes in for the kill.

The two scenes portrayed above are inextricably linked. The chapter heading 'corpses and cockfighting,' apart from being a piece of alliteration that rolls off the tongue and makes for an intriguing combination, is related directly to the Burnmoor Trod that joins Wasdale to Eskdale. The trod is also known as the Corpse Road or Corpse Trail because in the days before the churchyard at the tiny St Olaf's, Wasdale Head (the roof beams in the church are reputed to have come from a Viking long boat) was consecrated in 1901 the bodies of the dead were taken on the back of a horse or by horse and cart over Burnmoor and then Eskdale Moor for burial at the lovely little church of St Catherine's, set beside the River Esk in the heart of Eskdale. Swallows nest among the beams in the roof of St Catherine's porch and visitors are asked to keep the church door closed in case the birds get into the building and cannot escape. Fascinating old headstones in the churchyard bear the names of people from Wasdale Head (or Wafdale as it is inscribed on the stone) who were buried at St Catherine's after the funerals made their way over Burnmoor from Wasdale.

The cockfighting comes into it because the Corpse Road on the Wasdale Head side, near the location of some old and now broken down peat houses, was, according to Joss Naylor, a popular location for men from the valleys of Wasdale and Eskdale to engage in cockfighting. It was a handy meeting point and one from which policemen arriving on foot, push bike or on horseback could be easily spotted by the lookouts.

St Catherine's Church, Eskdale. The dead were carried here over Burnmoor from Wasdale Head for burial.

Tommy Dobson's last journey over the Hardknott Pass into Eskdale.

Joss Naylor, the photographer Val Corbett, myself and Joss's dogs Spy and Titch, made our way over the Burnmoor trod in early May on a bleak day ideal for experiencing the mood of the fell. As Val lingers to take pictures of a beautifully renovated little packhorse bridge, Joss and I stand out of the wind at the back of one of the peat houses and he tells me about old Bill Porter, huntsman for the Eskdale and Ennerdale Foxhounds, whom he knew as a lad.

"When I met up with him he was more or less retired and he used to invite us ovver on Boxing Day for the oppening hunt and they were good times really," recalls Joss. "He used to tell us aw sorts about what happened in the past and he used to tell us every place that foxes used to cub in Wasdale Head and that sort of thing. He used to tell us aw about Tommy Dobson's days (the previous huntsman who is buried, as is Bill Porter, in St Catherine's under a very elaborate headstone on which Tommy Dobson's head is carved in the stone together with a whip and hunting horn). It's a pity, but a lot of it's gone out of mi head and it hasn't been documented and handed down.

"He told us about cockfighting here (referring to the peat houses). He always had

The interior of St Olaf's Church. The roof beams are reputedly from a Viking long boat.

Logo for the column, occasionally using characters from the bar at The Wastwater Hotel, which appeared on a weekly basis in The Whitehaven News.

The sign that says it all. Stay to the right if your destination is Eskdale.

Ritson's Bar at The Wasdale Head Inn.

A shepherd and his Herdwick at Eskdale Show.

gamecocks at Brantrake. He said this was an ideal place for cockfights because the men would come up from Eskdale and out of Miterdale and Wasdale and mebbe Nether Wasdale, and it was a good look out point. The police in them days would either have to walk or come on horseback or cycle.

"I can always remember meeting Bill Porter going up the common there one night about half past six and I said 'where you off?' and he said he was gonna stop the weekend with J.R. Whiting. 'I've just fetched him a game cock,' he said, and he oppened the bag and showed us and it was a black-red yan, a real bonny cockerel, it was all dubbed and it had great big spurs, it's own that is, not fighting yans. It was a beautiful bird and it was with the hens for years and it would die of old age. It was the last one that J.R. Whiting ivver had. Garn back to the turn of the last century there would be a fair bit of cockfighting going on in them days."

Can he recall it happening in Wasdale?

"No, not officially," replies Joss. "But I know places where it did because I've dropped on it when I've been out on long runs. But them days are long past because there are too many people on the fells walking about. It did take place and it was a way of life even though it was against the law. It got people out and one valley mebbe fought against the other . . ."

Was there, I wondered, great rivalry between Wasdale and Eskdale?

"No," says Joss, "there was none because Wasdale was far superior. They had the best fighting cocks, the best sheep and ivverything. And the dogs? Well, they could bark when they were asked and be quiet when they were told."

So there was rivalry?

"Yes there was a bit of rivalry, but it was all good natured, aye. There'd be money on the outcome of cockfights. It would be the talk in the pubs. There's no crack in the pubs today."

That certainly wasn't always the case. My research among the bound copies of *The Whitehaven News* uncovered a column written in the 1950s by the then editor of the newspaper, one Willie Newell, writing under the pseudonym 'Copeland'. The column was headed 'Let's have a crack' and its pleasing little logo was a pen and ink drawing of four men, two of them smoking pipes, gathered round a table in a cosy bar. Occasionally the column would be entirely devoted to the supposedly fictional and entertaining world of The Fighting Cock Inn and would feature the locals at the bar who were named as Satty (short for Satterthwaite), Joe Thwaites, Speddy, Batey, t'Parson, Richardson and landlord Wilson. I have no doubt that the bar in question was in fact that at The Wastwater Hotel, Ritson's Bar as it is now and The Huntsman as it was then and that the landlord referred to was none other than the popular figure of Wilson Pharaoh.

The writer, of course, would be familiar with the bar and local characters and events through his friendship with the one time owner of the hotel and bar, J.R.Whiting (see Chapter 1). I do not think it would be a coincidence that the name of the inn was 'The Fighting Cock,' an indication perhaps that cockfighting was still on the go back then. In fact, news reports in the same newspaper refer to police apprehending up to 30 men caught red-handed at a cockfight near Broughton Moor. The men were later fined between £3 and £10 at Cockermouth court. Fourteen live game birds and one dead one were recovered and six of the birds were equipped with steel fighting spurs.

Joss also remembers the days when Herdwick sheep would be taken over the Burnmoor Trod to Eskdale Show.

"If the show was at Eshdell there'd be fower lots come ovver here – Ennerdale ovver Black Sail, Buttermere ovver Scarth Gap, Borrowdale ovver Styhead and then there'd be all the ones out of Wasdale Head, tups to be hired out and sold. Most of them had their faces washed and they would have raddle* (a special dye to give tups a ruddy colour) on them and it would be just nice now to see the fower flocks coming up this path past the peat houses. You can imagine it. But it's a tradition that's gone and there's very little that's been documented about it. There were hundreds of Herdwicks at Eshdell and they were spectacular. They would come ovver from Styhead and Buttermere and stay the night at Wasdale Head and then they stopped at Eshdell as well on show night and the shepherds would have a singsong and a booze up and come back the following day. They were always very special

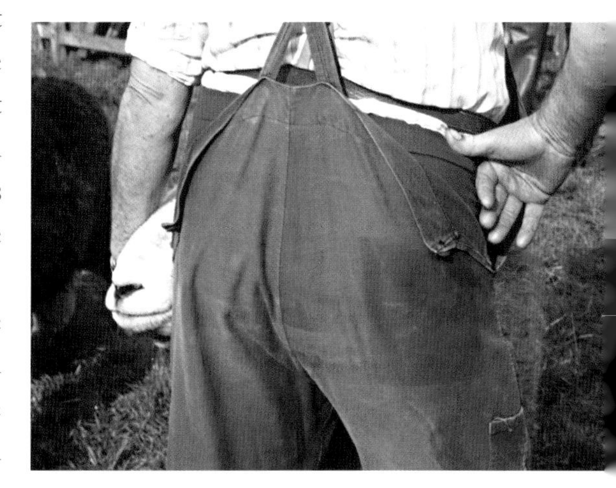

occasions. There were lads who liked their pop and there was a great atmosphere. All in all those frae Buttermere would have been gone for the best part of fower days ya way or another.

"Me and mi father were the last persons to walk ovver here with sheep and rams to Eshdell Show. That was in 1949. We cem up here (by the peat houses) and there was quite a lot of sheep about and he said 'you just go on in front, whistle and mek a bit of noise and then they won't get mixed'. Once we got out on to the moor there was nothing really to bother them. The tups and the sheep he was tekking ower held together well. The dog he had wid 'im knew its job. Mi dad often used to meet Eshdell shepherds at Burnmoor Tarn.

"We stayed with Jimmy Possy at Brook House and it was a nice sunny morning on the day of the show. We would only bring 15-20 tups back wid us and we would tek mebbe 80 ovver. I can always remember we stopped at the Burnmoor pub and I had a bottle of cider and father had an Export. Sid Cross and Hargreaves (keen mountaineers in their day) were there then and it was only a year later that Hargreaves got killed in the Alps and Sid Cross had moved to Dungeon Ghyll at Langdale. There was always lads who wanted to sing and entertain. There just isn't that around here any mair. Yance ower in Wasdal' they were nearly all Tysons and Wilsons, generations of them. They've all moved away and died out. As far as characters and that goes I'm afraid they've gone and they'll nivver return. Kids aren't brought up on the hills anymore. The old ways bred character. Time teks care of ivverything, which is awfully sad."

Joss's father Joe Naylor originally came from Caldbeck. He was shepherd for two and a half years for Mr R.M. ("Dick") Wilson at Middle Row, Wasdale Head and afterwards, in 1928, took over the farm himself. He farmed there until 1958, running it in tandem with Row Head for the final seven years of his working life. Joss has enormous respect for his father and describes him as the cleverest person he ever knew.

"He had the best head on him of any person," he says. "He had 4,000 sheep and he knew ivvery yan o' them. And he was a great fella, a sound personality and ah nivver heard him say a wrang word about anybody."

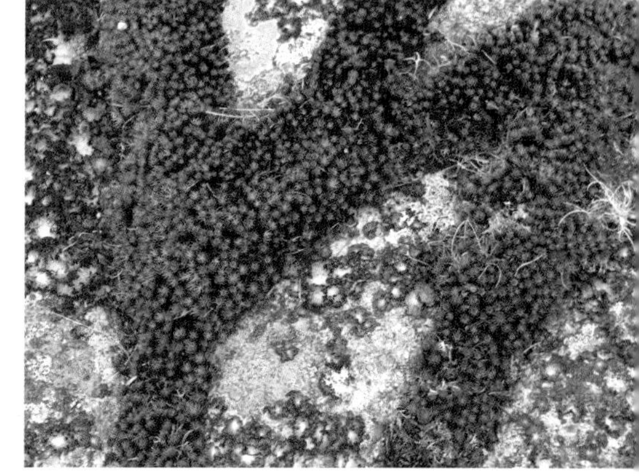

Joss is now the last living person to have brought Herdwicks over Burnmoor from Wasdale to Eskdale for the show and 60 years on from that date in '49 he is on the look out for stones and one particular rocky outcrop that carries a story. We move away from the Corpse Trail and Eskdale Moor on to another path, beneath Eskdale Fell, that Joss says is known as The White Cross Path, so called because a landlord of The Woolpack in the early days, Johnny Armstrong, painted white crosses on stones on the route over the moor in the hope that it would lead walkers directly to his pub in the Eskdale valley.

Joss inspects a number of stones on the path and fears that the white crosses may have been washed away after being exposed to the elements off the Irish Sea for many years. But then, to his delight, he finds one on the sheltered side of a rocky outcrop a few hundred yards beyond the wooden Lambford Bridge. He also identifies this same outcrop as the one that he believes holds a secret.

"It would be in the 1920s," Joss reveals. "Ned (Edward) Nelson had been at Eshdell Show and he had walked his tups over Burnmoor with mi dad. Ned was at Gatesgarth, Buttermere, before the Richardsons went there and he had sold quite a few and had hired a lot out and had done well for hissell at Eshdell. On the way back they stopped for a rest and old Ned was sitting on this crag and counting his money. He had spread his money out on top of this rock and a gold sovereign slipped from his hand and disappeared down a crack in the rock. It could have been this yan," said Joss, indicating

Colourful lichen on a rock.

The white cross on the rocky outcrop on the White Cross Path. The crosses were not religious but were intended as a marker to his pub, The Woolpack, by the then landlord Johnny Armstrong. Joss Naylor reckons that this particular outcrop holds a gold sovereign accidentally dropped into a fissure by the shepherd Ned Nelson.

a deep, but very narrow fissure in the rock out of which it would be impossible to retrieve a coin. "There's no way he could get it out so it'll be there to this day," Joss adds.

On the top of the moor near the tarn are the remains of a large, rectangular sheepfold. This, apparently, was known as the 'pund fold', so named because there was a system in place for anyone retrieving a sheep from the fold to pay £1.

We head back towards the Corpse Trail and as the weather begins to worsen it brings home the reality of how soul destroying it must have been to walk the several miles over the exposed heights of the trod as part of a funeral cortege. No one has much of a say on the date of his or her death and, not surprisingly, the majority would prefer to carry on living as long as possible. So the chances of a coffin being taken over Burnmoor on a terrible mid winter's day were very real; heaven forbid that there was a white out, they might all have perished.

Among its many virtues the rowan will apparently guard you and your animals against evil spirits and its magical powers are especially potent in the high fells where it can grow in the most unlikely places, hanging over a waterfall on a fell beck or prising its way out of rock. Such trees are known as 'flying rowan.'

John Richardson (1817 – 1886) of St John's in the Vale, in an article on funeral customs wrote: ' . . . they were very particular at funerals about going the right way to church. From every hamlet and homestead, to the parish church, was a particular road or path, called a corpse road, and so exact were they on these occasions, to keep upon that path, that in time of flood, a funeral party has been known to wade knee deep through the water, rather than deviate a few yards to the right or left . . .'

It is inevitable perhaps that where there is a corpse trail there is also a ghost story and Burnmoor trod is no exception. The story goes that one winter the horse carrying the coffin of a young man became alarmed, made a bolt for it and disappeared into the mist. The horse could not be found and the young man's mother was so overwhelmed with grief that she wasted away and died the following winter. As the funeral party for the mother made its way over Burnmoor the grey mare carrying her coffin suddenly galloped off. It must have been habit forming.

While the search for the grey mare proved fruitless they did, however, come across the brown horse carrying the coffin of the son. Spooky or what? I think 'or what.' The grey mare was never seen again, but there are, apparently, walkers who have heard hoof beats on the moor as the mist comes down. Joss, Val and I heard or saw nothing relating to coffins, corpses or hoof beats on the day we were there, but we did have a hair-raising moment when a low flying jet exploded deafeningly out of nowhere as it crested the brow on the Wasdale side of the tarn. Any lower and we would have been able to count the fillings in the pilot's teeth.

The 'pund' fold with Burnmoor Tarn in the background.

During a walk over Burnmoor to Eskdale on the Corpse Trail, Joss paused to have his photograph taken with two walkers, the Rev Jon Wilkinson and a walking friend Gael Dowdeswell. Joss is always very sociable with walkers he meets on the fell and Spy and Titch do not have a problem with photographs for the family album.

The story of the ghostly coffin-carrying horse is probably a bit far fetched and equally unlikely is the sexist tale of the rowan tree by the side of the corpse trail. The Norsemen, ancestors of many of the families that still inhabit the high Lakeland fell farms, believed that the rowan was a sacred tree. The name rowan comes from the Old Norse for the tree, raun or rogn. The rowan is also prominent in Norse mythology as the tree from which the first woman was created.

Among its many virtues the rowan will apparently guard you and your animals against evil spirits and its magical powers are especially potent in the high fells where it can grow in the most unlikely places, hanging over a waterfall on a fell beck or prising its way out of rock. Such trees are known as 'flying rowan.' A website that I referred to added: 'Whatever your connection to the Rowan be sure to look out for the changes that will occur as a result of any communication with this tree. It should not be underestimated and its influence will bring about a quickening of your energy on many subtle levels. For this reason it has always been used by the wise ones (by magicians and druids for staffs for example) and revered as a powerful influence and should be treated with the greatest respect.'

This, in part, explains why I have not one but two rowans in the garden of my home at Keswick, one at the front and the other at the back. The protection and powers are a bonus, the real reason they are there is because I have always thought the rowan, or mountain ash, with its green foliage and clusters of red berries, is a beautiful tree. It is a tree that has energy and something about it and is ideally suited to the Lakeland

An attractive packhorse bridge on the Wasdale side of the Burnmoor Trod.

The 'pund' fold at Burnmoor, looking back towards Wasdale.

landscape. Joss thinks so too and has planted more than his fair share near his Low Greendale home.

Rowans grow close to the corpse road from Wasdale to Eskdale and on one occasion in the distant past, or so the story goes, a horse bearing a coffin containing the body of a woman strayed marginally from the trod and jolted against a rowan. The impact resulted in the woman being miraculously restored to life. Some years later she 'died' again and her coffin once more made its way over the moor on horseback to Eskdale. But this time her husband – clearly not enthused at the possibility of a second coming – noted the closeness of a rowan to the side of the trod and gave a cautionary message to his son who was leading the horse: "Tek care o' yon rowan John," he said.

And the woman went to her grave.

*Raddle. Joss is referring to the rud that is used to colour Herdwick tups for show purposes. The tups are coloured up with Herdwick Red, or rud, a distinctive powder that is sprinkled on to the sheep and then rubbed in liberally with the hand. The rud originates from the West Cumbrian iron ore where the miners were known as the 'red men' because of the colour of their skin after working in the mine. Joss recalls that in his day a supplier provided the rud: "A laal fella cawd Eric come round and he travelled for Fell Dales for years and he used to supply the ruddle. It's bad to get now and it's fairly expensive stuff."

JOSS AND JACK 11
When shepherds meet

Sampson's Bratfull. A pile of stones dropped from the apron of a giant on Stockdale Moor.

Shepherds' meet. Joss Naylor, Jack Ellwood and dogs outside the barn at Bowderdale. Photograph by Mary Naylor.

Joss Naylor and Jack Ellwood relax in the sunshine at the entrance to the old barn at Bowderdale, Wasdale. They are doubtless engaged in one of those seemingly endless conversations that take place from time to time among like-minded Lake District shepherds. And if you are not entirely conversant with the vagaries of that famous breed, the Herdwick sheep, or the intricacies of Cumbrian dialect (as she is spok) then perhaps it's better that you keep your distance and admire from afar as these two lads enjoy the crack.

But should you approach and be bold enough to interrupt their conversation you will find them welcoming, friendly and engaging. And, provided you can understand a word of what is being said, you had better be on your guard (especially if you are a visitor) because old Jack and young Joss might just be tempted to tell you a tall story or have a little joke at your expense. But it will all be in the best possible taste and with no malice in mind whatsoever, that's the Cumbrian way.

The photograph of Joss and Jack was taken by Joss's wife Mary and sits in pride of place on a windowsill at their home, Low Greendale. Joss tells me of the 'phone conversations he receives from old Jack in which his more elderly compatriot – 15 years his senior – will talk at length about putting the world to rights, spouting his views and criticisms down the wire from his farm at Scalderskew, way up on the fell and sandwiched between Swainson Knott, Ponsonby Fell and Stockdale Moor. The moor, incidentally, is home to the wonderfully named Sampson's Bratfull, an unimpressive pile of stones in the middle of nowhere and apparently dropped from the apron of a giant – so legend has it – as he strode across the moor on what must have been a dark and stormy night. Did he, I wonder, shout into the night like his distant relative in Jack and The Beanstalk:

Fee-fi-fo-fum!
I smell the blood of an Englishman,
Be he 'live, or be he dead,
I'll grind his bones to make my bread.

Unless you prefer to believe in giants and what they carry in their aprons across storm-blown fells late at night, Sampson's Bratfull is the site of an ancient barrow, or grave, this area being strewn with antiquities and signs of ancient settlements.

Jack Ellwood himself probably feels a bit like an ancient settlement these days. He was born, he thinks, in September 1922 and has been slowed in his progress of late by a double hip replacement that developed the added complication of a blood clot. But neither clot nor new joints has stopped him from working on the farm and the fell, with the help of a quad bike and a cacophony of sheepdogs. His Methuselah-like appearance is encouraged by a flowing white beard that gives him the look of an ancient god or, at the very least, a wise old sage.

But the Norse features and the voice, the dialect, his manner and his sense of humour are unmistakeably Cumbrian.

Reaching Jack's farm at Scalderskew is in itself something of an adventure. The farm is way out in the wilds and to reach it you go to Gosforth, head inland and where the road forks right across a bridge to Wasdale you carry straight on along a rutted track that runs alongside the fast-flowing waters of the River Bleng. From here you gradually rise through Blengdale Forest on a rough track until - thinking that

Scalderskew seen from the fell.

you are lost – you emerge from the woods. If this was America and deep in the Georgia wilderness you might be tempted to start thinking in terms of Deliverance, the Cahulawasse River and duelling banjos. But a sign pointing the way to Scalderskew brings you back to reality and you eventually find yourself looking out over fields to the fells beyond. The farm is situated on a slope in the lee of Scalderskew Wood. It stands on its own at the end of the track, a huddle of buildings, but your eyes are drawn not to the farm but to what comes out of it as you make your way towards it, half a mile away across the fields. A pack of dogs, too many to count precisely, stream out of the farm entrance and sweep down the fields towards the oncoming car. Scalderskew dogs makes for an interesting slant on reservoir dogs and the welcoming party give every indication of being feral. And then they are upon us, barking loudly and racing across in front of the wheels and I put my foot on the brake, fearful that I might run one over.

"It's aw reet," says Joss, "Keep your foot down, they'll git oot o' t' way."

He is right, they are quick and their reactions are quicker, but I'm still reluctant to go any faster than a slow crawl as we continue uphill and into the farmyard pursued and surrounded by all these whirling dervishes from the sheepdog world, one of which has only three legs.

A Scalderskew dog.

The River Bleng makes its way through Blengdale Forest.

A crow's nest in desolate Blengdale.

This is my second time at Scalderskew. The first occasion was on a magazine assignment with the artist Keith Bowen. When we entered the farmyard that day, surrounded as ever by the dogs of war, I suggested to Keith that he get out first and knock on the farm door. He reminded me that it was my idea to visit Scalderskew in the first place and if anyone was going to be bitten it was going to be me and not him, thank you very much. Fortunately the dogs' barks were indeed worse than their bite. In fact they were quite a friendly bunch of rag, tag and bobtails once you became acquainted. Although, having said that, one or two gave the distinct impression of being more aloof and the type that might prefer to snap first and ask questions later.

Joss doesn't bother with a knock on the door. He opens the back door and walks in, shouting a 'hello' as he goes. Jack is in a small living room, next to the glow of a welcoming coal fire. The main purpose of the visit, from my standpoint, is to witness at first hand a conversation between Joss and Jack, reminiscent of that in the Bowderdale barn photograph taken by Mary. Inevitably the conversation, after the opening pleasantries, turns immediately to the sacred subject of sheep and, for some reason best known to Jack and Joss, their teeth and mouths. This leads to them comparing notes on the respective well being of their own gnashers.

"You can't beat a good set of false uns," says Joss at the outset of a conversation that was to encompass such subjects as Jack's upbringing, family history and a surprise discovery, how to steal cream off the top of the milk, hard work as a hired lad, spectacles, cameras in the sky, mortality, kidology, shepherds' meets, dogs, drink, mending a broken leg and, last but not least, the years when there were at least seven golden eagles in Blengdale.

"Have you got false teeth Joss?" I ask.

"Aye," says Joss, "I got aw mine out ya day. I'd come back from the fell and the buggers were aching and I said to Mary 'ring t'dentist' and I went through and he said 'what do you want?' and I said 'I want aw mi teeth out.' Anyway he injected us and pulled the bottom uns out. Well, the stuff hadn't worked and it hurt like hell. And do ya know when I was coming back frae Whitehaven aw mi mouth went numb. I went back a week later to have the top uns out. He injected us and the phone rang. He went and answered it and was away for a while. When he cem back mi mouth was numb and he took them out and I didn't feel a thing."

Before he developed any teeth (subsequently loosened and then removed some years down the line after flying off the back of a motorbike following a birthday celebration) the babe Ellwood came into this world at Underwood Farm, situated under the Pennines and near the charismatic Cross Fell which in ancient times was known as 'Fiends' Fell' and was said to be haunted by evil spirits. In more recent times a shepherd searching for sheep on Cross Fell in the late 1980s found more than she bargained for, firstly a cloud or disc which hovered over the fell before disappearing, unusual tracks that caused one of her collies to bolt and, last but not least, the sight of five black clad figures about eight feet tall which stood motionless for about a minute before melting away.

The River Bleng near the head of Blengdale.

Jack Ellwood at Scalderskew.

Back in the world of humankind, Jack Ellwood was part of a large family, seven sons and one daughter born to Tom Ellwood and his wife Victoria (nee Richardson).

"Is thoo a Richardson?" asks Jack and when I reply in the affirmative he adds: "Where are you frae then?"

"Keswick," I say. "But there's a Robinson connection on my grandmother's side of the family. Came from out Bampton / Helton way."

"Aye, there's Robinsons mixed in wid our lot. I saw the family tree," says Jack.

"Ah tell you what," injects Joss with a laugh. "You two buggers must be related!"

I think this observation comes as something of a surprise to Jack and myself, but meks us think. Moving swiftly on, Jack says that he went to Milburn School as a lad.

"It wus the best spot ivver, I liked that school," he added, in marked contrast to Joss who positively hated his school days. "And when I left school I went to work for mi father's cousin, John Ellwood at Howrigg. Well, I worked like hell for nowt. Joss'll tell ya, they were hard fellas and they sent you theer to break you in like a bloody hoss. There's nee wet days and at half past four in the morning you'd be up. Aye, they were hard fellas . . . what you lot should have had (directed at me). Have you got a job or are you just garn round talking to us lot . . ?

"Any way another thing was at breakfast he'd always scrape the cream off the milk and he had it hissell. He did that cos he was boss. He wasn't any better than t'rest of us, just boss. And I thowt to hell wid this, why shouldn't I have it? So ya day I went in early and his daughter Ruth said 'there'll be trouble' and I said 'well, we'll see . . .'

"Well, he come in and the cream had gone and I said it's too bloody late unless you eat me. I got a telling off and he told me nivver to do it again."

Joss remembers it was all horse work in those days, no tractors or quad bikes.

"It would be half past four in the morning when they were getting up to git the hosses ready at Middle Row," he remembers. "They would cut the grass until half past seven and then they would give the hosses some feed and they would be in the stable until 11.30 and then they went out and turned hay and scaled hay. They put in long days did them hosses. When the oil runs out in another 20 years or so we'll mebbe see things garn back that way again."

At some point I give Jack a copy of the book *Ivver Sen* which contains a chapter on Joss. As Jack squints at the cover Joss says to him: "You'll enjoy that Jack. Have you still got mi glasses? I give him a pair of bloody glasses about five year ago so he could read. He'd nivver bloody read for 20 years!"

Jack searches round for them to no avail and wonders if Duncan, his son, might know where they are. I can only imagine that the glasses are a sight for sore eyes – apologies for the terrible pun – if they are anything like the spectacles I have seen at Low Greendale and which belong to Joss. Big round hoopla-like frames and guaranteed to make their wearer look at the very least like a studious owl. In fact I seem to recall Mary saying that they were safety glasses.

From looking for spectacles we move smoothly on to the realm of surveillance. Joss and Jack play hell about all the paperwork that's needed in farming these days and the endless scrutiny involved.

"You can go abroad easier than it is to sell a bloody cow," says Jack.

"Aye, and they'll have a camera in the sky counting how many sheep you've got," adds Joss.

"The world's gone mad when they're watching folk like that."

"They can put your post code in Jack and someone can sit and watch yer aw day."

The conversation takes a bit of a maudlin turn when the two shepherds move on to the subject of death.

"We're aw alike when we're young," pronounces Jack. "We aw think we'll live for ivver and that we'll be aw right. Don't we? But it doesn't work like that."

Joss: "It's the luck of the draw on the day."

"You're right Joss. If your number comes up you're gone. I've known a lot of young fit fellas and they're just bloody dead. And that's it."

On a less sombre note, Joss remembers the shepherds' meets at Wasdale in years gone by.

"Arthur Ellwood (Jack's uncle) brought Herdwicks over from Eskdale for years," he says. "From Taw House he used to fetch all the Eskdale sheep ower. He used to come out by the Woolpack and used the white cross path where Johnny Armstrong put a white cross on the stones to mark the way. And then he would pick up the Burnmoor trod and drop into Wasdale . . ."

Jack: "They talk about dogs being good today but what beats me is the shepherds went back o' dark and they were drunk. The fella was drunk, but not the bloody dogs. The shepherd counted his sheep when they left, when they were still sober, and they didn't pick any up on the fell on the way back and all the sheep landed."

Joss: "The dogs knew the job."

Joss goes on to recall with affection an old shepherd called Arthur Coward who farmed at Gill Bank, at the head of Eskdale: "He used to drink tea aw day. What a dog fella he was, he always had great dogs."

"I nivver seen him hit them," adds Jack. "Patience? He had more bloody patience than we'll ivver have. If he went to the fell and the dog didn't deuh right he would stop and tek the time to mek it deuh right. He used to fetch them down from Gill Bank to the pub at Boot, leave them on the road in the dark with the sheep standing there on their own and the dogs watching them."

"He was a kind fella," says Joss. "And he would git aw maks o'folk to ga and help him."

"I wish he was here now," says Jack. "When he was failing I went to Gill Bank to collect a sheep and when I went in the house a fella cawd Jimmy Poss' was theer. I asked Jimmy 'How is he?' And Jimmy said 'Oh, he's doing a lot better.' And there was a cry from upstairs: 'Is I buggery!' He died soon after."

This brings to mind a wonderful story told to me by Betty Birkett (nee Richardson) the sister of the former Blencathra huntsman, Johnny Richardson, both of whom feature prominently in the book *Ivver Sen*. Two brothers called Benson farmed and grew old together at Hollins, Eskdale, and over the course of a lifetime they became known, not by their names, but as 'Yan' (meaning one in the dialect) and 't'Other' (meaning, of course, the other). One of the brothers died and the story has it that the remaining sibling went to a neighbouring farm and told of his brother's sad demise with the words: "t'other's died . . . there's only yan left."

It occurs to me that if there had been a third brother he would probably have been known as 'The Other Yan.'

In those days the shepherds did not worry over much about the finer points of medical science for man or beast and would often resort to home-spun methods of treatment. This was also true of the aforementioned Bensons.

"Yan of the Bensons was gitting ower a gate when he fell and brok' his leg," recalls Jack Ellwood. "Uncle Arthur was theer at the time and Benson went yam wid this brokken leg and he got some tar and sticks, set the leg, went to bed and the tar clogged up the bed."

Joss also tells the tale of old Billy Phillips "a one-off frae Gosforth," who used to help the Naylors at Middle Row and who also worked at the nearby Wastwater Hotel. "He once tried to convince a poorly visitor, who was suffering frae a cold, that the best cure was to eat a lump of coal out of the fireplace in the bar," says Joss.

Outside the farmhouse window there are bird feeders. A conversation about wildlife on the fells and the important role previously played by gamekeepers leads to mention of the golden eagles that once lived and nested in Blengdale. The valley is remote and rarely visited and when Joss, the photographer Val Corbett and myself went there one April, we did not see another soul. An occasional wheatear put in an appearance and, in a gully hidden from view until you were upon it, crows had nested in the boughs of a rowan tree hanging over a small beck. The nests seemed entirely appropriate to the starkness and loneliness of the valley. Apart from a couple of small stone sheepfolds and rocky hides built into the side of the fell for shooters on the look

Where golden eagles nested.
Crags in Blengdale.

out for wild dogs in the distant past, the area gave little sign of human presence. This was probably why the golden eagles chose to make their home there on the crags overlooking the source of the Bleng.

"There were seven golden eagles in Blengdale at ya time," says Jack. "We come here (to Scalderskew) in 1964. In the 1950s a fella cawd James Hewetson wrote in *The Whitehaven News* that there were eagles in Blengdale and we thowt he was imagining things. I had only bin here three days when I saw this bird way up in the air and it barked like a dog. Eagles ga sort of 'wup!' (Jack makes a sound like a dog). And I looked at this bird and it was an eagle and ah thowt 'by God, old Jimmy's bin right aw along.'

"After that they used to come and tek rabbits. I can nivver say for sure that they nivver went wid a lamb, but they used to come at lambing time and ga wid the after birth. They used to catch foxes. There wus seven eagles at ya time and the funniest thing is that if you lived amang them they're not frightened. But if you git folk coming with funny coloured bloody clothes I reckon the birds are frightened.

"These eagles they reared two and when the young started flying they went up that hawse off Birk Crag and they used to feed 'em there. They would ga with the remains of a dead sheep and perhaps an odd grouse. Then it got out that there was eagles in Blengdale . . . when was that Joss? About the early Eighties?"

"Aye," says Joss. "It was 1981. Do you remember that big snow Jack? They covered the nest up in Birk Crag. They moved to Rossett Ghyll the following year and they reared yan. And then after that things seemed to ga wrong. I often used to see them in Netherbeck, they seemed to sit about a lot."

Joss and Spy stride out through Blengdale.

Jack: "They do. And if they are settled and you come across them all of a sudden they fly straight up. I've nivver seen a bird that does that, they ga straight up. There was a cow deed and there was such a bloody row. There was carrions and there was ravens and they were fighting over this cow and there was this greet big bird amang them and it was an eagle. Any way they saw me coming over the gate and the others are off, squawking and flappin' away. But this eagle went straight up in the air. How the hell they've got the power to do that because they don't seem to flap their wings. It just went straight up . . . "

Joss: "They were part of our way of life. People should have just shut up and let them be. If they'd left them alone they'd probably still be theer noo."

As it was, news of the eagles in Blengdale became more widespread. The birds were watched and monitored by conservationists who built a hut – the remains of which are still there – in the valley. But the eventual demise of the eagles in Blengdale was not down to over zealous bird watching and wider public interest.

I understand that men with guns blasted them out of the sky or poisoned them and that the wings of at least one of these marvellous birds of prey were paraded round a pub.

Joss and the author in a sheepfold on the approach to Blengdale.

VIVA ESPAÑA 12
Citrus heaven

The orange grove. The oranges reminded me of baubles on a Christmas tree.

Photography by Keith Richardson

There is no mistaking the long-legged, rangy figure of Joss Naylor striding around in the supermarket car park, just off the dual carriageway at Punta Prima along the N-332 coast road, our meeting point on my second morning in Spain. I am there for three weeks, spending time with Joss generally getting to know him better, walking the hills, visiting bars and restaurants, and picking an exquisitely tasty orange or two straight off the tree in the endless groves of oranges and lemons that stretch inland on the Costa Blanca. And all this in a Mediterranean environment far removed from his lifelong stomping ground of Wasdale where the screes take a nosedive into the ice-cold depths of Wastwater from the heights of Illgill Head.

Joss goes to Spain from time to time in the winter months to escape the worst of the Lake District weather because if he doesn't it could have serious implications for his health. He was 73 at the time of writing and for a number of years had been troubled with circulatory problems in his lower limbs and feet. The warm weather in Spain keeps the condition at bay although even there, on cooler days and nights, he occasionally has to wrap his feet in a couple of layers of thick woollen socks.

"I had no actual pain in mi legs at first but mi feet were splitting oppen and there were black spots appearing," explains Joss. "I had this for three or four winters back home and it was just like walking on red-hot cinders, as though someone was pressing a red-hot poker on your feet."

If he is in a land where the temperature persistently falls below 10 degrees the circulatory problems start to kick in when the blood runs cold. He needs to visit Spain to, as he puts it, keep things right.

"I don't have a problem when I'm out here," he says. "Having said that this winter's bin cold, I think it's bin the coldest winter for 44 years. I've had to wrap them up of a night just to be on the safe side. One of them was burning a bit and if it starts burning you know summat's happening so I wear of couple of pairs of thermal socks when I'm out."

Joss loves his lifestyle in Spain and reckons that the warmer climate can put another

10 years on your life. Provided, that is, you don't kill yourself tumbling down a mountain, falling off a bike or being hit by a car while cycling. But we'll return to that a little later in the piece.

I was there in January 2009 and my HQ was an apartment in a hotel overlooking the coast at Mil Palmeras. The weather was fine most of the time with just a single dramatic storm one night that had the palm trees by the pool bent almost double in the wind. Giant waves, spurred on by thunder, noisily attacked the shore while lightning flashed across the horizon out at sea. It was not a good night to be alone in a small boat in the Mediterranean without a sou'wester.

The days were generally sunny and mild and some without a cloud in the brilliant blue sky. It was, in fact, ideal for fell walking and exploring the surrounding hills and countryside. Once I had started driving on the correct side of the road in a metallic grey hire car and going anti-clockwise around roundabouts, life became a whole lot less stressful for everyone – not least other motorists coming in the opposite direction. However, I quickly discovered that Joss's navigational skills on the roads and in finding the start points for walks were considerably less efficient than they are in the Lakeland fells he knows so well. He was the one who had been coming to this part of the world for the best part of nine years but, unfortunately, our combined linguistic skills were not exactly wide ranging and tended to be restricted to one word. Worse still, it appeared to be the same word, 'hola', and this term of greeting, while it rolls smoothly off the tongue, can only get you so far when you are attempting to ask for directions on how to find your way to the foot of a mountain. Mind you, it might also help if you actually knew the name of the mountain you were headed for.

We invariably got lost, sooner or later, and I did not fully appreciate how many dead ends, one-way streets and vacant parking lots there are in the historic city of Orihuela which, for some reason, we always seemed to find ourselves driving around, striving to find a way out. We had no trouble at all in entering the city but – like minnows trapped in a jam jar – could not find the exit route or, at least, the one we wanted. At one point Orihuela became synonymous in my tortured mind with Hell, a recurring nightmare from which there was no escape as the Devil in Chief (Joss the navigator) spiked me with his pronged instructions to turn left, right and then, when it was all too late and we had missed a turn "Damn! We should have gone down theer."

On one occasion I recall pointing out to Joss that I could have driven from Keswick to London in the time it had taken us to locate the starting line for a mountain a relatively short distance away. We also visited more than our fair share of industrial units where the walking is not noted for its scenery, ridges or summits. Strangely enough a lot of the starting points for walks were churches or cemeteries – I'm not entirely sure if any significance can be attached to that – and one of the cemeteries in question had four strands of barbed wire on a fence around the top of its high wall.

"They mean to keep 'em in round here . . . " observed Joss with one of his characteristic one-liners.

As Joss and I sat outside a bar one evening, enjoying the final warmth of the sunset and drinking coffee and brandy after a day in the mountains, I noticed that the peak of his purple baseball cap bore the name El Campello.

What does it stand for? I asked.

"I haven't a bloody clue," replied Joss. "There's nobody belted us for wearing it yet so it must be harmless." It transpires that Campello is the name of a resort north of Alicante.

While Joss's command of the road system and his ability to distinguish between left and right was questionable, there was no stopping him when he left the tarmac behind, hit the plains or the hills and felt the good, honest earth and rock beneath his feet. At one stage on a walk around a salt lake near Torrevieja, Joss knelt and looked at hoof prints left in the clay soil of the path and declared that the horse must have been there earlier that day. It was the same with the shredded pinecones he came across in a wood high on a mountainside. Joss reckoned that the squirrels had not been there for some time as the scales from the cones, scattered about the woodland floor, were old. Is Joss really a Native American, I wonder? And does this make me The Lone Ranger to his Tonto? Kemo Sabe?

Somehow we always found our way to the top of a mountain – any mountain we could locate in fact – and to this day some of those peaks remain largely anonymous to me despite some half-hearted research as to their location and identity. In the end I resorted to giving them entirely new names of my own creation and so, for example, a particularly testing mountain – for me at least, but not for the mountain goat that is Joss Naylor – became known as 'The Formidable Peak.' All I can tell you is that it was close to Callosa de Segura and not a million miles from Orihuela.

Looked at from afar The FP bore a passable resemblance to Blencathra. Its distinctive shape and ridges were instantly recognisable from a distance across the fertile plain that stretches from Elche in the north to Murcia in the south and even in the dry conditions and on solid rock some of the climbs onto which Joss and I ventured were considerably more worrying than Sharp Edge.

Joss's fell walking and rock climbing style is simple. He rarely stops and goes straight up. It is almost as though he is on a mission. Sometimes he will pause to allow you to catch up, but no sooner have you reached his high point than he's back on his feet and off again, leaving you panting and sweating in his wake. You get 15 minutes or so, very little more, for your food and drink on the summit and then you're off again. Hi-ho. He also has the potentially irritating habit of whistling rather aimlessly as he walks and climbs. Every time I hear him burst into tune I start to think of it as his 'Happy Wanderer' moment. Val-deri, val-dera, my knapsack on my back . . . personally I'm far too fazed by the exposure of the drops on either side, the steepness of the climb and my heavy breathing, to attempt any carefree melody, whistled or hummed.

"Is it any particular tune?" I asked him one day as we scaled the heights.

"Not really," he replied. "It's all self-composed stuff."

Joss, the born leader, was invariably out there in front with yours truly bringing up the rear. But then keeping your distance from Joss on a walk, especially in the

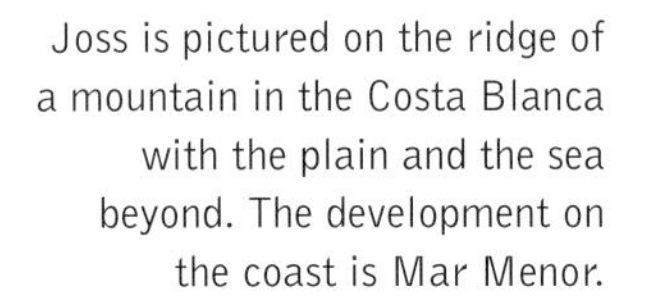

Joss is pictured on the ridge of a mountain in the Costa Blanca with the plain and the sea beyond. The development on the coast is Mar Menor.

morning, does have its advantages. One is that he positively honks of garlic. This might have something to do with the fact that he buys it in bulk at the Saturday market and crunches his way through a clove or two every morning. Walking too closely in the slipstream of Joss Naylor's garlic fumes is not recommended. But if it becomes too overpowering you can always reach down and run your fingers through the stems of the Rosemary shrubs that grow in profusion on the hillside and take a deep breath from the traces of the sweet aroma left on your fingers.

Many of the mountains are similar in stature to those in the Lake District, but instead of cairns to mark the way there are thin strips of parallel yellow and white paint stencilled at regular intervals on the rock. Someone has gone to a fair amount of trouble in establishing and marking the trails. The mountaineers, or someone else around here, must also have an interesting sense of humour. A metal container with a glass front and back, about three foot by two, and held in place with stones on its roof, is situated on the ground near the summit of one peak. It houses an irreverent nativity scene in which plasticine-like figures of Mary and Joseph and the donkey, wise men and assorted angels appear to share their domain with a urinating cowboy and a defecating hill walker, bottom bared and crouching. Oh well, it takes all sorts . . .

Once you reach a summit the plain stretches out before you, a mixture of agriculture and isolated pockets of industry. For the most part it is rich, green, fertile land on which there are thousands upon thousands of acres of orange and lemon groves, stretching as far as the eye can see and interspersed with other crops in a fascinating patchwork quilt of fields growing almonds, olives, broccoli, potatoes,

The Formidable Peak.

lettuce, artichokes, pomegranates and palm trees.

But it is not all Eden. The hills are dangerous and must be treated with respect. Some of the drops are spectacular and the exposure on awesome cliffs, ravines and gullies is enough to leave you dizzy and all too aware of the consequences of a trip or fall into oblivion. My first attempt at The Formidable Peak was an abject failure. After toiling upwards in Joss's wake through rock, tree and scrub for about a thousand feet the path suddenly took us across a rock face to a ridge. Looking out over the ridge, beyond the safe confines of the gully out of which we had emerged, and into a yawning drop below, I got a severe attack of the hebee jebees. From our position on the exposed ridge we were to traverse to another ridge, beyond which I couldn't see the route ahead. The fear of the unknown – what lay beyond the next ridge – the exposure and the drop were all carving massive fault lines in my confidence. In short I was out of breath from the climb so far, apprehensive (let's face it, I was scared) and when Joss reassuringly announced that the worst was beyond the next corner where wires had been attached to the rock as an aid, that was it . . . this, after all, is a man who has made a career of climbing down hazardous and highly exposed rock faces in the Lake District, to rescue sheep.

A fierce looking Joss is pictured on top of one of the mountains we climbed in the Costa Blanca.

"I can't do it," I said. "I've come here to write a book, not kill missell or end up in hospital."

Joss, to his eternal credit, was very understanding. No pressure, he said, if it doesn't feel right we should go back down. And that was it. I retreated and in doing so felt uneasy at my lack of bravado. Descending was probably the wise thing to do under the circumstances but I felt, rightly or wrongly, that I had let Joss and myself down. If he cursed me under his breath I didn't hear it. My emotions - fear, sense of relief and then shame - were all soon replaced by a growing resolve not to let this thing beat me. It suddenly became quite important to make amends, to prove a point.

Back at the foot of the climb, a thousand or so feet below, I trained my binoculars on the point where I had turned back. Two young Spanish climbers, the only other people on the mountain, were making light of the descent and I came to the conclusion that it might not be as bad as I had first thought. Heavens, if they can do it why can't I? Being able, even from this distance, to get some idea of what lay ahead diminished my fear of the unknown. And so I resolved to try again. On the car journey home, after we had climbed a summit less fraught with danger, I told Joss of my intention. Two days later we returned to The Formidable Peak and this time I was more prepared and resolute, employed the old 'don't look down' trick, and climbed out and across the pitch that had given rise to my concerns. It was a great feeling to have met my fears head on and triumphed. We then followed a spectacular ridge walk all the way to the top and there was a spring in my step. But I still couldn't keep up with Joss who loped ahead at a deceptive pace, whistling as he went.

The good life for Joss as he poses for my camera on the beach at Mil Palmeras in January.

Joss had been laid low by a virus and had not done any running or fell walking since we last went on the fells together from Wasdale Head in the late Autumn of the previous year. But this had not prevented him from climbing on his bike and facing the hazards of the open road in Spain. Joss goes cycling with a friend, Don Lupton, on Wednesdays and Sundays.

"I've had a lot of bad luck on the cycle," says Joss. "I've come off about seven bloody times and each time the road gets harder. At least I haven't brokken owt as yet. I've had a bit of skin knocked off and ended up with a couple of black eyes, but apart from that I've been all right. The worst time was when I somehow managed to ride into the back of Don. If you can survive all the cycling accidents there's a good chance you'll put 10 years on your life out here. I'm trying to concentrate a bit more now, stop thinking that I'm Lance Armstrong.

"But it brings reality home when you are on the bike. One day I thought I was going along quite reasonably. I was in middle gear and moving away nicely and this bloody young lad flew past us like a bullet. And this bike I go on is a flying machine, drop handlebars, the lot.

"There was ya time I was following Don and going like hell and I didn't notice this corner with a great big ravine beyond it. I couldn't slow down in time, was heading for this ravine and I had to jump ower the handlebars. I landed on the road and the pain was serious. I wear a helmet but that didn't stop us gitting two black eyes. I was like a bloody panda and when we went to a Chinese restaurant that night this lass said: 'An old man like that . . . he doesn't ride a bike does he?' The cheeky bugger."

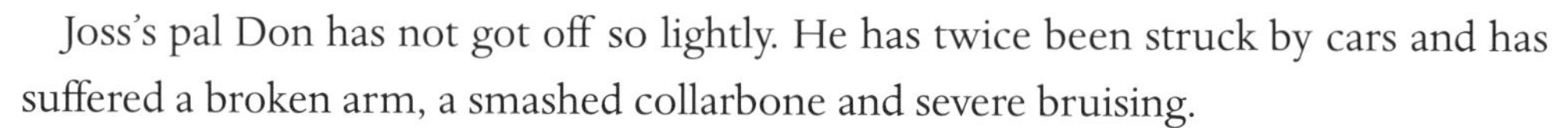

Joss's pal Don has not got off so lightly. He has twice been struck by cars and has suffered a broken arm, a smashed collarbone and severe bruising.

"The second time he got snottered," says Joss, "this car came flying round a corner and as I looked up he was sailing through the air. The bike went 20 metres and landed on top of a fence. Don ended up behind a crash barrier but where the car had hit him it took his calf muscle off. It was mair or less hangin' by a piece of skin and there was a fair bit of flesh left on the car's headlight. But give the hospital their due . . . they did a fantastic job on him."

The ex-pat way of life in Spain is interesting to observe. It's not entirely my cup of tea and I think I would become homesick after a month or so. However, it clearly does have its benefits, not least the climate and I would gladly exchange the Lake District and its rain and cold winds for a January spent on the Costa Blanca or some other warmer location, especially the Caribbean.

Joss is pictured outside the Calle Guilpiles complex where he and his wife Mary have an apartment. A firm called the Praetorian Guard provide the security for the complex and it would appear that they have used some of their spears for fencing.

The fancifully designed estates on which people live in their various enclaves on the Costa Blanca seem to go on forever. Giant cranes break the horizon. Each estate has its own unique brand of architecture and colour scheme; some I can only describe as being Salvador Dali-esque in design. The estates are usually situated in secure compounds behind high walls or fencing with sliding metal gates to admit vehicles. You need a special key code to gain entry. I note from a sign on a prison-like iron-barred gate to the rear of the complex, Calle Guilpiles, where Joss and his wife Mary's apartment is situated, that it is guarded by a security firm called the Praetorian Guard. It must be reassuring to know that your property is being protected by a company that takes its lead from an elite force once used by Roman emperors. Joss says that instances of vandalism have gone down since the Praetorian Guard went on duty. Perhaps it's the prospect of crucifixion that deters young offenders. Even so, the dry stonewall Joss built on the estate in a small area of parkland – a little corner of Cumbria - was subject to vandalism and Joss had to reinforce the top of the wall with concrete to prevent further damage.

Joss's wife Mary loves the way of life, helping out in the community's library, reading a lot, enjoying the sunshine on the apartment balcony, going on outings and gentle walks and occasionally painting. On the walls of the apartment are Mary's pictures of St Bees Head and Wasdale. There is also a portrait of Joss in which he looks a little startled.

On Saturday mornings she and Joss go to a local market. In the evening they will eat at home and Joss concludes his dinner with four small squares of chocolate and a glass of red wine, a forerunner to the cloves of garlic the next morning. On a Friday they will venture out to a nearby English restaurant / bar, Maggie's, for dinner. On the day I arrive the specials board at Maggie's was offering kippers with tea, bread and butter and a Sunday roast that can be eaten in the restaurant or delivered piping hot to your apartment door.

While Joss clearly enjoys his lifestyle in Spain ("out here it's a great way of life," he says) I get the impression that he does occasionally miss the Lake District and Wasdale Head and wonder how he feels when the time comes to leave the lakes for a break in Spain and the warmer climate?

"It's an upheaval really," he says. "You get into your ways and then you're off again. The biggest job when you leave home is leaving the dogs. You feel sorry for them because they know you're going before you set off (the dogs are looked after by their farmer son Paul at Wasdale when Joss and Mary are holidaying in Spain). One died a few years ago when I was out here. The day it died I knew that there was summat wrong . . ."

For me it was an enjoyable but strange experience being out in Spain during January. Many of the properties were unoccupied in the area where I stayed and I could take a walk in the evening without seeing a soul. It was, quite literally, soulless and felt like a ghost town; a complete contrast I imagine to the summer. I also had the length of a nearby beach entirely to myself. In the morning, on my way to meet Joss, I would come across the occasional pair of Nordic walkers striding out, other less energetic types going to the communal rubbish skip at the roadside or emptying their dog on some wasteland and returning home with the day's newspapers. And then, in the afternoon, some sought a change of scenery at the pubs or bars

Joss looks as though he is about to post a letter through this wonderfully bright red and white door of a house that we came across during our travels on the Costa Blanca.

for a quiet drink in the sun that might just develop into a full-blown session stretching out into the evening and night. Joss and I, after a walk, occasionally called in at a bar called 'The Odd Couple' – it seemed appropriate - where the owners had just printed their own calendar, complete with naked male customers discreetly arranged on, beside or behind strategically placed objects.

On our walk round a salt lake near Torrevieja the path took Joss and I near to orange groves. The oranges were clearly ripe and were so full, round and . . . well, deep orange, that they looked like king-sized baubles on a Christmas tree. The orange trees themselves were not particularly large and almost appeared overwhelmed by the burden of the fruit. The floor of the grove was littered with fallen oranges. It all had an unreal quality, that of a particularly rich oil painting.

Joss ventured off the path and plucked an orange from a bough, prised it open with his fingers and took a deep, juicy bite. He said it was "magic," a word he frequently uses. I tried one for myself and the taste was out of this world. All I can say is that until you have eaten a ripe fruit fresh off the tree in the sunlit Costa Blanca then you have never ever enjoyed the true pleasure of eating an orange. This was citrus heaven.

It certainly beats nicking a turnip from the edge of an old farmer's field in the Lake District as we used to as kids, or perhaps a stick of kale for its sugary content.

With just a handful of days to go before my departure from Spain, Joss gave me a perfect example of the accident-prone side of his nature. He took a tumble on the descent from a mountain and was left in a heap by the side of the path. Joss, as usual, was some distance in front when it happened. The steep path had loose stones that

Joss runs along the beach at Mil Palmeras.

could be treacherous underfoot. And as he looked round to see where the hell I'd got to his feet went from under him and he landed awkwardly on his knee. In fact he somehow contrived to sit on the joint in falling and felt it give and tear open on impact with the ground.

I saw him crumple followed by an anguished shout of: "Oh, mi bloody knee . . ." or words to that effect.

When I reached Joss he was clearly in serious pain. The damage was to his right knee, the one with which he has had a lot of trouble down the years. He hasn't any cartilage in the knee – it was surgically removed years ago – and bone grates on bone with every step.

He sat by the path for a while and I urged him to just settle for a while before attempting any movement. Eventually he was able to flex the knee gently and got to his feet. He hobbled off the mountain – with me a few paces in front for a change – and for the next few days he was out of action. The injury had stiffened up and he was reduced to a limp with a lot of discomfort on every footfall. When I phoned him from the UK a week or so later he reported that he was on the mend.

It came as a relief to know that Joss would be able to continue running and walking the mountains he loves, especially those back home in Cumbria, and that I had not been indirectly responsible for ending the active life of a Lake District legend.

Although Joss appears to be pulling a face as he bites into an orange, I can assure you that the taste was wonderful.

JOSS AND FAMILY
Bowderdale and beyond 13

Joss and Mary Naylor spent most of their working and married lives, almost 40 years, at Bowderdale, a beautiful whitewashed 18th Century farmhouse flanked by Yewbarrow and Middle Fell in the midst of the Wasdale Valley. In the distance to the back of the farmhouse is Red Pike and to the front are marvellous views down over Wastwater and across the lake to the spectacular screes. It was an idyllic location for Joss and Mary to raise a family but there was a time when Bowderdale and the Naylors had the company of one or two other inhabitants – one of them most certainly unwelcome – who might have been there for a couple of centuries at least.

The view from the pasture at Bowderdale out over Wastwater.

Bowderdale was haunted and in the dead of night Mary and Joss had close encounters with visitors from what we can only presume was the spirit world, for want of a better description. And on one of those occasions Mary was justifiably terrified.

I have always been sceptical about ghosts, demons and things that go bump in the night but in the light of what Joss and Mary told me about events at Bowderdale, it has certainly made me think again. When two people as down to earth as Joss and Mary tell you they have seen something out of the ordinary you are inclined to believe them.

After a honeymoon in Wales in the cold, stark winter of 1963 the newlyweds moved into Bowderdale on March 12 that year after their wedding in February. They had lived for a short time, after returning from Wales, with Joss's brother Scott and his wife Cathy at Middle Row (where Joss was born and raised) and had the option to stay at Middle Row. Scott and Cathy were moving to Row Head to take over from Joss's parents, Joe and Ella, who were retiring and going to live at Low Greendale.

But then Bowderdale suddenly became available for a farm tenancy and Joss and Mary jumped at the chance, preferring Bowderdale's more remote location to Middle Row, right next to the Wasdale Head Inn.

And so they began their new lives together, running a fell farm and determined to make a go of things with Mary out to prove herself to Joss's mother Ella who had not, initially, approved of the marriage. Joss and Mary were very much a team in every sense with Mary also involved in farm work as well as running a home, raising the children and looking after visitors. Bowderdale's guests loved to stay in the accommodation on the farm with its views over the lake and hills. Being on a working farm was all part of the appeal.

But then the Naylors got a visit from two unexpected non-paying guests in the shape of ghosts. Mary and Joss cannot put a precise date on it, but the children were young at the time and while the ghostly visits certainly did not exactly shatter the way of life at Bowderdale, Mary found it disturbing for a while, especially if she was in the farmhouse on her own with the young children when Joss was away on running trips that could take him to other parts of the UK if not the world.

"I saw this lady in our bedroom at Bowderdale," Mary said. "We had moved from the bigger bedroom into a smaller room and it was in the very old part of the house, previously the servants quarters. We had a chair in the bedroom, an ordinary chair next to the bed. I had gone upstairs to bed and was wide-awake, I wasn't tired or anything – Joss was asleep beside me – and I was just lying there on my side and I suddenly saw this white figure. It was a lady with a baby in her arms."

As Mary told me this I felt the nerves quicken on the back of my neck.

"She was in a rocking chair. She was in the place where our chair was but it was now a rocking chair. She had very long dark hair and she was so peaceful that I wasn't frightened at all. In the end I just fell asleep watching her. Joss had seen her before but didn't like to say anything unless I thought he was being a bit daft. But then I mentioned it and he said that he had seen her. We didn't see her a huge amount, just odd times. I saw her more than once, two or three times perhaps, and she was always with the child. Joss had only seen her standing there at the foot of the bed."

Joss added: "It was in the top part of the old house at Bowderdale. There was a woman in her middle 20s and she had her hair up in a bun and was wearing a long frock. I looked at her for two or three minutes and then she just disappeared. Ah nivver said owt to Mary for a long time but then thowt ah better had just in case she appeared again, but Mary mentioned it fust. Three or fower year later she was there with a laal kid, sitting in this armchair in a corner of the bedroom, just rocking it to sleep. Mary watched it until she fell asleep hersell.

"There was nowt else until we moved the bloody bed. Then Mary woke ya night and the curtains were standing straight out in the bedroom and she felt as though some bugger was trying to suffocate her. She was terrified. Any way I got up and put the light on and we moved the bed back to where it was and there hasn't bin a problem since."

Mary took up the story: "We only moved the bed in the first place because we bought this three piece wardrobe and we couldn't put it next to the wall because of some radiator pipes – so we put the bed over there and the wardrobes on the back wall. On the night it happened Joss was asleep – I was always later than him going to bed - and I got into bed, lay down and after a while I just felt my pillow moving. I was still awake. The pillow seemed to be pushing up against my face and it wasn't a pleasant experience. We had curtains tied with ribbon and I just sort of looked and the curtains were standing straight out in the room and there was smoke, in the shape of a figure, and I was terrified. I have never ever been frightened of anything in my life, except that.

"I had no light at my side of the bed - we had only just moved it that day - and I shouted out to Joss to put the light on. When he put the light on the curtains were down and it was gone. We moved the bed back the next day and I never saw that again. But at the time it was very, very frightening. It was sort of looming over me and the pillow was pushing up against my face. I was a bit uneasy for a while because Joss was away running and I would be in the house on my own with the kiddies. It was eerie the first few nights he was away but whatever it was it didn't come back again. The second apparition had to be a different one. We moved the bed back the next day and we never saw it again."

Joss Naylor most definitely believes in ghosts and does so because he believes the evidence of his own eyes. Joss says that he has now seen ghosts, spirits, apparitions or what ever you prefer to call them, on separate occasions and in entirely different circumstances, including one on the summit of a fell. He is convinced that when he was running over the fells at the break of day on one of his long distance epics he came across someone who was not, strictly speaking, of this world.

"We were coming up on to the top of Cold Pike and it was about half past five in the morning," he explains. "It was storming like hell and mi pacers were struggling a bit and they were behint us. As I ran towards the cairn there was this lad standing there. He was youngish, mebbe 27 or 28, fairish complexion and light sandy hair and he had on red clothing and a pair of good, strong climbing boots. I said 'by the heck, you've had a good start this morning' but when I got to the cairn there was no bugger there. I can see the bloke yet . . . "

Interestingly, Joss also had a dream about 20 years or so ago concerning a freestanding boulder at the foot of Bull Crags, Mosedale. I was on a walk with Joss out of Mosedale to Black Sail when he told me about it. As we made our way out of the valley he said: "There's a stone over there called the Y boulder (it gets its name from the distinctive Y shaped cracks on one side of the boulder). The rock is only about 12 feet high but a lot of climbers use it for bouldering and there could be as many as 13 laal routes on it. In mi dream I was out for a run. I often ran round this spot when I was at Wasdale Head. I could see these ropes on the rock and when I went round the back there was this fella hanging on the rock face and the rope had got round his neck and he was hanging in it. He was dead and it's debatable whether he had set it all up to commit suicide or it was an accident. It was so vivid and clear. I can still mind it now. And you wonder where on earth these sort of thoughts come from when you're dreaming."

The Y boulder.

Joss Naylor as a young man. When Mary Naylor first saw him it wasn't love at first sight.

Mary Naylor (nee Downie) is originally from the North East and despite all the years she has now spent in Wasdale and Cumbria, still has a hint of Geordie in her voice; although it is often mistaken for an Irish brogue. After a couple of other jobs in the area, at Workington and Egremont, Mary eventually came to work for Joss's mother Ella at Row Head Farm where much of the work centred on visitors, cleaning and preparing rooms and serving meals.

"The very first time I saw Joss a whole crowd of cats came to the back of the house at Row Head followed by Joss's dogs and Joss," she recalls. "The dogs were chasing the cats. I didn't really know who he was then but that was the first time I saw him. The cats would escape over the wall or whatever and he went up the beck edge."

Was she suitably impressed?

"No," Mary replies. "There was this very hairy man in a pair of cut off shorts. No I didn't think a great deal of him. It wasn't love at first sight. I suppose then I must have met him in his mother's house. I can't really remember but he must have come to the house and then eventually he asked me if I'd like to go to a dance. So we went to a dance in Gosforth Village Hall on a Saturday night. I couldn't really understand anything he said. I just couldn't find a little gap between one word and another and didn't know what he was saying. And so that's how it started.

"We met in July and by October that year (1962) we decided to get engaged but Joss's mother wasn't very happy about it. We were actually going to get married in October but his dad persuaded him to wait until later on and we got married in the February. So that was it."

Mary was thrown in at the deep end on the farm.

"Because Joss's mother didn't think I was farming stock I had to learn to do everything that she probably had to do because she wasn't all that keen on us getting married," says Mary. "She was very difficult. She was a very domineering character. Most of the time she was friendly with me, probably because I was as strong as she was and she admired somebody with strength. I stood up to her all the time and never let her get away with anything. She seemed to admire it, but she was such a really strong woman and it made life difficult for a lot of people.

"Anyway I had a new life to live and had a lot to learn. So I had to learn to cook, to milk cows, make butter, all sorts of things, everything a farmer's wife does. And there were the visitors to look after. I even sheared sheep once and that was when Joss got sunstroke shearing outside in the sun and he couldn't carry on. So while he went to lie down I decided to shear the sheep. Unfortunately I didn't realise I'd picked the big wethers which are the biggest sheep apart from the rams. I used hand shears and had a rough idea what to do because I had watched Joss doing it. I had been told that you never ever let the sheep go once you start. You hold it there until you get the whole fleece off and I did. But I nearly killed myself in the process."

Joss and Mary Naylor with their baby daughter Gillian.

On another occasion Mary skinned a calf that had died.

"I just had an ordinary knife and I kept that skin for years. I've never been worried about gory things," she added. "It was a hot day and it had to be done. I was always ready to jump in and help do everything."

Joss's parents Joseph and Ella Naylor had four children, Joss, Margie, Scott and Jim. Joss is the last surviving member of that group and Joss and Mary have two daughters, Gillian and Sue and a son, Paul, all of whom were raised at Bowderdale. Gillian is now an artist, Sue is a social worker while Paul farms at Bowderdale. Joss and Mary now have five grandchildren, Craig, Denise, Lochlan, Ella and Alice. All the time that Joss and Mary were bringing up their children Joss was becoming increasingly involved in fell running. He was also suffering from his back problem.

Joe Naylor and his lads, Scott and Joss.

"His first run just before we were married was the Ben Nevis race," Mary remembers. "He probably ran at home in the Mountain Trial before I met him. After that he did have a hard time because of his back. He got severe cramp all of the time. It was not unusual for us to be waiting at the end of a race and he didn't come in when we expected. He had collapsed with the pain on the run, become unconscious and then come round, got up and carried on. We always knew something had happened. He would pass out half way through the race because of the pain from severe cramp. For a lot of years he got cramp, probably because of trapped nerves. This was before and after his operation to remove the discs from his back. He also used to use those Charles Atlas arm strengtheners to build himself up.

"He was constantly in a huge amount of pain. At one point in the early days he literally could not sit up and get out of bed. He used to have to roll over onto the floor and get up on his hands and knees. One day, quite by accident, I just happened to touch his back at a particular point when he was standing there and he just dropped to the ground. I had obviously touched a pressure point that had this effect on him.

"But he doesn't bother about things like pain. He just blanks it out and carries on. He has suffered a lot of pain and just ignores it. I don't think he got used to it but he just seemed to be able to close his mind off. It's a case of mind over matter. He has always wanted to carry on and so he just blanks it out until he's finished. I think there are very few people who can do that. He's very determined."

After ascending and descending 72 Lakeland peaks in 23 hours 11 minutes in the summer of 1975 (his marathon version of the Bob Graham Round) Joss told a *Daily Mail* reporter: "To outsiders, running up and down mountains probably looks either crazy or impossible. To those who don't understand, it's difficult to explain. But all my life I've awakened at dawn to look at this beautiful country around me. I have grown up to know every inch of the mountains and their moods. I see in them the beauty that the tourists come to look at, but I also see their vicious side that defies attempts to tame them. It's the old battle, man against nature. At the start of this run I paused for a moment on Skiddaw at first light. I had seen it like this so often before, the world stretched out 3,000 feet below in the sunlight. I could see the course in front of me and I found something new in the triumph of actually being there.

"I don't fear 40. I am capable of carrying on for years yet. It's a question of applying

Joss's father Joe making his way over the packhorse bridge at Wasdale Head.

your mind for weeks ahead and convincing yourself you cannot fail. I literally switch off my mind when I'm running. I have no thoughts at all. I was troubled with a bit of cramp at the start but I told myself that it was impossible for my body not to achieve the target I'd set it. I couldn't imagine giving in, that possibility didn't exist. This was certainly my last long-distance run. I feel I will never be able to better it, although I shall carry on fell running as a hobby."

Mary helped out on many of Joss's long distance runs and provided the food and drink for the support team and the pacers.

"I used to feed them all," she says. "Everyone who helped got fed, sandwiches, cake, and trifles. I used to make loads of trifles and on one run he did – I think it was the Wainwrights – he used to travel with Sue and she got messages back to me to say what he fancied. I would take cooked food and have it ready for them wherever they were."

Despite the physical problems and the pain Joss had to endure, Mary was never overly concerned for his well-being. All that has changed as Joss has grown older, but has not really moderated his ambition to continue doing long runs, the 60 peaks at 60 years of age and the 70 at 70 and this year's run, at the age of 73, to celebrate 50 years of fell running and taking in Souther Fell, Blencathra, Skiddaw, Grisedale Pike, Wandhope, Whiteless Pike, Robinson, Dale Head, Grey Knotts, Brandreth, Green Gable, Great Gable, Kirk Fell, Pillar, Scoat Fell, Haycock, Seatoller, Cat Bields, Glade How, Buckbarrow and back home to Greendale Bridge. How many people do you know who could run 20 peaks at that age?

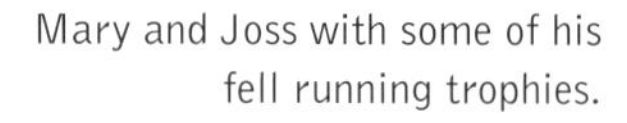

Mary and Joss with some of his fell running trophies.

Joss with Paul and Susan.

Joss affectionately describes Mary as The Management. Mary, for her part, feels that she is not so much The Management as The Managed.

"I was never concerned in the early days when he was a younger man," she says. "The only thing I get concerned about now is his age. He thinks he's younger than he is. One of these days it might not just come off right and if he had some injury or something that he couldn't put right he would hate himself. He could not live like that. Over all the years I've never bothered about him running but he's 73 now and if he has a serious accident he would hate to have to sit in a house chair bound or whatever. I don't think he actually thinks about this but the consequences are not good if it happens."

I sense that Mary is probably wasting her time in sounding her warning notes.

"People think I'm the boss," she adds by way of confirmation, "but he takes no notice of me whatsoever. He just doesn't. It doesn't matter what I say he doesn't take any notice of me and he wants to do what he wants to do. Joss is quite happy on his own.

"He's a one off. I don't think you'd find anyone quite like him. He's a very strong willed, determined man and considering he couldn't really do anything before he had his operation it's just like a dream he has and he's carried it on right through his life. He's not an easy man to get on with all the time because he is so determined and single-minded. He doesn't really think about what other people think. Basically he's only got it in his head what he wants to do. He's not sidetracked in any way and is very focussed."

What drives him?

"He loves the mountains," she replies. "He loves to be up there. He'll go up there on rubbish days when no one else would be out but he'll just set off and he's done it for years. I actually think the running was a by-product of him wanting to be up there. In the beginning he couldn't run very well but he wanted to be up there in the mountains. He simply has to be up there . . ."

Joss himself freely admits to being a solitary figure and is at his happiest when he is on the fells.

"Ivvery day ah spend hours on mi own," he says. "I have done aw mi life. I don't like being amang crowds and I don't like standing about amang people. I don't like going to shows or going shopping or owt like that. It's just the way you are. I'm at mi happiest when I'm running on the fells on mi own with a couple of dogs."

Personally I have likened Joss to the raven. All his life Joss and the high mountains have been as one. In much the same way that the raven tends to hold fast to the fell tops, swooping, gliding and cawing – with that highly distinctive raven croak – Joss is at his most content in the fells, racing along a ridge, his loping gait eating up the miles and his mind up there in the mist and the cloud, appreciating the mountains and the sense of wild solitariness, and distancing himself from the clamour of the town and people.

It is perhaps no coincidence that one of Joss's favourite birds – he loves all wildlife while reserving a special hatred for crows because of what they do to newborn lambs – is the raven, a bird that appears to have a strong sense of aloofness and a passion for high places.

"There's summat about a raven," adds Joss. "There was ya night ah was comin' ower Black Sail and you could have heard a pin drop. There was two ravens flying at mebbe 10 feet above us in the gloom and you could hear the wings cutting the air. Hell, it was eerie."

While Joss's continual efforts to push back the boundaries in running at an increasingly grand age is a cause for concern for Mary, his involvement in the sport has clearly had its plus points, not least a sense of pride in his achievements in running and in raising money for charity, but also in terms of the people Joss and Mary have rubbed shoulders with at various award ceremonies and the like.

"We had a lovely time when we went to the Guildhall in London," Mary recalls. "That was very good for the simple reason we went with Eric Wallace and the camera crew from Border TV. They had put Joss in for this award. We went down to London with them and Eric Wallace was a fantastic man. He was great company. We went to this awards ceremony and we all had minders. There were all sorts of people there and me and Eric went over to chat to Eric Morecambe and he was fantastic, really down to earth."

Eric Wallace – the same Eric Wallace who was a lifelong fan of the movies of Luis Bunuel and who had the name 'Eric Wallace' stitched into every single stripe of his pinstripe suit – was a regular visitor to Bowderdale with his Border TV crew. Eric was a lovely man, still remembered with a great deal of affection, and he would report on various stories about Joss and his exploits for the Lookaround programme, or Border Crack and Deek About as it was known locally.

Another visitor was the TV presenter and entertainer Stuart Hall who came to Bowderdale to make a programme about Joss.

"Joss was actually dipping sheep at the time," says Mary, "and I think Stuart got a bit wet on that occasion. Joss got quite a bit of dip on him, but he took it all in good heart. He was a very nice man. No side to him at all, which is nice."

Mary was also a big fan of the athlete and newspaper journalist Chris Brasher (see Chapter 5 headed The Runners).

"Chris Brasher did the most fantastic articles on Joss," Mary adds. "Nothing was too much trouble to him as far as Joss was concerned. But Chris, surprisingly for an athlete, was a smoker and he made a promise to his wife that he wouldn't buy any more cigarettes. He didn't – he used to cadge them! And the day I stopped smoking he was really desperate for one and said 'you can't have stopped Mary, who am I going to get cigarettes off now'?"

Earlier this summer Joss's daughter Gillian completed the Coast-to-Coast cycle ride for charity. The ride ended at Whitehaven and Joss and Mary drove to the town to meet her at the finishing point. At one stage Joss became impatient and was convinced that they must have missed Gillian and that she had been and gone.

"I remembered all the years when Joss was running and me and the kids went along to the race and waited, waited and waited," said Mary. "So I said to Joss 'do you remember all the years me and the kids sat for ages in a car when it was pouring down waiting for you to come in and now we're getting our own back – you're going to have to sit there and be patient.' And he was. But he had never ever done it before, never had to sit and wait for other people. So we sort of got our own back on him – just the once!"

THE LONGEST DAY
The King of the Fells 14

It is 6am on the longest day. The midges are up early, but their breakfast isn't carrying a lot of meat. Joss Naylor, nine stone wet through and as lean and brown as a piece of dry cured bacon, is flexing his leg muscles at the roadside at Mungrisdale and looking round a little anxiously for a likely place, the back of a wall perhaps, to empty his bowels.

With him on the road are two fellow runners, Barry Johnson and Peter Ferris, Joss's dog Spy and Peter's dog Gerry – someone makes a crack about Gerry and the Pacemakers – and the entire group is coming under the focus of a camera crew led by writer and broadcaster Eric Robson who is making a special film on the aforementioned Joss. The lad himself has just discovered that the drop on the far side of a wall goes straight down to the beck and he has to look to the fell and the bracken band for cover.

Mungrisdale at 6am and on photo call before the start are (left to right) Peter Ferris, Joss and Barry Johnson.

Joss and his team on the ascent of Grisedale Pike. In the front is Richard Askwith, author of the book 'Feet in the Clouds.' Photographs: Tony Greenbank.

It is Sunday, June 21, 2009 and Joss Naylor, aged 73 and a bit, is about to set off on a run to celebrate his 50 years of fell running and to raise money for charity. But first things first and, not to put too fine a point on it, some things are better out than in when it comes to setting out on a long distance run over the Lakeland fells.

Mission accomplished, Joss and his pacemakers / companions and the dogs set off up the side of Souther Fell, a fell where, down the years, a ghostly Roman army has reputedly been seen marching across the bow-like slope. Over 14 hours later a very real Joss Naylor will run down to Greendale Bridge, next to his home in Wasdale, to complete a 35-mile run that the Roman legions at their best would be hard put to better. It has taken in over 16,000ft of ascent and 20 Lakeland peaks including Souther Fell, Blencathra, Skiddaw, Grisedale Pike, Wandhope, Whiteless Pike, Robinson, Dale Head, Grey Knotts, Brandreth, Green Gable, Great Gable, Kirk Fell, Pillar, Scoat Fell, Haycock, Seatoller, Cat Bields, Glade How and last, but not least, Buckbarrow.

Fully fit men half his age would struggle to complete a day like this on the fells, but

Joss takes it all in his stride, despite problems with cramp and back spasms.

Along the way the run also becomes something of a celebration of Joss's life, a sort of 'This is Your Life' on the run, so to speak, with friends and family turning up at different rest and refuelling points along the route and, at one stage, his daughter Gillian, grandson Lochlan and granddaughter Alice running alongside Joss as he descends Dale Head for a brief stop at Honister. Joss's wife Mary, is waiting there with a car boot full of food and drink for runners and supporters; undeterred by a couple of day trippers who ask her if there is a car boot sale. My request for a third cherry-laced rock bun, I have successfully munched my way through two at previous stops at Braithwaite and Newlands Hause, is given the cold shoulder by Mary and I don't push my luck.

Joss's daughter Sue is on hand to massage her father's legs and troublesome back. At one point Joss is flat out on his stomach on the rough stone of Honister car park while Lochlan holds his legs, Colin Dulson applies pressure to the small of the back and Barry Johnson, standing astride Joss, lifts his upper body off the ground by the arms and shoulders creating an arc for the back. It looks painful to say the least. While it is designed to ease the back, the Honister treatment looks like the hands-on equivalent of a Medieval rack and Joss is grimacing in agony.

"Mi back isn't letting us go," he says when I ask him a daft question on how he is feeling. "Mi back's tight. It's just a bloody nuisance because mi legs are dead with it."

"You'll get through it," I say, the font of all knowledge relating to running and back

Joss takes a drink at Newlands Hause watched by the cameraman and Barry Johnson.

Joss leads the way on to Souther Fell at the start of the run with Barry Johnson (left) and Peter Ferris and the dogs Spy (front) and Gerry.

problems and someone experienced (not) with a 35-mile run over the fells and its impact on the body.

"Aye," says Joss, "but it should be a pleasure not bloody torture."

Billy Bland, the fell runner from Borrowdale, is at Honister to greet Joss and he tells me: "You'll not stop him, the only way he'll not git to t' other end is if he dies."

Billy, like all other fell runners, is full of admiration for Joss and what he has achieved.

"He was the man to aim at when I started," Billy says. "He was the daddy of them all and he is the grandfather of fell running. Joss is the man and he obviously brought a lot of people into it, including missel', comin' from the same sort of background. Joss was looked up to by a hell of a lot of people. He still is. In his time they couldn't beat him.

"It's marvellous that he's still wanting to do it. I take mi hat off to him. His determination is second to none, ten times more than I would have done. He's always had problems from a kid so he'll have grown up with aches and pains and I suppose that gives him the ability to put up with it."

It is about 2pm on a Sunday afternoon and Honister is bouncing, there are people everywhere, including a group of very lively female fell runners who call themselves the Fells Angels; I love the title and their motto 'catch us if you can.' These young women were practising for a charity run across the fells following in the footsteps of Billy Bland's record run of 13 hours 53 minutes that he set in 1982 for the 72-mile Bob Graham Round. There was talk of Joss Naylor, if he was particularly good, being recruited as an honorary angel for the occasion when 72 angels would each run a mile in relay fashion.

In the middle of all this feverish activity, Joss Naylor, clad in a peaked cap, T-shirt beneath a checked woollen work shirt, and shorts that are soon to be joined by what appear to be moth-eaten dark blue long johns, hauls himself off the ground and sets off again on his own mountain epic, this one in aid of the Eden House Children Hospice, part of the Eden Valley Hospice. With him on the last leg to Wasdale are Peter Nelson, Steve Steel, John Slater, Kate Charles and Peter Ferris.

And the same question is probably on everyones' lips. How does he do it?

Peter Ferris is going the distance with Joss, while Barry Johnson accompanies him for the first leg of the run from Mungrisdale to Braithwaite over Souther Fell, Blencathra and Skiddaw and then across the 'Bad Lands', the swampy area at the head of Bassenthwaite. This was before Joss headed off from the car park at Braithwaite Institute, the second stop point of three on the run, for the demanding ascent of the pyramid that is Grisedale Pike, with the words "we'll go and knock hell out of it."

Peter Ferris is telling me that the first leg of the run was very pleasant considering it was a bit misty when Joss's sudden departure, he's up and off without a bye or a leave, almost catches him by surprise.

"He's off again, I'd better go . . ." says Peter, jumping to his feet as Joss is already loping across the A66. Time waits for no man and certainly not for Joss Naylor when he has a mountain in his sights.

We get in our vehicles to follow and I catch up with Barry Johnson for a chat at the second checkpoint, Newlands Hause, where Barry is to rejoin the run for the third leg, and one of his comments is highly pertinent in the light of the subsequent back treatment at Honister.

"We were on a long run over the fells when Joss asked if I had any food left," Barry recalls. "I said I hadn't but I did have some gel. 'Is it any good?' he said. 'Yeah,' I

said, 'it'll give you an energy boost.' When we reached Langstrath Joss turned to me and said: 'I could do with that gel now.' And with that he lay down on the ground, took his shirt off and said 'just rub it in there.' He thought it was gel for rubbing in his back and didn't realise it was for swallowing with water!"

A family affair. Joss makes his way off Dale Head on the descent to Honister. With him (left to right) are his grandson Lochlan, daughter Gillian and grandaughter Alice. And, of course, the ever attentive Spy.

Daughter Sue gives her dad a leg massage in the car park at Honister.

Photography by Tony Greenbank

Barry, a leading sports consultant who is 69 but going on 50 in appearance, has been a running companion and friend of Joss Naylor's for many years. What does he think is Joss's motivation?

"This has been his life," he replies. "He gets such a big kick out of doing it. We were just talking about it this morning. Once you start out on one of these long events you get into a frame of mind that is your own. It's hard to explain exactly what it's like but you are totally and absolutely immersed in your own thoughts and you are on a real high. It's almost like floating. If you get it right there is a point on an event like this where you are just running on a high and even after 60 – 80 miles you can still feel that it is fantastic. It's brilliant. And when you see Joss in full flow there is nothing quite like it, the number of lads that he will burn off. He just goes at his own pace, nice and steady, never stops and he whistles as he goes . . .

"I have a great deal of respect for Joss. He inspired me to start running and he's a great inspiration, a great mentor. He's a solid, fantastic Cumbrian character who's got a massive heart. He is more than a mentor, he's more than a motivator and he does that with so many people. He's just a good bloke, a good solid bloke that you can trust and rely on and have a good time with. You'd invite him to any occasion. I've run hundreds and hundreds of miles with him and I'll have drunk gallons and gallons of beer with him and it's always good crack, it's always funny. You can have serious conversations with him. I'm never stuck for a word with him, he's that sort of guy.

"It would faze a lot of people out would this run. The leg that we have done this morning is a tough run. We did it in training with a lad, a good runner from Pooley Bridge, Rainer Burchett. He's one guy who has run every London marathon (the first was in 1981). We went over that section with Rainer running his little socks off and we did it in 4hrs 20 minutes. We did it in 4 hours today and Joss has just floated

through. For somebody to do that at 73 years of age is just amazing.

"We were having to rein him back on that first part of the run because he'll suffer later on. His back'll go and his knees'll go. He'll slow down and if he gets too far ahead of schedule that comes on a lot quicker. So he's got to be fairly patient. As soon as Joss feels bad he starts to stoop, he really goes down, right over the top and you've really got to stretch him out (vis-à-vis the back stretch at Honister car park)."

Barry remembers that he and Grant Edmondson ran the Lakes, Meres and Waters in under 24 hours and were absolutely chuffed at their achievement, and then along came Joss and slashed a further four hours-plus off their time.

But Barry is quick to point out that running with Joss is not all about times and targets. Running with Joss has another dimension.

"You can go out with lads and they'll never notice their surroundings," he says. "They'll run it and they'll want to run it fast and they've done this race and they've done that race and the other race. You go out with Joss and we'll sit and we'll look at the clouds, the sun, listen to a sky lark or take in the musty smell of sheep or the aroma of bracken as you are running through. We did the Coledale Horseshoe last Tuesday and there were these amazing foxgloves and we stopped to look at them. To have that sort of affinity with Joss and with nature, to be on that wavelength, is amazing. You get immense pleasure out of it.

"I did one run with Joss, 55 summits at 55, and we were coming off Haystacks, nearing the end of the run at Loweswater and Joss said: 'I'm just going down here and I'll see you at the bottom' and with that he disappeared. He came back up and he had a sprig of white heather – which you very rarely see in Cumbria - and he said 'that's for Val'." Barry's wife, Valerie, is the daughter of Gerald Hayes, the late lamented and celebrated former landlord of the Twa Dogs Inn, Keswick.

Barry was the manager at Whitehaven Sports Centre when he first got to know Joss. It was the late 1960s, early 70s.

"I put on a series of lectures," Barry explained. "I had people like Fred Trueman and George Best and I interspersed these well known sports personalities with local heroes and Joss was one of them. Joss just walked in and talked about fell running and everybody was bloody entranced by it. It was magic."

Joss inspired him to take up running and Barry later organised a charity fun run in which Joss and Whitehaven's Olympic track athlete John Kirkbride took part.

"There were 300 in the fun run and John Kirkbride won it and Joss was second," Barry explained. "Brian Bone interviewed Joss for BBC Radio Carlisle and he said 'Now then Joss, you've had a good run but I'm a little bit surprised you were in second place.' He was expecting Joss to say 'well, it's John Kirkbride I was up against,' but Joss said 'I'll tell you the reason why I was second, I've just run in from Wasdale.'

"'You've what?' Says Brian.

"'I've just run in from Wasdale and I've got to run home as well, mi sheep'll be waiting for mi.'

"So the interview finished," Barry added, "and Joss wandered off and got in his car!"

Barry and I break off to investigate the contents of Mary Naylor's 'car boot sale' at Newlands Hause. There is enough food and drink to keep an army on the move over the Alps. What's on the menu?

"Whatever they want," says Mary, who points out that Joss did not sleep particularly well the previous night because of Three Peakers making their way continually up and down the Wasdale Valley in the small hours on their way to and from Scafell Pike. "Trifle with strawberries. Egg mayonnaise and corned beef mush. Tomato soup in case Joss wants some because he likes his tomato soup."

At this stage I'm still good for a second rock bun. But I'd better make the best of it, because it's to be my last.

Joss and his team are making their way off Whiteless Breast before climbing through the bracken to Newlands Hause and the second stopping point. Among those looking on as the runners (Peter Ferris, Richard Askwith, Dan Tindall, Scott Umpleby, Joss and the dogs Spy and Gerry) stream down the fell, before making the tortuous ascent to the Hause, is Colin Dulson, who is to accompany Joss on the next stage together with his son Lochlan. Colin tells me a somewhat alarming anecdote.

"Joss was training for the Wainwrights with a guy called Andy Ligema and myself," he tells me. "Joss was in a pair of shorts and training shoes and nothing else. We had done about 30 miles one evening and it was getting dark and we got to the top of

Billy Bland (in the yellow top) chats in the car park at Honister.

Joss in profile.

Photography by Stuart Holmes

Illgill Head and Joss suddenly produced a chocolate Brazil nut from somewhere and said: 'Does anybody want one of these?' At which point Andy and I looked at each other and said 'I don't know where you've been keeping that but you can have it yourself, we don't want it'."

Still on the subject of food, Colin recalls that Joss had some rather peculiar requirements when staying overnight in a bivouac.

"He'd try to get you to mix pot noodle with chocolate blancmange in the same bag, claiming that it all went down the same way and it didn't matter," says Colin.

"But he's great company on the hills. He doesn't talk about running very much. Wildlife, politics . . . he's a man of usually few words but they're either funny or very to the point. There is a reckless side to him and a real tough side to him as well.

"He has some interesting ways of motivating people, along the lines of 'follow on and if you want to you'll keep up, if not it'll hurt.' It's a head game. There's a picture of him which I really love and the caption someone has put on it reads 'get stuck in and mek them sweat.' Which is one of his sayings along with 'if they're gonna beat me they're gonna have to work for it.'

"He has that tenacity to stick at it. When he did the Wainwrights I remember them wanting to shut the van doors and take him off and not allow him to carry on because his face and hands were swollen, his feet were knackered and he was losing weight. His muscles were being eaten away on the side of his arms and he was in a real mess after seven days non-stop running. Quite incredible, but he would have dropped down dead rather than not do it."

Colin says that he has been trying to encourage Lochlan, who is Joss's grandson, to go for a run with Joss. The 50 years of fell running celebration had provided the ideal opportunity.

"There is a strong resemblance between Joss and Lochlan," he adds, "especially if you look at pictures of Joss in his youth and compare them with Lochlan as he is now. And if you look at Lochlan's hands you'll see the Naylor vice like grip."

Eric Robson's camera crew is moving around the fells following Joss's run, he is filming the event for a Striding Edge DVD on Joss to be entitled 'Iron Joss.' Before the start of the run and in the intensely itchy minutes of the midge attack at Mungrisdale,

Eric says of Joss: "He's impossible. He can't exist can he? I mean, they call him the Bionic shepherd, Iron Joss and all the rest of it, and he hates those phrases. I've never known anybody who had such an understanding of how he works. He has a way of tightening down the screws on pain, on weakness. He is so focussed that he would be bound to succeed in any walk of life."

Out with the cameras on the fell and also being eaten alive by midges is David Powell-Thompson, former Head Teacher at Eskdale School, and a friend and running companion of Joss Naylor. After the run and over a pint at the bar of The Strands Inn, Nether Wasdale, David is making an observation on Joss's interesting sense of fashion when it comes to running.

"He's got a lumber jack's shirt on, leggings that have more holes than fishnet tights and one of the runners says to him 'ever tried Lycra? And Joss replies 'no – I'm more for free and easy.'"

David started working as a researcher for Eric Robson for his 'Out of Town' TV series and was instrumental in bringing Joss's 60 at 60 run to Eric's attention (a film 'Naylor's Run' was the end result) and David and his wife, Margaret, also became involved in helping to fund raise for Joss and the Multiple Sclerosis charity he supported for that particular event.

"During the filming I found Joss totally inspirational," David recalls. "So much so that I went off and bought my first pair of Walsh's (running shoes). I was a rock climber, not a fell walker or a runner. I felt a bit embarrassed going into the shop because I was 51 at the time. They used to be blue and silver – I've still got my first pair – and started doing a bit of fell running on Sunday morning. There was Joss, Peter Ferris and anyone else who would come along. We used to set off together, the three of us and within 100 yards I was by myself. But I kept going and when I was 60 I did the Joss Naylor Challenge from Pooley Bridge to Greendale in 15 hours 54 minutes and I only did it because of Joss. He was so inspirational while Peter Ferris was a rock, guiding me along.

"I've got a huge amount of admiration for Joss. He's so gentle with people, he'll be there for you, guiding you along on a run. But he's as tough as bull's lugs you know. We were out training and I felt wretched; you have good days and you have bad days.

We got to Styhead and I said 'I'm not feeling good, I'm going to drop into Wasdale Head and pick up the car' and he said 'all right, I'm going on.' This was about four o'clock and he didn't come in until half past seven, he'd gone right round the skyline and back home."

David, 63, with his long, ginger and bronze-tinted curly hair (too many holidays in Greece under the sun) his beard and sawn-off Levi shorts, never ceases to be tickled by some of the things that Joss comes out with.

"We were coming down off Gosforth Crags one day, down towards Bowderdale," he says, "and we were running along and there's this ewe with a tip lamb. And as he ran past the tip he said 'you know, you're the spit of your father.' He knew the sheep so well he could see in that young lamb the image of its father. Just amazing.

"And he'll talk to everyone on the fell. Lots of people know him and he'll treat them all like long lost friends."

I did not put a clock on the precise time Joss and the runners and the dogs finally arrived at Greendale Bridge to conclude his 50 years of fell running epic – it was sometime after 8p.m. and he'd been running for over 14 hours, virtually non-stop – but I remember being struck by the sight of the runners as they streamed off Buckbarrow, an irrepressible force with Joss Naylor out in front. For some reason, as they got ever nearer, it made me think of how it must have appeared to locals in the dark days of the Border Reivers when marauding bands appeared over the hill to raid their farmsteads.

But the only attackers on this warm summer's evening in Lakeland were the bloody midges as Joss Naylor ran in to the cheers and applause from a small gathering of family, friends, supporters, and film crew. Joss gave his wife Mary a kiss and an embrace and she then broke open a bottle of bubbly that everyone enjoyed out of white plastic cups. After the initial hubbub and excitement on the completion of the run, Joss and Mary (Spy had earlier been enticed away by his dinner) made their way down the road to Low Greendale. As they did so Margaret Powell-Thompson suddenly produced a crown out a bag, as you do, and placed it triumphantly on Joss's Head.

It looked kind of comical to see a man in his early seventies wearing shorts, thermal leggings (complete with holes) and a lumber jack shirt worn over a T-shirt walking along the road in deepest Wasdale on a drizzly Sunday night with a highly colourful and very tall velvet crown on his head. Even allowing for the fact that this was the longest day and Shakespeare's Midsummer Night's Dream was in rehearsal over the hills at The Theatre by the Lake in Keswick, it wasn't something you see every day. It certainly wasn't conventional.

But then Joss Naylor is not a conventional man, anything but. He is extraordinary in many ways and even if he does not personally care for the phrase, he is, indisputably, King of the Fells.

Joss's training shoes drying on a fence top at Low Greendale.

STATISTICALLY SPEAKING

The following is not an entirely comprehensive list of the events that Joss took part in over the years. It does, however, include the vast majority of what might be termed his most significant runs. At one stage Joss held no fewer than 11 records.

Joss's fell running achievements include the following:
1971: 61 peaks in 23hrs 37mins.
1972: 63 peaks in 23hrs 35 mins.
1975: 72 peaks in 23hrs 11 mins (involving 108 miles and 38,000 feet of ascent and descent).

Other fell running achievements include:
1971: The Three Peaks (Ben Nevis, Scafell Pike and Snowdon) in 11hrs 54 mins.
1974: Pennine Way in 3 days and 4 hours.
1983: Lakes, Meres and Waters circuit of 105 miles in 19hrs 20 mins 14 secs.
1986 (aged 50): Completed the Wainwrights in 7 days.
1996 (aged 60): Ran 60 Lakeland fell tops in 36 hours.
2006 (aged 70): Ran 70 Lakeland fell tops in under 21 hours covering more than 50 miles and ascending more than 25,000 feet.

THE ENNERDALE HORSESHOE FELL RACE:

At one stage in his career Joss won an amazing nine Ennerdale Horseshoe Fell races on the bounce. He was only prevented from going for 10 successive victories because of injury. Joss at one point held the record with a time of 3hrs 30mins 40 seconds, a record that was set in 1972. Kenny Stuart subsequently bettered this in 1985 when he ran 3hrs 20 mins 57 secs.

Ennerdale Horseshoe Fell Race is 23 miles with 7,500 feet of ascent and descent. The route starts at the western end of Ennerdale Water and takes in Great Bourne (2,020ft) and then, along a ridge route, Red Pike (2,479ft), Black Beck Tarn (1,600ft) and across to Green Gable (2,628ft). The next target is Kirk Fell (2,630ft) followed by Pillar (2,927ft) Haycock (2,618ft) Iron Crag (2,077ft) Crag Fell (1,700ft) and back to the finish at the original starting point.

The origin of this exacting fell race was a very strenuous walk by groups or individuals seeking to improve on their personal best. The course was well established before the 1st World War and the walkers had developed from the more conservatively-dressed to those who wore a sort of one piece woollen garment and raced around as quickly as they could. It was not formally organized until that first event of 1968, organised by Joe Long and Frank Travis. Here are the details of Joss's nine consecutive wins:

Saturday, June 8, 1968 (the first Horseshoe Fell Race)
1. J Naylor, WCOC, 4hrs.
2. C Fitt, Kendal, 4hrs 3 mins.
3. M Davies, Reading, 4hrs 8mins.

Joss comment: *"I was determined to win it. I battled it out with Mike Davies and Chris Fitt and just before the end they both seemed to die. Lucky for me! I think this was the run that really got me into fell running."*

Saturday, June 14, 1969
1. J Naylor, WCOC, 4hrs 8mins 25 secs.
2. WA Walker, Kendal, 4hrs 42 mins.
3. C Firstbrook, Man YMCA, 4hrs 52mins 10secs.

Saturday, June 13, 1970:
1. J Naylor, Kendal, 3hrs 53 mins 20secs.
2. D Weir, PFOC, 4hrs 12mins 40secs.
3. A Heaton, Clayton-Le-Moors, 4hrs 16mins 20secs.

Saturday, June 12, 1971:
1. J Naylor, Kendal, 3hrs 35mins 40secs.
2. D Weir, Rucksack C, 3hrs 57 mins.
3. M Nicholson, Kendal, 3hrs 57 mins 50secs.

Saturday, June 10 1972:
1. J Naylor, Kendal, 3hrs 30mins 40secs.
2. D Weir, Rucksack, 3hrs 51secs 10secs.
3. D Cannon, Kendal, 3hrs 54mins 40secs.

Saturday, June 9, 1973:
1. J Naylor, Kendal, 3hrs 33mins.
2. D Weir, Sale, 3hrs 51mins 10 secs.
3. H Walker, Blackburn, 3hrs 53secs.

Saturday, June 8, 1974:
1. J Naylor, Kendal, 3hrs 32 mins 42 secs.
2. M Short, Horwich, 3hrs 40secs 32 secs.
3. A Churchill, C-Le-M, 3hrs 40mins 51secs.

Saturday, June 14, 1975:
1. J Naylor, Kendal, 3hrs 30mins 55secs.
2. J Norman, Altrincham, 3hrs 45mins 40secs.
3. H Walker, Blackburn, 3hrs 46mins 22 secs.

Saturday, June 12, 1976:
1. J Naylor, Kendal, 3hrs 46mins 8secs.
2. M Short, Horwich, 3hrs 57 mins 32 secs.
3. H Blenkinsop, Kendal, 3hrs 58mins 17secs.
On the day of this particular event, the ninth Ennerdale Horseshoe Fell Race, it was announced that Joss Naylor had been awarded the MBE for his services to fell running. On that day he also set a Veterans' 0/40 record.

THE FOUR LAKE DISTRICT 3,000ft peaks:

June 1970. Start and finish at Keswick. Skiddaw, then along the road to Seathwaite, Borrowdale. Via Taylor Gill, Corridor Route, Deep Ghyll to Scafell. Via Foxes Tarn and Mickledore to Scafell Pike (Broad Stand was out of bounds). To Esk Hause, Angle Tarn, High Raise, Wythburn, Steel End to Helvellyn. Down to Thirlspot and along the road back to Keswick.
Total time: 8hrs 20 mins. Distance 45 miles.

61 PEAKS:

1971: 61 peaks in 23hrs 37mins.
Saturday and Sunday, July 26/27, 1971.
Starting and finishing at Brackenclose, Wasdale Head. Total distance approximately 90 miles, ascent and descent of 34,000ft. Assisted on the fells by Alan Heaton (Accrington), Ken Heaton (Hapton), Stan Bradshaw (Padiham), Danny Hughes (Gosforth), Allen Walker (Whitehaven), Mike Nicholson (Windermere), Frank Milner (Ossett), Ted Dance (Chapel-en-le-Frith) and Peter Walkington (Skelmersdale). Assisted at check controls by Janet and Frank Travis (Seascale), Fred Rogerson (Windermere) and Tommy Orr (Whitehaven).

FIRST SECTION: Start from Brackenclose at 11.06. Accompanied by Danny Hughes.

1. Yewbarrow	11.34.
2. Red Pike	12.00.
3. Steeple	12.13.
4. Scoat Fell	12.16.
5. Pillar	12.31.
6. Kirk Fell	13.00.
7. Great Gable	13.23.
8. Green Gable	13.38.
9. Base Brown	13.41.
10. Brandreth	14.02.
11. Grey Knotts	14.07.
Stop: Honister Hause	14.13 – 14.30.

Joss comments: *Start delayed one hour (should have been 10.00) due to low clouds, rain and high wind. High winds encountered on Gable and Brandreth. A whirlwind, picking up small stones, made going difficult on Aaron Slack. Base Brown an additional summit. In cloud most of the way.*

SECTION 2: Accompanied by Danny Hughes and Alan Heaton.

12. Dale Head	14.48.
13. Hindscarth	14.58.
14. Robinson	15.10.
Stop: Newlands Hause	15.20 – 15.23.

Joss's comment: *A fast run with a following wind.*

SECTION 3: Accompanied by Alan Heaton.

15. Aikin Knott	15.43.
16. Scar Crags	15.55.
17. Causey Pike	16.02.
18. Sail	16.22.
19. Crag Hill	16.29.
20. Wandope	16.35.
21. Grasmoor	16.49.
22. Sand Hill	17.10.
23. Hobcarton Crag	17.13.
24. Grisedale Pike	17.25.
Stop: Lairthwaite Road	18.02 – 18.20.

Joss's comments: *High winds, gusty at times. Had there been rain, there would undoubtedly have been exposure risk. Causey Pike an additional summit.*

SECTION 4: Accompanied by Ted Dance, Mike Nicholson and Peter Walkington.

25. Skiddaw Little Man	19.10.
26. Skiddaw	19.24.
27. Great Calva	19.58.
28. Blencathra	20.54.
Stop: Threlkeld	21.17 – 21.40.

Joss's comments: *Hard going due to heather on climb up to Blencathra. High winds.*

SECTION 5: Accompanied by Allen Walker, Frank Milner, Ken Heaton and Stan Bradshaw.

29. Clough Head	22.20.
30. Great Dodd	22.53.
31. Watson Dodd	23.07.
32. Stybarrow Dodd	23.19.
33. Raise	23.35.
34. White Side	23.49.
35. Helvellyn Low Man	00.02.
36. Helvellyn	00.10.
37. Nethermost Pike	00.20.
38. Dollywagon Pike	00.34.
39. Seat Sandal	01.06.
Stop: Dunmail Raise	01.30 – 02.05.

Joss's comments: *Heavy rain and strong crosswinds. Shivers – combination of cold wind and rain affected legs. Tea delivered by Fran and Stan to Grisedale Tarn. Stan lost his watch, which was found by a woman from Wigan! Change of clothes.*

SECTION 6: Accompanied by Allen Walker, Peter Walkington, Frank Milner and Stan Bradshaw.

40. Steel Fell	02.30.
41. Calf Crag	03.00.
42. High Raise	03.37.
43. Sergeant Man	03.48.
44. Thunacar Knott	03.59.
45. Pavey Ark	04.07.
46. Harrison Stickle	04.23.
47. Pike o' Stickle	04.35.
48. Loft Crag	04.40.

Stop: Old Dungeon Ghyll 04.58 – 05.36.

Joss comments: *Heavy rain at Dunmail cleared on leaving. Stan and Frank with tea at Thunacar. Dawn breaking.*

SECTION 7: Accompanied by Ted Dance, Peter Walkington, Allen Walker and Alan Heaton.

49. Pike o' Blisco	06.25.
50. Cold Pike	06.47.
51. Red How	07.10.
52. Crinkle Crags	07.35.
53. Shelter Crags	07.46.
54. Bowfell	08.09.
55. Esk Pike	08.29.
56. Allen Crags	08.44.
57. Great End	09.05.
58. Ill Crag	09.21.
59. Broad Crag	09.34.
60. Scafell Pike	09.46.
61. Scafell	10.18.
Brackenclose	10.43.

Joss comments: *Hard slog to the summit of Blisco on wet rock. Broad Stand very greasy – rope brought by Peter proved useful. All summits in cloud. Insufficient time to do Lingmell. Home base a welcome sight!*

63 PEAKS:

1972: 63 peaks in 23hrs 35 mins.

Schedule for the ascent and descent of 63 Lakeland fells walking and / or running in 24 hours.

Saturday / Sunday, June 24/25 1972.

Start 10am. Start and finish: Brackenclose Road, Wasdale Head (map ref 182074).

Total distance 92 miles approx. Total ascent / descent 35,000 ft.

Joss Naylor, of Wasdale and the Kendal A.C.

Accompanied on the fells by: Alan Heaton, Stan Bradshaw and Michael Meath (all Clayton-le-Moors Harriers), Donald Talbot (Rucksack Club), Peter Walkington (Bolton United Harriers), Neil Shuttleworth (Bolton United Harriers), Allen Walker, Eric Roberts and Jim Strickland (all Kendal A.C.), Chris Brasher, Ian Macintosh and David Locke (all Ranelagh Harriers).

Assisted at the checkpoints by Janet and Frank Travis and Margaret and Fred Rogerson. Photographed at every opportunity by Tommy Orr, of Whitehaven, and the N.B.C. of America.

FIRST SECTION:

Depart Brackenclose at 10am to arrive at Honister Hause at 12.57pm.

11 summits. Time: 2hrs 57 mins (1971 attempt 3hrs 7mins). Accompanied by P Walkington and I Macintosh. There was a good turn out to see Joss off and wish him well. A signal from Harry Griffin and Joss is off to flying start and in 25 minutes is at the top of Yewbarrow. All summits are in cloud. Stan Bradshaw is at Black Sail with a brew of tea and Jim Strickland joined in there.

A six-minute stop at Honister Hause for refreshment (1971 – 17 mins).

Brackenclose Road	10.00.
1. Yewbarrow	10.25.
2. Red Pike (W)	10.50.
3. Steeple	11.03.
4. Scoat Fell	11.07.
5. Pillar	11.21.
6. Kirk Fell	11.52.
7. Great Gable	12.14.
8. Green Gable	12.21.
9. Base Brown	12.29.
10. Brandreth	12.43.
11. Grey Knotts	12.48.
Honister Hause	12.57.

Joss's comments: *Mist down to 1,000ft. Light rain. Conditions bad underfoot, stones very slippery, but we were running well. Took a bad line off Green Gable to Base Brown. Seemed to get amongst all the stones and rocks. Mist very thick at this point.*

SECOND SECTION:

Honister Hause (depart at 1303) to Newlands Hause (arrive at 1358). Three summits. Time 55 mins (1971 attempt 50 mins). Accompanied by P Walkington and D Locke.

Honister Hause.	13.03.
12. Dale Head	13.21.

13. Hindscarth 13.32.
14. Robinson 13.46.
Newlands Hause 13.58.

Joss's comments: *Climbing well, winds gale force and very heavy rain on Dale Head and Fleetwith. Lost a few minutes. Peter beginning to weaken. Took a good line to Newlands Hause.*

THIRD SECTION:

Newlands Hause (depart at 13.03) to Lairthwaite Road, Keswick (arrive 14.62). 11 summits. Time 2hrs 41 mins (1971 attempt 10 summits 2hrs 39 mins) Accompanied by D Locke and A Heaton.

Newlands Hause 14.01.
15. Aikin Knott 14.23.
16. Scar Crags 14.35.
17. Causey Pike 14.41.
18. Sail 15.00.
19. Crag Hill 15.06.
20. Wandope 15.11.
21. Whiteless Pike 15.18.
22. Grasmoor 15.37.
23. Sand Hill 15.55.
24. Hobcarton Crag 15.58.
25. Grisedale Pike 16.10.
Lairthwaite Road 16.42.

Joss's comments: *Rain stopped, conditions rather better. Had a bad patch coming off Causey Pike. Left knee stiffened up on descent and didn't release on the better going. Had ligament trouble on all descents to Braithwaite. Ran the road to Lairthwaite with ease.*

FOURTH SECTION:

Lairthwaite Road (depart 16.55) to Threlkeld (arrive 20.05). 4 summits. Time 3hrs 10 mins (1971 attempt 2hrs 57 mins). Accompanied by M Meath, D Talbot and N Shuttleworth.

Lairthwaite Road 16.55.
26. Skiddaw Little Man 17.51.
27. Skiddaw 18.05.
28. Calva 18.37.
29. Blencathra 19.30.
Threlkeld 20.05.

Joss's comments: *Bad section. Got a chill at Lairthwaite. Had too much to eat. Had to stop four times with cramp, lost a lot of time. Took the wrong turn off Blencathra and came down Doddick Fell. Had a nice warm cup of tea at Threlkeld and felt much better.*

FIFTH SECTION:

Threlkeld (depart 20.17) to Dunmail Raise (arrive 23.50). 11 summits. Time 3hrs 33 mins (1971 attempt 3hrs 50 mins). Accompanied by A Walker, E Roberts and N Shuttleworth.

Threlkeld 20.17.
30. Clough Head 21.02.
31. Great Dodd 21.29.
32. Watson Dodd 21.37.
33. Stybarrow Dodd 21.50.
34. Raise 22.03.
35. Whiteside 22.11.
36. Helvellyn Low Man 22.23.
37. Helvellyn 22.28.
38. Nethermost Pike 22.38.
39. Dollywagon Pike 22.45.
40. Seat Sandal 23.31.
Dunmail Raise 23.50.

Joss's comments: *Feeling strong and going well again. Mist down to 1,000ft. Lost Neil Shuttleworth going on to Clough Head. He had my cagoule, sweets, glucose etc. Started to rain, very cold. Eric gave me his cagoule to keep me warm. Pitch dark coming off Dollywagon and the heavens opened. Stan Bradshaw at Grisedale Tarn with a cup of tea. Conditions too bad to do Fairfield, Hart Crag and Gaterigg Man. Managed to get into workmens' hut on Dunmail Raise. Dry clothes and feet up for the first time. A good tonic at this stage.*

SIXTH SECTION:

Dunmail Raise (depart 00.15 to Old Dungeon Ghyll (arrive 03.37).
9 summits. Time 3hrs 22 mins (1971 attempt 3hrs 31 mins) Accompanied by A Walker, E Roberts and P Walkington).

Dunmail Raise 00.15.
41. Steel Fell 00.40.
42. Calf Crag 01.00.
43. Sergeant Man 01.50.
44. High Raise 01.59.
45. Thunacar Knott 02.14.
46. Pavey Ark 02.31.
47. Harrison Stickle 02.45.
48. Pike o'Stickle 03.01.
49. Loft Crag 03.10.
Old Dungeon Ghyll 03.37.

Joss's comments: *Conditions very bad. Too many cairns on Sergeant Man, difficult to find the right one. Rain coming down in sheets, gale force winds. Just managing to keep body heat. Dawn starting to break at Thunacar Knott. It took two hours before it was light enough to manage without torches. Had a lot of pain in my kidneys – taken too much salt. Drank water to get rid of pain.*

SEVENTH SECTION:

Old Dungeon Ghyll (depart 04.03) to Brackenclose (arrive 09.35). 14 summits.

Time 5hrs 32 mins (1971 attempt 13 summits 5hrs 7 mins).
Accompanied by A Walker, D Locke and C Brasher.

Old Dungeon Ghyll	04.03.
50. Pike o' Blisco	04.55.
51. Cold Pike	05.16.
52. Red How	05.41.
53. Crinkle Crags	06.07.
54. Shelter Crags	06.18.
55. Bowfell	06.41.
56. Esk Pike	07.00.
57. Allen Crags	07.20.
58. Great End	07.45.
59. Ill Crag	07.54.
60. Broad Crag	08.04.
61. Scafell Pike	08.15.
62. Scafell	08.44.
63. Lingmell	09.10.
Brackenclose Road	09.35.

Total time: 23 hours 35 minutes.

Joss's comments: *Water everywhere. Rain seems to get worse if that's possible. Going well up Blisco – home in mind. Allen Walker navigating very well under terrible conditions. Stan on Esk Hause with tea. Alan Heaton and Donald Talbot took over the pacing. Broad Stand was like a waterfall, had to go by Lords Rake to Scafell, but managed to get down Deep Ghyll to Lingmell. Came out of the mist, the valley was a welcome sight. Home base at last!*

Fred Rogerson, organiser, writes: An even bigger turn out of people came to see the finish and to cheer Joss home in appalling weather. A quick retreat was made to Bowderdale where ample fare, both liquid and solid was available. Words to describe this new record are hard to come by. To say that it is a superhuman feat of endurance seems inadequate. Yet how better can one describe it? Had the weather been more kind and the moon shown its face I have no doubt that the target of 65 fells would have been achieved. Thanks to all who accompanied Joss on the fells in the true Wakefield tradition and to Janet, Margaret and Frank who worked at top speed to recharge Joss and his companions under great difficulty because of the weather. Scorched by spot lamps and flood lamps, poked at by cameras and microphones, cigars and chewing gum all round, yet sticking it through. Full marks also to our PRO Tommy Orr. A momentous day.

Chris Brasher wrote: 'That is how he broke the record. It stands now at 63 peaks, 34,000 to 35,000 ft of climbing (Leith Hill standing on top of Ben Nevis, standing on top of Everest). The distance is about 92 miles; the time 23hrs 35mins. Joss went home and had a bath; his wife, Mary, fed all the helpers, 14 or 15 of us, and then we cured our dehydration over pints and pints of beer. And then we went home and Joss went off to milk the cows. And still it rained.'

THE WELSH 1,000 METRE PEAKS. June 1972:

Start from Aber and follows a route via Aber Falls to Carnedd Llywelyn, then Carnedd Dafyddm crossing the A5 and keeping east of Tryfan and Glyder Fach to reach the road at Pen y Pass. Then up the PYG track to the railway, doubling back to Crib y Ddysgl, Return to railway and Snowdon summit. Total time: 3hrs 37 mins. Distance 25 miles.

THE 'VAUX' LAKE DISTRICT MOUNTAIN TRIAL:

September 1974. At this stage in his career Joss had won the event on six occasions, including four successive wins. He also started as last man away in this handicap event and overhauled every other competitor on four occasions. The course varies each year and competitors do not know the route until their own start time on the day of the event. The distance is usually about 17 miles and involves the ascent and descent of some 7,500 ft.

Sept 1974. Venue at Coledale Inn, Braithwaite, near Keswick.

10.07	Coledale	grid ref 229234	Hotel yard.
10.41	Stream junction	190229	Hobcarton Gill.
11.01	Sheepfold	179215	Gasgale Gill.
11.42	.1772	197186	Knott Rigg.
12.37	.2143	235163	High Spy.
13.17	.1821	212200	Aikin Knott.
13.39	.1863	211214	Outerside.
13.50	Coledale		Field behind hotel.

Total time: 3hrs 43 mins 50 secs. Approx distance 17 miles.

THE PENNINE WAY, June 1974:

Day 1:

ARR	DEP		Dis	Time	
	03.05	Kirk Yetholm			
06.15		Chew Green	24 ½	3hrs	10mins.
06.55	07.05	Byrness Road	5		40.
08.24	08.37	Bellingham Road	12	1	19.
10.00		Ladyhill	12 ½	1	23.
10.55	11.30	Steel Hill car park	7 ½		55.
15.00	15.15	Slaggyford	19	3	30.
16.25	16.30	Alston	6	1	10.
17.05	17.15	Garrigill	4		35.
21.22		Dufton	16	4	07.

Overnight stop of 5hrs 48 mins. 106 ½ miles. 16hrs 49 mins.

Day stops 1hr 28 mins.

Day 2:

ARR	DEP		Dis	Time	
	03.10	Dufton			
05.50	06.05	Saur Hill Farm	13	2hrs	40mins.
06.35	06.50	Holwick Head	4 ½		30.
08.05		Road B6276	8	1	15.
08.44		Balderhead	3		39.
Approximate half way stage					
09.50	10.20	Road A66	4	1	06.
11.45		Tan Hill	7	1	25.
12.45		Keld	4	1	00.
14.20	14.45	Thwaite	3	1	35.
16.50		Gayle	11	2	05.
18.00	18.10	Kidhow Gate	5	1	10.
19.40	19.55	Horton	9	1	30.
22.15		Dale Head	5	2	20.
00.10		Tennant Gill	4	1	55.
Overnight stop 5 hrs.			80 ½	19	10

Day stops 1hr 50 mins.

Day 3:

ARR	DEP		Dis	Time	
	05.10	Tennant Gill			
06.20	06.25	Malham	5	1hr	10mins.
06.53		Airton	3		28.
07.50		Gargrave	4		57.
08.20		East Horton	3		30.
09.50		Lothersdal	6	1	30.
10.41		Ickhornshaw	3		51.
11.52	12.12	Pondon	6	1	11.
15.20	15.30	Callis Wood	12 ½	3	08.
17.15		Whitehouse	7	1	45.
18.40	18.55	Road A640	5	1	25.
19.42		Road A62	3		47.
20.55		Road A635	3	1	13.
23.45		Crowden	8	2	50.
Overnight stop 3hrs 35mins.			68 ½	17	45

Day stops 50mins.

Day 4:

ARR	DEP		Dis	Time	
	03.20	Crowden			
05.15	05.20	Road A57	7	1hr	55mins.
07.41		Edale	9	2	21.
			16	4	16.

Day stops 5 mins.

Final totals:

Overnight stops 14hrs 23mins. 271 ½ miles. 58 hours.

Day stops 4hrs 13mins.

Overall total time: 3 days 4hrs 36 mins.

Pennine Way support team: Bill Bird, Chris Brasher, Geoff Ball, Graham Dugdale, Alan Evans, Brian Evans, Dave Ludd, Ken Ledward, Ian Milne, Ian Munro, John Offley, Shay O'Gorman, Tommy Orr, Mike Parkin, Margaret Pope, Peter Trainor, Allen Walker, Tim Walker. Assistance was also given by Messrs Townsend and Milligan at Kirk Yetholm, Mr and Mrs Howe at Dufton, Mr and Mrs Moon at Malham, Dave Cooper at Crowden and George Walker.

Joss and Pete Trainor on the Pennine Way.

72 PEAKS

1975: 72 peaks in 23hrs 11 mins. Total distance 108 miles approx and 38,000 feet of ascent and descent. Support team on the fells – Eric Roberts, Dave Ellison, Alan Evans, Peter Walkington, Rod Pashley, Chris Brasher, Ken Ledward, Mike Nicholson, Mike Pearson, Pip Ledward, Allen Walker, Neil Shuttleworth, John Franklin. Assisted at road points by Fred and Margaret Rogerson.

SECTION 1:

Accompanied on the fells by Eric Roberts and Dave Ellison. Start at Lairthwaite, Keswick at 7.07am.

1. Lonscale Fell	07.44.
2. Skiddaw Little Man	07.57.
3. Skiddaw	08.07.
4. Little Calva	08.28.
5. Great Calva	08.40.
6. Great Scafell	08.53.
7. Knott	08.57.
8. Coombe Height	09.07.
9. Blencathra	09.50.
Threlkeld	10.08.

***Joss's comments:** John Birney on the summit of Skiddaw with a welcome drink. Brilliant sunshine. Stopped for a few seconds to look at the skyline ahead wrapped in a blue haze. The fells seemed much further away than they actually were. A change of shoes at Threlkeld as my left foot was troubling me.*

SECTION 2:

Accompanied by Peter Walkington, Alan Evans and Rod Pashley.

Depart from Threlkeld at 10.16am.

10. Clough Head	10.55.
11. Great Dodd	11.10.
12. Watson Dodd	11.15.
13. Stybarrow Dodd	11.23.
14. Raise	11.31.
15. Whiteside	11.38.
16. Helvellyn Low Man	11.45.
17. Helvellyn	11.50.
18. Nethermost Pike	11.58.
19. Dollywagon Pike	12.06.
Stop: Grisedale Tarn	12.12 – 12.14.
20. Fairfield	12.33.
21. Hart Crag	12.41.
22. Great Rigg Man	12.58.
23. Seat Sandal	13.19.
Dunmail Raise	13.30.

***Joss's comments:** Set off in a hurry from Threlkeld. Pacers had no time to get drinks etc. Becoming very hot. Dehydrated going over Helvellyn, cramp in both legs. No water anywhere, just had to keep going until Grisedale Tarn. A welcome drink and cramp soon goes but leg muscles very sore.*

SECTION 3:

Accompanied by Mike Nicholson and Ken Ledward. Depart from Dunmail Raise at 13.34.

24. Steel Fell	13.55.
Stop: Midway between Steel Fell and Calf Crag	14.00 – 14.09.
25. Calf Crag	14.20.
26. High Raise	14.43.
27. Sergeant Man	14.48.
28. Thunacar Knott	14.56.
29. Pavey Ark	15.00.
30. Harrison Stickle	15.07.
31. Loft Crag	15.14.
32. Pike o' Stickle	15.19.
33. Rossett Pike	15.46.
Stop: Rossett Gill	15.48 – 15.55.
34. Bowfell	16.15.
35. Red Howe	16.58.
36. Cold Pike	17.07.
37. Pike o'Blisco	17.23.
38. Crinkle Crags	17.54.
39. Shelter Crags	18.09.
40. Esk Pike	18.37.
Stop: Esk Hause shelter	18.40 – 18.40.
41. Allen Crags	18.56.
42. Great End	19.11.
43. Ill Crags	19.20.
44. Broad Crag	19.27.
45. Scafell Pike	19.39.
46. Scafell	19.52.
47. Lingmell	20.18.
Stop: Wasdale	20.37 – 20.49.

***Joss's comments:** Decided not to stop at Dunmail for food. Went up Steel Fell with ease. Stopped on level ground between Steel Fell and Calf Crag for food and a drink and enjoyed it. More of a day for sun bathing than running.*

Head down and off again. Seemed no time until Esk Hause shelter where Mike Pearson was waiting with a drink. Run from shelter to Wasdale very enjoyable. Not a breath of wind, not a cloud in the sky. Arrived in Wasdale only to be eaten alive by midges. They must have moved south from Scotland.

SECTION 4:

Accompanied by Allen Walker and Neil Shuttleworth.

48. Yewbarrow	21.24.
49. Red Pike	21.58.
50. Steeple	22.13.
51. Scoat Fell	22.23.
52. Pillar	22.37.
53. Kirk Fell	23.16.
Stop: Beck Head	23.29 – 23.33.
54. Great Gable	23.50.
55. Green Gable	00.03.
56. Base Brown	00.17.
57. Brandreth	00.37.
58. Grey Knotts	00.46.
Stop: Honister Hause	01.00 – 01.08.

Joss's comments: *The light began to fail going up Yewbarrow. I was going quite well. Put on my shirt at the top for the first time but felt uncomfortably warm. Enjoyed going over Red Pike, Scoat Fell and High Crags. All the sheep were silhouetted on the skyline. Never seen so many up there. Could not use our torches for the shadows from the moon. Welcome cup of tea at Beck Head provided by John Franklin.*

SECTION 5:

Accompanied by Chris Brasher, Allen Walker and Eric Roberts.

59. Dale Head	01.33.
60. Hindscarth	01.49.
61. Robinson	02.10.
Stop: Newlands Hause	02.25 – 02.31.

Joss's comments: *Change of socks. A nice short section. I started with pain around my kidneys. Making nice time in not very good light.*

SECTION 6:

Helped and encouraged by all. Great support.

62. Aikin Knott	03.01.
63. Scar Crags	03.20.
64. Causey Pike	03.30.
65. Sail	03.55.
66. Crag Hill	04.01.
67. Wandope	04.11.
68. Whiteless Pike	04.21.
69. Grasmoor	04.48.
70. Sandhill	05.11.
71. Hobcarton Crag	05.14.
72. Grisedale Pike	05.30.
Stop: Road / fell	05.59 – 06.01.
Lairthwaite	06.18.

Joss's comments: *Light gets worse going to Aikin Knott, use torches for the first time. We turn back for Scar Crags and suddenly a ball of fire appears in the sky. The light was so intense that to look at it for more than a second or two gave you blotches before your eyes. In brilliant sunshine from Causey Pike to the finish. We are soon on top of Grisedale Pike, back pain still bad but oh . . ! What a fantastic morning!*

It makes you appreciate being alive when you have run through the night. Feet burning going down Grisedale Pike. A change of shoes at Braithwaite – a nice run along the road to Lairthwaite – and it's all over in 23 hours 11 minutes.

Words don't seem enough to express my thanks for the great work you all did for me during the 24 hour run. None of these records would have been possible without the cheerful and willing help from fellow fell runners who turn out so often in all weathers. I feel proud to have such friends. I hope to be able to help others in the future who wish to have a go and, in the meantime, to meet you all at other events in this great sport of ours.

Sustenance: *During the run Joss ate and drank the following at different stages – boiled sweets, tea, sugar, cake, pie and beans, sandwiches, Complan, cereal, chocolate, egg and beans, rice pudding. Not necessarily in that order!*

Running time	21hrs 59 minutes.
Road stops:	40 minutes.
Fell rendezvous:	32 minutes.
TOTAL	23hrs 11 minutes.

Harry Jarrett, West Cumbria.

Question: Do you like running at night Joss?
Answer: Aye, I don't mind. It's better wid a moon. I know that night we did 72 peaks it was strange because you'd have thowt you could have done with a light but you put the light on and the shadows were somehow against yer. We decided to do widdout but going up on to Gable was a bit black.

'THE FOURTEEN PEAKS:'

The Welsh 14 Three Thousanders.
Successful attempt on the record by Joss Naylor, Wasdale and Kendal AC. Sunday, June 17, 1973. Time: 4hrs 46 mins. Previous record: Eric Beard 5hrs 13 mins in 1965. From Snowdon (3,561 ft) to Foel Fras (3,092 ft). Approx 22 miles.

FIRST SECTION:
Snowdon to Nant Peris. Approx four miles.
Accompanied by Joe Craven.

Snowdon	10.00.
Crib Y Ddysgl	10.05.
Crib Goch	10.17.
Nant Peris	10.43.

Joss's comments: *Very cold and misty on the top of Snowdon. Lost some time going into Crib Goch. Got crag fast. Reached road in 35 minutes.*

SECOND SECTION:
Nant Peris to Ogwen. Approx 9 miles.
Accompanied by Adrian Watson (to Glyder Fach) and Chris Cole (from Glyder Fach to Ogwen).

Nant Peris	10.43.
Elider Fawr	11.24.
Y Garn	11.40.
Glyder Fawr	12.09.
Glyder Fach	12.19.
Tryfan	12.32.
Ogwen	12.46.

Joss's comments: *Very hard to climb Elider Fawr. Having difficulty on descent as I had bruised my right heel on Saturday. The mist cleared going on to Glyder Fach. Had difficulty going on to the summit, a rope is really needed. A good descent and run over to Tryfan. Down to the road in 15 minutes.*

THIRD SECTION:
Ogwen to Foel Fras. Approx 9 miles.
Accompanied by Allen Walker (Ogwen to Foel Fras) and by John Jones and two farmers (Carnedd Llywelyn to Foel Fras).

Ogwen	12.46.
Penyrole Wen	13.15.
Carnedd Dafydd	13.50.
Yr Elen	14.05.
Carnedd Llywelyn	14.20.
Foel Grach	14.30.
Foel Fras	14.46.

Total time: 4hrs 46 mins. Distance: 22 miles.
Joss's comments: *Very hot and humid going out of Ogwen and cold wet mist on Penyrole Wen. Got cramp on Carnedd Dafydd. Cold got into my legs. Allen took a good line to Yr Elen in thick black mist. Had difficulty getting off Carnedd Llywelyn and lost a few minutes. Mist very black. Met John Jones coming off Foel Grach and a good job as he knew the ground and helped with navigation.*
Joss was assisted by Joe Craven, Adrian Watson, Chris Cole, Allen Walker and John Jones.

THE WASDALE FELL RACE, July 1973:

Starting from Brackenclose Hut, Wasdale.
10.00 Brackenclose.
10.36 Whinn Rigg.
11.26 Seatallan.
12.08 Pillar.
12.44 Great Gable.
13.10 Esk Hause walled shelter.
13.31 Scafell Pike.
13.48 – 13.55 Brackenclose via Lingmell spur.
Total time: 3hrs 48mins 55 secs. Approx distance 21 miles.
Joss's comments: *Cool and fairly clear for most of the event, some cloud between Seatallan and Pillar. Kirk Fell is traversed on the Ennerdale slope for this event. No rest halts en-route.*

THE LANGDALE FELL RACE, September 1973:

Starting from the car park at Dungeon Ghyll Hotel, Langdale.

10.00 Car park.

10.30 Thunacar Knott – via inlet of Stickle Tarn.

11.05 Esk Hause walled shelter.

11.20 Bowfell.

11.35 Crinkle Crags.

11.52 Pike o' Blisco.

12.05 Cattle grid under Blake Rigg.

12.08 – 12.20 to car park.

Total time: 2hrs 8mins 20 secs. Approx distance 17 miles.

Joss's comments: *Weather cloudy during early stages, clearing, warm. No rest halts en-route.*

THE MANX MOUNTAIN MARATHON 1976:

Start from Market Square, Ramsey. To: North Barrule, Snaefell, Carraghan, Colden, Slieau Ruy, Dowse, St John's, Sllagu Whallian, South Barrule, Cairn. Bradda Head, to a finish in Port Erin. ***Total time:*** 4hrs 23 mins 35secs. Distance 30 miles.

COAST TO COAST RUN:

June 26/27 1976.

Joss Naylor completed a Coast to Coast run for charity from Ravenscar to St Bees, 149 miles in 40 hours, including the trans-Yorkshire Lyke Wake Walk in five hours.

THE WAINWRIGHTS 1986:

A complete traverse of all the summits listed in the seven Lakeland guidebooks written by Alfred Wainwright. 214 tops visited in 7 days.

DAY 1:

Start at the Moot Hall, Keswick 0400 hrs Saturday, June 26, 1986.

1. Whinlatter	04.56.
2. Lords Seat	05.23.
3. Barf	05.20.
4. Broom Fell	05.33.
5. Graystones	05.46.
6. Ling Fell	06.00.
7. Sale Fell	06.20.
Stop: Pheasant Inn	06.27 – 06.33.
Stop: Robin Hood jnct	07.00 – 07.05.
8. Binsey	07.32.
Stop: Binsey Cottage	07.38 – 07.42.
Stop: Orthwaite	08.00 – 08.01.
9. Bakestall	08.47.
10. Skiddaw	09.07.
11. Skiddaw Little Man	09.19.
12. Carl Side	09.31.
13. Long Side	09.36.
14. Ullock Pike	09.42.
15. Dodd	10.10.
16. Latrigg	10.57.
Stop: Latrigg car park	11.05 – 11.20.
17. Lonscale Fell	11.52.
18. Great Calva	12.42.
19. Great Cockup	13.19.
20. Meal Fell	13.34.
21. Longlands Fell	13.55.
22. Brae Fell	14.29.
23. Great Sca Fell	14.34.
24. Knott	14.58.
25. High Pike	15.25.
26. Carrock Fell	15.50.
Stop: Round House	16.10 – 16.35.
27. Bowscale Fell	17.40.
28. Bannerdale Crags	17.52.
29. Mungrisdale Cmn	18.12.
30. Blencathra	18.33.
31. Souther Fell	19.03.
Stop: A66	20.10 – 20.11.
32. Great Mell Fell	20.30.
33. Little Mell Fell	21.10.
34. Gowbarrow Fell	21.30.
Stop: Dockray Royal	21.45 – 05.00.

DAY 2:

Start Dockray Royal Hotel	05.00 hrs.
35. Hartside	05.46.
36. Sheffield Pike	06.09.
37. Glenridding Dodd	06.29.
38. Birkhouse Moor	07.22.
Stop: Glenridding	07.44 – 07.55.
39. Arnison Crag	08.18.
40. Birks	08.40.
41. St Sunday Crag	09.02.
42. Seat Sandal	09.33.
43. Greatrigg Man	10.04.
44. Stone Arthur	10.15.
45. Heron Pike	10.34.
46. Nab Scar	10.47.
Stop: Rydal	10.54 – 11.15.
47. Low Pike	11.41.
48. High Pike	11.55.
49. Dove Crag	12.09.
50. Little Hart Crag	12.27.
51. High Hartsop Dodd	
52. Middle Dodd	13.03.
53. Red Screes	13.15.
Stop: Kirkstone Inn	13.25 – 13.40.
54. Caudale Moor	14.10.
55. Hartsop Dodd	14.26.
56. Grey Crag	15.23.
57. Thornthwaite Crag	15.42.
58. Froswick	15.57.
59. Ill Bell	16.09.

60. Yoke 16.18.
61. Troutbeck Tongue 16.52.
Stop: A592 17.19 – 17.27.
62. Wansfell 18.00.
63. Sow Howes 18.50.
64. Sallows 19.10.
Stop: Kentmere 19.45 – 04.00.

DAY 3:

Start at Kentmere 04.00.
65. Shipman Knotts 04.42.
66. Kentmere Pike 04.58.
67. Grey Crag 05.45.
68. Tarn Crag 06.00.
69. Selside Pike 06.42.
70. Branstree 06.59.
71. Harter Fell 07.23.
72. Mardale Ill Bell 07.59.
73. High Street 08.12.
74. The Knott 08.26.
75. The Nab 08.56.
76. Rest Dodd 09.19.
77. Rampsgill 09.46.
78. Kidsty Pike 09.53.
79. High Raise 10.02.
80. Wether Hill 10.25.
81. Loadpot Hill 10.39.
82. Arthur's Pike 10.58.
83. Bonscale Pike 11.09.
84. Steel Knotts 11.43.
Stop: New Martindale Church
11.59 – 12.40.
85. Hallin Fell 12.55.
86. Beda Fell 13.30.
87. Place Fell 14.18.
88. Angle Tarn Pike 14.51.
89. Brock Crag 15.10.
Stop: Hartsop 15.30 – 15.45.
90. Hartsop Above How 16.20.
91. Hart Crag 17.02.
92. Fairfield 17.48.
93. Dollywagon Pike 17.57.
94. Nethermost Pike 18.12.
95. Helvellyn 18.24.
96. Catstycam 18.40.
97. Whiteside 19.10.
98. Raise19.95.
99. Stybarrow Dodd 19.40.
100. Watson's Dodd 19.49.
101. Great Dodd 20.00.
102. Clough Head 20.20.
Stop: Wanthwaite 20.43 – 20.48.
103. High Rigg 21.36.
Stop: The Nest A591 22.00 – 05.10.

DAY 4:

Start at the Nest at 05.10 hrs
104. Walla Crag 05.25.
105. Bleaberry Fell 05.50.
106. High Seat 06.05.
107. Raven Crag 06.28.
108. High Tove 07.03.
109. Armboth Fell 07.17.
Stop: Watendlath 07.47 – 07.58.
110. Grange Fell 08.18.
111. Great Crag 08.44.
112. Ullscarf 09.37.
113. Steel Fell 10.24.
114. Calf Crag 10.57.
115. Gibson's Knott 11.21.
116. Helm Crag 11.36.
Stop: Easedale 11.45 – 12.25.
117. Tarn Crag 13.20.
118. Blea Rigg 13.48.
119. Silver How 14.22.
120. Loughrigg Fell 15.12.
Stop: Loughrigg 15.31 – 16.04.
121. Black Fell 16.55.
122. Holme Fell 17.52.
Stop: Pierce How Beck 18.20 – 18.35.
123. Wetherlam 20.28.
124. Swirl How 21.01.
125. Great Carrs 21.07.
126. Brim Fell 21.38.
127. Coniston Old Man 21.47.
128. Dow Crag 22.20.
129. Grey Friar 23.28.
Stop: Wrynose Pass 00.55 – 05.00.

DAY 5:

Start Wrynose Pass 05.00.
130. Lingmoor Fell 05.35.
131. Pike o'Blisco 06.41.
132. Cold Pike 07.08.
133. Crinkle Crags 07.45.
134. Bowfell 08.21.
135. Esk Pike 08.47.
136. Allen Crags 09.08.
137. Rossett Pike 09.43.
138. Pike o' Stickle 10.40.
139. Loft Crag 10.48.
140. Harrison Stickle 11.05.
141. Pavey Ark 11.18.
142. Thunacar Knott 11.31.
143. Sergeant Man 11.48.
144. High Raise 12.00.
145. Sergeant's Crag 12.36.
146. Eagle Crag 12.46.
Stop: Stonethwaite 13.10 – 14.30.
147. Rosthwaite Fell 15.17.
148. Glaramara 15.59.
149. Seathwaite Fell 17.00.
150. Great End 17.44.
151. Lingmell 18.25.

152. Scafell Pike	18.50.
153. Scafell	19.23.
154. Slight Side	19.56.
155. Hard Knott	20.13.
Stop: Hardknott Pass	21.23 – 21.55.
156. Harter Fell	22.40.
157. Green Crag	23.41.
Stop: Woolpack Inn	01.25 – 06.09.

DAY 6:

Start Woolpack Inn	06.09.
158. Whin Rigg	07.40.
159. Illgill Head	07.57.
Stop: Brackenclose	08.12 – 08.36.
160. Yewbarrow	09.25.
161. Red Pike	10.16.
162. Pillar	10.52.
163. Scoat Fell	11.19.
164. Steeple	11.25.
165. Haycock	11.46.
166. Seatallan	12.22.
167. Buckbarrow	12.38.
168. Middle Fell	13.15.
169. Caw Fell	14.22.
170. Lank Rigg	15.22.
171. Crag Fell	16.06.
172. Grike	16.17.
Stop: Anglers' car park	16.57 – 18.03.
173. Hen Comb	18.56.
174. Gavel Fell	19.24.
175. Blake Fell	19.40.
176. Burnbank Fell	19.53.
Stop: Waterhead	20.15 – 20.30.
177. Fellbarrow	21.13.
178. Low Fell	21.40.
Stop: Kirkstile Inn	22.02 – 23.30.
179. Mellbreak	00.29.
Stop: Sheepfold Mosedale	01.40 – 04.30.

DAY 7:

Start sheepfold at Mosedale Beck	04.30.
180. Great Borne	05.15.
181. Starling Dodd	05.51.
182. Red Pike	06.21.
183. High Stile	06.45.
184. High Crag	07.10.
185. Haystacks	07.58.
186. Kirk Fell	09.05.
187. Great Gable	10.10.
188. Green Gable	10.25.
189. Base Brown	10.43.
190. Brandreth	11.14.
191. Grey Knotts	11.29.
192. Fleetwith Pike	12.04.
Stop: Honister YHA	12.32 – 13.42.
193. Castle Crag	14.15.
194. Catbells	15.25.
195. Maiden Moor	16.04.
196. High Spy	16.31.
197. Dale Head	17.15.
198. Hindscarth	17.37.
199. Robinson	18.11.
Stop: Newlands Hause	18.46 – 19.07.
200. Rannerdale Knotts	19.52.
201. Whiteless Pike	20.45.
202. Wandope	21.12.
203. Grasmoor	21.41.
204. Grisedale Pike	22.41.
205. Hopegill Head	23.12.
206. Whiteside	23.33.
207. Eel Crag	00.39.
208. Sail	00.53.
209. Knott Rigg	01.47.
210. Aikin Knott	02.10.
211. Scar Crags	02.42.
212. Causey Pike	03.02
213. Outerside	03.33
214. Barrow	04.07
FINISH: Moot Hall, Keswick	05.25 hrs.

Joss's comments on the latter stages of the event, taken from 'Joss Naylor MBE was Here', an account of the Wainwright run:

'The hands were even more swollen and now, after a long time in the hammering rain, my face was swollen also. I heard someone remark "that doesn't look like Joss Naylor." Gillian once again did the nursing to my feet. I was happy to continue in the road shoes, I'd hardly slipped at all during the wet section of the day and the only real problem had been on the descent of Melbreak when I'd had to use Colin's shoulder to steady myself.

'I was to be accompanied on this next section by one of Britain's best ever fell runners, Billy Bland from Borrowdale . . . Billy was heard to say that the only way to get me to give up on this attempt was to knock me out with a pill. Billy and I chatted almost non-stop, he pointing out places of interest, places he had known since he was a lad . . .

'Neil Shuttleworth joined us for the run which was to finish off Robinson in a mighty thunderstorm. I was glad to get to the van and prepare for the last section . . .

'As evening drew on the weather started to improve, but my pace didn't: long, slow sections. Ground I could fly over was covered now at walking pace, feet swelling more and the inside of my mouth felt really sore; it wasn't easy to talk. Met Tony Rathbone who was out from Keswick taking photographs. He wished me well and told the lads to buy me a drink on him at the finish. It was a good surprise to meet Peter and Barbara Nelson and Mike Pearson, we started to look like a fell-walking group. I felt relaxed and

we chatted cheerfully, many of my aches suddenly disappearing as I realised just how close I was. . . .

'Not often do you get a group of happy souls sauntering along the ridges of the Newlands Fells at 0200hrs. All the team had been on the route somewhere during the last 30 minutes and it was great encouragement to see all those smiling yet very tired faces . . .

'Along the last section of roadway we met a small group of home going partygoers who may have wondered why our little group had seemed so happy and cheerful. I didn't realise at the time but the group held back to let me jog in solo to touch the Moot Hall and be congratulated first by my wife Mary.

'In the 7 days, 1hr 25 minutes since leaving the Moot Hall I'd visited 214 Lakeland tops, the ascent was approximately 121,000 ft – equal to in excess of four ascents of Mount Everest, and the approximate distance of 391 miles is equal to nearly 15 London marathons. The time taken from summit 1 to summit 214 was 6 days, 23 hours, 11 minutes.

'I'm not a great one for words. To find words to express my gratitude to those who took part is beyond me. Those who know me well will sense what I want to say. I don't show my feelings but I do feel things deep inside me. I'm a man for doing, not saying . . .'

THE JOSS NAYLOR LAKELAND CHALLENGE:

This is Joss's idea of a fun run. The route for the first run of the Joss Naylor Lakeland Challenge was established by Joss in 1990. The run is from Pooley Bridge to Greendale Bridge, Wasdale. It traverses 31 summits and covers a distance of some 48 miles with a total ascent of 16,000 feet (more than the height of Mont Blanc). In very bad weather and with a strong South West wind Joss, who was 54 in 1990, completed the run in 11 hours and 30 minutes.

The challenge is to veteran runners over the age of 50 to complete the run within set times relating to their age and sex: men 50-59, 12 hours; women 50-59, 14 hours; men and women 60-64, 18 hours; men and women 65 plus, 24 hours. Chris Brasher gave engraved pewter tankards to the first 20 runners to succeed, provided they raised at least £100 for the charity of their choice. The tradition is ongoing with a new sponsor.

60 PEAKS AT 60

1996 (aged 60): Ran 60 Lakeland fell tops in 36 hours.

The Joss Naylor 60 peaks at 60 years
Starting at 0300 hrs on Saturday, June 22, 1996 from Walna Scar, Duddon.

SECTION 1:

Pacers: Dave Nuttall, Tim Raw, Ken Linley, all Black Combe Runners, and Joss's dog Fly.

1. Dow Crag	00.39.
2. Coniston Old Man	03.54.
3. Brim Fell	04.00.
4. Great Friar	04.24.
5. Great Carrs	04.34.
6. Swirl How	04.38.
7. Wetherlam	04.56.
Arrive Three Shires	05.21.

SECTION 2:

Pacers: Hugh Simmonds , Kendal Athletic Club (right through) Jonathan Lagoe and Dave Nuttall (8-13), Billy Bland, Borrowdale Fell Runners (13-20), Anne Stanford (20-27), Irving Block and Dave Findlay, Cumberland Fell Runners (20 to Buttermere), Stewart Young, Brian Taylor, Paul Murphy (23 to Buttermere), Janet Sutcliffe (24 to Buttermere), Allen Walker (28 to Buttermere).

Fell support: Bivouac on Allen Crags, Ken Ledward, Borrowdale Fell Runners, and at Styhead with Mike Pearson, Keswick Athletic Club; Ian Roberts and Andy Bradley

Cumberland Fell Runners. Refreshments at Gillerthwaite: Debbie Watson; Broad Stand, Phil Allder, Kendal Mountain Rescue Team, Andy Clifford Kendal AC with Henry and Tom.

Start: Three Shires	05.23.
8. Crinkle Crags	06.06.
9. Shelter Crag	06.12.
10. Bowfell	06.30.
11. Esk Pike	06.45.
12. Allen Crags	07.00.
13. Glaramara	07.20.
14. Great End	08.04.
15. Ill Crag	08.15.
16. Broad Crag	08.22.
17. Scafell Pike	08.31.
18. Scafell	08.54.
19. Lingmell	09.29.
20. Green Gable	10.23.
21. Great Gable	10.35.
22. Kirk Fell	11.02.
23. Pillar	11.47.
24. Red Pike (W)	12.08.
25. Scoat Fell	12.18.
26. Steeple	12.22.
27. Haycock	12.37.
28. High Stile	14.14.
Arrive Fish Hotel	14.45.

SECTION 3:

Pacers: Colin Dulson, Cumberland Fell Runners, Tony Burton Patterdale Mountain Rescue Team. Fell support: Bill Hunter at Coledale Hause.

Start: Fish Hotel	15.03.
29. Sail	16.16.
30. Crag Hill	16.24.
31. Wandope	16.31.
32. Grasmoor	16.47.
33. Hopegill Head	17.18.
34. Grisedale Pike	17.36.
Arrive Braithwaite	18.15.

SECTION 4:

Pacers: Barry Johnson, Cumberland Fell Runners, Dr Dave Clarke, Phil Ledward, Borrowdale Fell Runners. Fell support: John Campbell on Skiddaw; Harold and Penny de Silva at Low Man; Val Johnson and Grant Edmondson, Cumberland Fell Runners, valley support.

Start: Braithwaite	18.29.
35. Skiddaw	20.23.
36. Skiddaw Low Man	20.30.
37. Blencathra	21.53.
Arrive Threlkeld	22.25.

SECTION 5:

Pacers: John Gay, Peter Hamilton (both Patterdale Mountain Rescue Team); Peter Todhunter, David, Donald, Jim Carr (Cumberland Fell Runners). Fell support: Rick Harrison, bivouac at Swirral Cairn; Ken Ledward, tent at Grisedale Tarn; Yvonne Armitage, Swaledale Outdoor Club, Dave Freeborn, John Williams, Mathew Cox, Patterdale Mountain Rescue Team, bivouac at Scandale Pass; Jacquie Freeborn, Patterdale Mountain Rescue Team, valley support.

Start: Threlkeld	22.52.
38. Great Dodd	00.49.
39. Watson Dodd	01.04.
40. Stybarrow Dodd	01.21.
41. Raise	01.48.
42. Whiteside	02.08.
43. Lower Man	02.35.
44. Catstycam	03.13.
45. Helvellyn	03.40.
46. Nethermost Pike	03.53.
47. Dollywagon	04.14.
48. St Sunday Crag	05.30.
49. Fairfield	06.17.
50. Greatrigg Man	06.36.
51. Hart Crag	07.16.
52. Dove Crag	07.33.
53. Red Screes	08.42.
Arrive at Kirkstone Pass	09.05.

SECTION 6:

Pacers: Peter and Barbara Nelson, Andy Ligema, Derek Fowler, Cumberland Fell Runners, Chris Mounsey Cumberland Fell Runners, Allen Walker, Colin Dulson, Cumberland Fell runners and others including Joss's daughter Gillian, Phil Allder, Mark Hartley and members and friends from Cumberland Fell Runners.

Start: Kirkstone	09.20.
54. Caudale Moor	10.12.
55. Thornthwaite	10.51.
56. Harter Fell	11.58.
57. High Street	12.58.
58. Kidsty Pike	13.36.
59. High Raise	13.52.
60. Rampsgill Head	14.04.
Arrive Side Farm	15.50.

OVERALL TIME from Walna to Side Farm 36 hrs 50 mins.

Summit of Dow (peak 1) to summit of Rampsgill Head (peak 60) 34 hrs 25 mins.

Estimated distance 176.85kil (110 miles) ascent, 10,252 metres / 33,636 ft.

Selected extracts from Joss's comments in the booklet 'Joss 60 at 60': 'On the Monday before the run I took a couple of gates to Drigg to help load some hogs on to a trailer. As I unloaded the gates I stepped back into a hole and felt my back go. I sat on the ground with the gate on top of me and cursed. On the Tuesday and Wednesday I tried to get a jog going and gave up before leaving the yard. I rested and felt much better on Saturday . . . met with Eric Robson and the Border TV team and my pacers at Walna Scar at 2.30am . . . on the ridge of Sail I started to feel the legs tighten and a sharp pain in the lower back, although I felt good overall I just couldn't lift the legs . . . soon after we got on to the serious climb on Skiddaw I was down on the ground and Barry (Johnson) had to give me a massage. The pain in my back came in spasms and I needed massage several times before we topped out on Skiddaw . . . the heaviness in the legs would not go away and coming down Hallsfell the feet seemed to have a mind of their own . . .

Only a short time in darkness but enough light to see the terrible erosion on Swirral Edge . . . the drop into Threshthwaite Mouth is rough and I found this and the climb out to Thornthwaite Beacon not easy at all . . . from Harter we turned about in the sun and with some of the best company a man could wish for . . . as soon as we turned on to the Kidsty Ridge we viewed one of the Riggindale eagles soaring just ahead of us . . . After a short break, and not a few wet eyes, I went over to be greeted by many supporters at Glenridding car park. Even Harold Iredale, who I'd first met when he was a young shepherd in Wasdale, now in his 80th year, turned out to give good wishes and congratulations.'

70 PEAKS AT 70:

Wednesday, July 5, 2006. Ran 70 Lakeland fell tops in under 21 hours covering more than 50 miles and ascending more than 25,000 feet

1. Flat Fell	01.52.
2. Blakeley	02.15.
3. Burn Edge	02.25.
4. Swarth Fell	02.31.
5. Latter Barrow	02.50.
6. Poukes Fell	02.55.
7. Lank Rigg	03.16.
8. Whoap	03.29.
9. Crag Fell	03.49.
10. Grike	04.02.
11. How Side	04.42.
12. Kelton Fell	05.05.
13. Godworth	05.13.
14. High Pen	05.27.
15. Gavel Fell	05.39.

Summit	Time
16. Banna Fell	05.49.
17. Floutern Cop	05.55.
18. Herdus	06.14.
19. Great Borne	06.24.
20. Starling Dodd	06.46.
21. Little Dodd	06.53.
22. Red Pike	07.11.
23. White Pike	07.15.
24. High Stile	07.26.
25. Grey Crag	07.30.
26. Gamlin End	07.46.
27. Seat	07.56.
Stop: Scarth Gap	08.04.
28. Haystacks I	08.19.
29. Haystacks II	08.21.
30. Green Crag	08.37.
31. Great Round How	08.50.
32. Grey Knotts	09.10.
33. Brandreth	09.19.
34. Green Gable	09.40.
35. Great Gable	09.56.
Stop: Styhead	10.10 – 10.20.
36. Tarn Crag	11.00.
37. Lincomb	11.05.
38. Unnamed	11.24.
39. Looking Stead	11.32.
40. Glaramara I	11.35.
41. Glaramara II	11.40.
42. Comb Head	11.49.
43. Dove Crag	11.56.
44. Rosthwaite Fell	12.09.
45. Heron Crag	13.11.
46. Sergeant Crag	13.25.
47. Low White Stones	13.59.
48. High Raise	14.05.
49. Sergeant Man	14.17.
50. Thunacar Knott	14.41.
51. Pavey Ark	14.47.
52. Harrison Stickle	15.04.
53. Loft Crag	15.15.
54. Pike o' Stickle	15.27.
55. Rossett Pike	16.10.
56. Allen Crags	16.49.
57. Kirk Fell I	18.34.
58. Kirk Fell II	18.43.
59. Blacksail Crag	19.02.
60. Looking Stead	19.17.
61. Pillar	19.54.
62. Black Crag	20.10.
63. Red Pike	20.32.
64. Little Scoat	20.49.
65. Steeple	20.56.
66. Great Scoat	21.03.
67. Haycock	21.19.
68. Seatallan	22.00.
69. Cat Beilds	22.20.
70. Glade How	22.30.
71. Buckbarrow	22.24.
Stop: Greendale	22.58.

For detail on the Lakes, Meres and Waters circuit in 1983 (105 miles in 19hrs 20 mins and 14 secs) see map on page 56.

The start of the Ennerdale Horseshoe Fell Race 1972. On the far left is Andy Church and then, from left to right, are Dave Cannon (No 28), Joss Naylor (No 31) Eric Roberts (immediately to Joss's left) Tom Sykes (No 55), Ken Ledward (No 67) Allen Walker (No 33) Jim Strickland (No 4 wearing a hat) and Danny Hughes (No 27). Alan Heaton was on the original line-up to Joss's right (pre start) but has become obscured behind other runners.

JOSS
Words of thanks

In sport, as in life, there are people who go out of their way to give you assistance. And it is certainly true that the people involved in fell running, past and present, and who know Joss Naylor, could not have been more helpful in providing information and images for this book.

In no particular order – there is no first over the line here – I would like to thank the following who helped me: Tommy Orr, Ken Ledward, Barry Johnson, Colin Dulson, Peter Ferris, Allen Walker, Kenny Stuart, Billy Bland, David Powell-Thompson, Mary Naylor, Fred Rogerson, Bill Teasdale, Rainer Burchett, and Brian Evans.

Many of the above agreed to help by becoming victims of my interviewing technique, while others – principally Tommy Orr and Ken Ledward - also provided a wealth of images and statistical information. I am indebted. Without their help this book would not have gone the full distance. Writer and broadcaster, Eric Robson, was once again immensely supportive and has the midge bites – suffered at the start and finish of Joss's epic run on the longest day – to prove it.

Ross Brewster, of Keswick, a man who was once advised by Joss Naylor to "git mair miles in them legs," provided the foreword for this book and also acted as proof-reader for the entire publication, so if there are any spelling errors or grammatical glitches, these are entirely the responsibility of Ross and his Grammar School education. Ross provided a great deal of encouragement and enthusiasm for the book and has also assisted with its promotion.

The words of the late, great Chris Brasher, as reported in *The Observer* newspaper and elsewhere, were of enormous help as was the reporting of Simon Winchester, for *The Guardian* (probably then *The Manchester Guardian*) at the time of Joss's entry in the Pikes Peak Marathon, Manitou Springs, in the 1970s.

Which leads me to appreciation of the work of the photographer Carl Iwasaki (*Sports Illustrated Magazine* / Getty Images) for his images of Joss taking part in the Pikes Peak marathon. Another photographer, the late Brian Duff, took the graphic photograph of Joss Naylor that provides the cover image for this book while Tony Greenbank and Stuart Holmes provided images of Joss's fell run on the longest day.

My thanks also to Patrick Cremer for his painting of three countrymen and a crazy looking dog outside a marquee at a Lakeland show, and to Jonathan Trotman for his portrait of Joss descending screes, a painting based on a black and white photograph by John Cleare.

If this book is a success then the photographer Val Corbett, who walked the fells with Joss, Titch and Spy and myself, in pursuit of the ever-elusive best light and the image to end all images, can take a large part of the credit for that. I believe the picture she took of Joss and his dogs standing on the rocky outcrop at Dore Head is a timeless classic.

Val has asked me to thank Spy and Titch for their company on the walks.

And finally, my thanks to the man himself, Joss Naylor, for living the life and for telling me about it and, last but not least, to Joss's wife Mary for the rock buns.

I think I had more than my fair share.

Keith T Richardson, August 2009.

JOSS
Dialect glossary

The following is a glossary of the dialect words in the order in which they appear. In a limited number of cases and to help the reader who is not familiar with the dialect, definitions also appear in brackets in the main body of the text.

Tek us: Take us.

Cem: Came.

Mebbe: May be.

I divvent know: I don't know.

Laal: Little.

Owt: Anything.

Fust: First.

Ga: Go.

Nivver: Never.

Wid it: With it.

Nee: No.

Varra: Very.

Nowt: Nothing.

Nowt ivver come of it: Nothing ever came of it.

Mi: My.

Ah larnt: I learned.

Yam: Home.

Ya: One. As in 'ya morning'.

Ah thowt: I thought.

Ovver: Over.

Ah nivver: I never.

Mair: More.

Ivverything: Everything.

Summat: Something.

Gev: Gave.

Aw: All.

Frae: From.

Tekken: Taken.

Whitehevven: Whitehaven.

Wucked: Worked.

Anaw: As well.

Caw it: Call it.

Theer: There.

Hod: Hold.

Oppen: Open.

Reet: Right.

Deuh: Do.

Git: Get.

Neebody: Nobody.

Scopped: Threw.

Fower: Four.

Thoo: You.

Deed: Dead: As in 'huh, might as well be bloody deed.'

Garn: Going.

Wus: Was.

Meks: makes.

Gonna: Going to.

Watter: Water.

Missell: Myself. As in 'freshened missell up.'

Amang: Among.

Cawd: Called.

Hissell: Himself.

Doon: Down.

Behint: Behind.

Wol: Hole.

Aboot: About.

Deuh summat wid it: Do something with it.

Ivver ah sen: I ever saw.

Telt: Told.

Dunno: Don't know.

Forrard: Forward.

Yance: Once.

Kessen sheep: One that is stranded on its back.

Brokken: Broken.

Togidder: Together.

Cleas: Clothes. As in 'beans (bones) was inside t'cleas'.

Thersells: Themselves.

Eshdell: Eskdale. As in 'hod reet fur Eshdel.' Keep to the right in order to get to Eskdale.

Aw maks: All makes, all sorts. As in 'aw maks o'folk.'

Facing page: Keith Richardson, Joss Naylor and Titch walk out of Wasdale Head into Mosedale.

WHAT THEY SAID ABOUT IVVER SEN

Keith Richardson's book 'Ivver Sen' – Lake District: *The life and times of the men and women who work the land* (published by River Greta Writer) won The *Lakeland Book of the Year* 2009. The artist Keith Bowen illustrated the book with pastel drawings of the central characters.

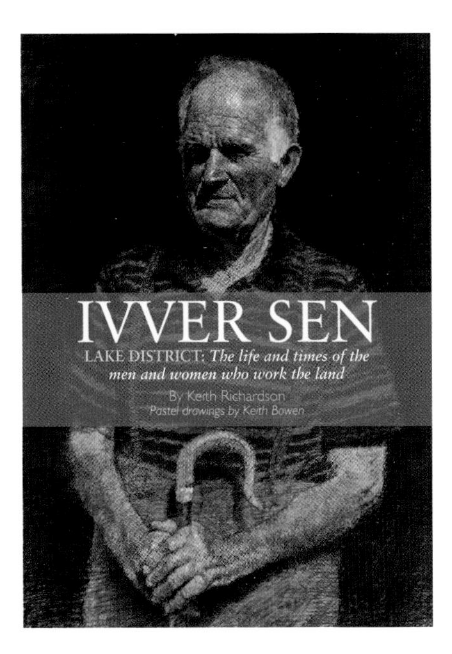

When it was decided to apply for World Heritage status for the Lake District it was on the basis of its cultural landscape.

In this fine, evocative book Keith Richardson puts figures in that landscape, figures that may reach for their pitchfork at the very mention of culture; but characters, faces that carry in their grain the Lake District's DNA.

When I first came to live in Wasdale some 20 years ago I was told that the characters had gone and the agriculture that sustained them was going to hell in a handcart, too. But the death notices were premature. Keith Richardson tracks the survivors in a volume that should be essential reading for the bureaucrats and politicians who have treated Lakeland's way of life with such careless disdain.

ERIC ROBSON,
writer and broadcaster.

Books about the Lake District are ten a penny. Often they do no more than recycle previous writing, books for the tourists, trotting out all the weary clichés, words and pictures that present a chocolate box image of the lakes and fells. Not so this book. Deep within the author was a yearning to write a book that would be a testimony to the heart and soul of his native county, seen through its personalities and their family histories... Keith Richardson has done a remarkable job in getting Lakeland characters to talk frankly in a book that tells it like it is, not in some contrived and cosmetic way.

ROSS BREWSTER,
News and Star.

Keith Richardson's tome is rich in every sense and a glorious celebration of a changing way of life... it is all the more appealing because of Keith Bowen's high-calibre pastel images, which complement the words wonderfully and paint a sensitive portrait of each individual.

Every picture really does tell a story. I must mention, too, the stunning landscape photographs taken by Val Corbett. All in all an award-winning gem if I ever did see one...

ADRIAN MULLEN,
The Westmorland Gazette.

By the same author

Companions of a Kind - *short stories.*

Ike - *biography of the West Cumbrian rugby league player Ike Southward.*
(Both books no longer in print).

Ivver Sen. Lake District: *The life and times of the men and women who work the land.*

www.rivergretawriter.co.uk

JOSS
Index

Joss, Spy and Titch climb away from Dore Head.

Overleaf: The unique walls at Wasdale Head.